To FR...

OK, You Dummies,
Up Against The Wall!

ENJOY THE BOOK!

Best Wishes,

OK, You Dummies, Up Against The Wall!

(From "Hey, is this thing loaded?" to "Hey is this thing on?")

The intriguing story of one man's unique career
change from FBI agent to entertainer

by Former FBI Agent

Rick Berger

To order additional copies of this book, contact:
Xlibris Corporation
1-888-795-4274
www.Xlibris.com
Orders@Xlibris.com
48983

Contents

Dedication

Writing this book has been an experience of sheer joy mingled with touches of exasperation. I could not have completed (or even started) this project without the help of my wife Audrey. Her patience and understanding were unwavering throughout the entire writing process. Her love has remained constant through both the times when I carried a gun as well as now, when I carry a puppet.

ACKNOWLEDGEMENTS

I wish to acknowledge all those who gave me the drive to forge ahead with my crazy career change. Included in this troop of stalwart "encouragees" is Mark Wade, the nation's premier kids' show ventriloquist. Thanks, Mark, for answering all of my questions, some dumb and some not so dumb. Thanks also to ventriloquist Jonathon Geffner who guided me toward the puppet makers who now create my little partners, first and foremost of whom is Mary Ann Taylor. Next on the bill is Guy Parker, president of Watersign Creative Recording. Thanks Guy, for your innovative approach to creating the musical accompaniments that enhance my shows. To Bob Statler, I tip my hat for introducing me to the world of magic and kick-starting my new career. I offer special thanks to my parents Sam and Ruth Berger, for getting me through the growing pains of growing up. A big kiss to my mother-in-law Thalia Maltz, who provided the inspiration for my character Ceil. A huge smile and an exclamation of "Wonderful!" for my good friend Jeff Simon, who is no longer with us, but whose legacy is the infinite batch of words and phrases that are the basis of many of my little friends' dialogs. My profound thanks to my sister-in-law Lynn Janiak for her superb editing, which included the deletion of most of my beloved commas. A debt of gratitude is owed to Paul Rapisarda, who constantly spurred me on (and inflated my ego) by declaring that I was truly a "Renaissance man." And finally, thanks to everyone who encouraged me by saying, "That's an interesting story. You ought to write a book!"

INTRODUCTION

"Are you the entertainer?" I looked around and over my shoulder, searching for the person who would answer, as I thought to myself, "Who me? No, I'm with the FBI." That's when it finally hit. I *am* the entertainer. From now on I would *be* . . . the entertainer. After all, that's what I always wanted, wasn't it? To be in show business, not just on the fringes of it but fully immersed in its magic. It was hard to come to grips with the truth. I was no longer Mr. FBI, the guy who was there to ask you some questions. In a flash I had lost my identity, an identity that for thirty years had defined just who I was on this planet. It was an identity that was never true, an identity that served as a role I played in a show that ran for over a quarter of a century. Yes, I am the entertainer and as Gypsy Rose Lee once said, "Let me entertain you."

"Life Is Not a Dress Rehearsal."
—Anonymous

"One of these days is none of these days."
—Even More Anonymous

PROLOGUE

The wind whistled its way through the walkways between the towers of the World Trade Center. It skimmed across shimmering ice patches that resembled miniature ponds dotting the plaza. A cold New York day had been delivered to all of us working in the city. It was the kind of day where I looked out of the FBI office window and was glad that I didn't have an outdoor job. I loved the outdoors on a warm spring day, but certainly not on this day in February. It was the twenty-sixth of the month. The year was 1993. On this day I was perfectly content to be sitting at my desk, writing a report. I anxiously watched the clock as the day progressed. That evening held the promise of a fun date with my wife Audrey. We would be attending a concert by rock oldies legend Gene Pitney at New York's famed Carnegie Hall. We looked forward to hearing him sing his hits from the 1960's, including one called "Town Without Pity." I had always enjoyed that song and often sang it in the shower. I knew that it had come from the movie *Village of the Damned* but never having seen the film, I couldn't quite grasp the meaning of the lyrics. Anyway, my plan was to carefully study how he sang the number, so that someday I would be able to perform it during one of my own shows.

As the morning drew to a close, there was a sudden ringing of phones on the agents' desks surrounding mine. Before I could ask what was going on, my phone rang. A fellow agent asked if I had heard an explosion. I told him that I hadn't. He said that he had just heard a report that something had happened at the World Trade Center and that there might have been an explosion caused by a bomb. The floor on which I worked had several windows facing downtown toward the World Trade Center. However, my desk was not located on that side of the building. I quickly got off the phone and headed toward the windows that faced the Trade Center. By then, a sizeable group of agents and support personnel had gathered at the windows. I could hear the shrill wail of sirens growing louder. I was able to secure a small open space near the lower left corner of the window. As I peered out at the scene I could see that whatever had happened was of a sizeable proportion. Racing toward the twin towers was a phalanx of emergency vehicles, their blinding red lights spinning and their reflections bouncing off the large windows of the banks and businesses which lined the streets. The Trade Center was six blocks away from the Federal Building which housed our office. Our location on an upper floor in the building enabled me to see a panorama of the downtown area. However, without binoculars it was quite difficult to make out any details.

The buzz throughout the office was that a bomb had gone off on one of the lower floors, perhaps the basement in one of the towers. Reports regarding injuries or damage to the building had not yet been received.

Since I was not assigned to any first responder type of unit, I knew that it was not my place to rush out of the office and report to the scene. If indeed a bomb had gone off, the FBI's bomb squad would immediately respond and upon arriving on site, would link up with the New York Police Department's bomb unit. Once at the scene, working jointly, they would secure the area and make every effort to ensure the safety of those individuals within the vicinity.

Within minutes our squad supervisor called a meeting to brief us on what had happened. He said that the first reports indicated that a bomb had gone off in the basement of one of the World Trade Center's towers and that at this point, our squad was not involved in the investigation. This was due to the fact that the squad to which I was assigned handled foreign counterintelligence matters. Since our expertise was related to espionage matters, only on special occasions where a need for increased manpower existed, would we be called upon to assist. In this case, we were, however, placed on a standby status, should our help be needed. This meant that we were to continue whatever we were doing, but when we left the office we were to report in every two hours to let them know our current location and where we could be reached.

Knowing that my services were not presently needed, I cleared my desk of all classified documents, locked them in a secure place, then checked once more to make sure it was okay to leave. Having received permission to go, I headed home to pick up my wife and bring her back to the city for the concert. Safety was on the mind of every New Yorker that evening. Many plans were cancelled due to the fear that this could be an act of terrorism leveled against the United States and that additional attacks could possibly follow.

I checked with Carnegie Hall and was told that the concert had not been cancelled. I was glad to see that as always, New Yorkers reacted with caution, but refused to bow to the actions of criminals and cowards. As I traveled home to New Jersey every radio station was broadcasting continuous news coverage of the event. The reports indicated that an act of terrorism was suspected. Back at my home in New Jersey, I was greeted by my wife, also a native New Yorker, who stalwartly insisted that no terrorist was going to ruin our evening. She understood that I would be checking in with the office every two hours. Bureau wives get used to this sort of procedure and accept it without question. Arriving back in the city that evening it was obvious that there was an air of caution hanging over New York.

Extra cops had been placed on duty in strategic places such as the tunnels and bridges leading into the city. Cars were moving at unusual paces. Some drivers seemed to be racing to get to their destinations while others appeared to be moving much more slowly than usual, perhaps in anticipation of some action up ahead which they might encounter.

We arrived at the theater with time to spare. Huddled against the frigid February night air the bustling crowd of Baby Boomers was abuzz with rumors and conflicting stories. However, the overriding attitude that swept through the group was one of defiance. Many expressed the belief that if this were terrorism, they'd be damned if they'd change their plans because of it. I felt a sense of pride in being an American, a native New Yorker and an FBI agent. I glanced at my watch. Time to call in again. I made a quick call to the office and was told that most likely no additional personnel would be needed until at least the next day but to continue to call in every two hours. Within minutes we were ushered into the theater.

As tickets were collected and ushers guided us toward our seats, I could hear the gist of the conversations turning from the topic of terrorism to discussions of rock and roll stars of the past, oldies shows that people had recently seen, and general New York chitchat. When Gene Pitney stepped out on stage and the drums and guitars smashed the air with a driving rock beat, all thoughts of terrorism vanished. It was time to rock and roll!

The concert was our escape. It was a couple of hours away from problems related to national security and terrorism. Our ears got a respite from the repetitive drone of radio and TV news reporters regurgitating information, which often proved to be mere speculation, regarding what had occurred at the Twin Towers. As we drove away from the city, we questioned whether buildings such as the Trade Center had enough protection. We speculated on the point that if this were an act of terrorism, perhaps a similar thing could be prevented from happening in the future if certain measures were taken. We concluded that after this security would surely be beefed up and that nothing like this would ever happen again. Ever.

After a final check-in call to the office, we headed back to New Jersey. As we exited the Lincoln Tunnel, rounding the familiar curve that led to the various New Jersey highways we could see in the rear and side view mirrors the two towers, the lights in their windows glistening brightly. As the image shrank to a tiny vignette, we knew that the days ahead would be busy ones for the FBI. Once at home I made my last call of the evening, checking in with the office one last time to see whether I would have to turn around and return to New York. I was told to get a good night's sleep, because starting tomorrow, most of the agents in the office, regardless of their current assignment, would be busy handling some portion of the investigation.

The following day, I arrived at work at 5:45 a.m. as I had each morning for the thirteen years that the FBI had been located in the office building at Federal Plaza in lower Manhattan. The reason for getting to the office so early was of course, dedication. Just kidding. That's not to say that I wasn't dedicated but the real reason was a simple matter of parking. Beginning at about 6:00 a.m. it becomes impossible to find a parking space in New York. For many of the agents who commuted to the city, the only solution to this problem was to arrive in the city extremely early. "What?" you ask. "Doesn't the government give you a place to park your FBI car?" The answer is a resounding *No*. There is simply not enough space in Lower Manhattan to park all of the FBI cars. The rule is simple: first come, first served. Get into the city early and you'll get a spot within walking distance of the office. Arrive any later and as they say in the Bureau, "your ass is grass."

As talk of the bombing at the Trade Center escalated, agents began to receive assignments related to the investigation. For many, the mission was hardly investigative, but rather a matter of providing security in and around the crime scene area. About midafternoon, I received a call from an agent who was involved in the search for evidence. He simply said, "Rick, this is Bob. Remember how to use a camera?" I immediately knew what my assignment was going to be. I assured him that for me, photography was like riding a bike. After all, my first job in the FBI was working in the photo lab. I assured him that I could produce some valuable shots of evidence and anything else that had to be photographed.

Bob and I arrived at the scene toward late afternoon and entered the basement through the parking garage. He said that evidence found so far pointed to the possibility that a vehicle carrying a bomb had blown up in the basement. As we approached the building, the February air whipped through the chasms of Lower Manhattan. Ice slicks on the sidewalks made walking dangerous. Bob explained that a hole had been blown through the ceiling of one of the building's lowest floors and that we would be working with a team which was gathering evidence from the floor of the basement. One portion of the area that had blown up was located directly below the outdoor plaza between the towers. The powerful blast had blown a large hole in the ceiling through which you could see outside.

The most direct way to get the pieces of evidence out of the building was through the gaping hole and the best way to do this was not exactly a high-tech method of evidence retrieval. The team below on the basement floor had a large plastic bucket. As they sifted through the debris, they would place any objects of interest into the bucket, which was attached to a long rope that ran straight up through the hole. The agents two stories above on the outdoor plaza would grab the rope and raise the bucket up, take out the objects, then lower the empty bucket back down to the agents below. The team on top would record and photograph each piece. Another team would then take the pieces to a location where they were analyzed, cataloged, and stored for future retrieval as evidence.

Bob and I began looking for a way to get from where we stood, about two flights below the plaza, to the area above on the plaza where the hole was located. Having been to that very spot many times before, I remembered the location of an outdoor escalator, which ran up the side of the building. When Bob and I reached the escalator I stopped briefly at the bottom step. My mind flashed back to the blistering days of summer when I had stood on those same gleaming metal steps. It was here that I would meet my wife, who would join me for an outdoor lunch as we enjoyed the concerts held there in the shadows of the skyscrapers. We always laughed at how the sound bounced between the two towers making most of the songs inaudible. We didn't care if the acoustics were not quite up to Carnegie Hall standards. It was still a fun way to spend lunchtime in New York.

On this wintry day, the power to the escalator had been shut off and the stairs were covered with sheets of plywood to prevent anyone from attempting to use it as a staircase. The escalator and its handrails were coated with a heavy glaze of ice. However, looking around, I realized that this escalator was the only way to reach the crater on the plaza. Bob said that we would be replacing the previous team of agents who had been hauling the bucket up. They had left a short while before. It was now our turn to continue the process.

The heavily iced sheets of plywood made the escalator look like an Olympic bobsled run. It was apparent that the only way to get to the top was to scale the sides of the escalator where the rubber handrails ran. The left rail was completely iced over making it impossible to climb. The right one however, showed more promise since there were several areas which were free of ice and could possibly provide some traction. As the sun crept behind the silver spires of the Trade Center, we began to shimmy up the right side of the escalator. I thought back to my days of training at the FBI Academy. "Sure," I thought, "they taught us how to rappel down the side of a building, but that was on a warm, dry Virginia morning." We were not really trained to climb icy handrails in subzero cold. It didn't matter because one way or another, we were going to make it to the top.

As we crept over the topmost portion of the escalator, practically falling onto the cold concrete of the plaza, Bob and I shook hands. I imagined that he, too, was already thinking, "Great, we made it. Now, how the hell are we going to get back down later?"

Walking slowly across the outdoor plaza we made our way over to the crater and like Tom Sawyer and Huckleberry Finn looking down into a fishing hole, we carefully leaned over the edge. Two floors below was a scene looking every bit like a Hollywood movie set. Lit by the glare of shielded work lamps hanging on long thick electrical cables were five or six agents, each sporting a navy blue raid jacket with bold yellow block letters on the back which in no uncertain terms spelled out FBI. A couple of them were precariously perched on broken concrete beams jutting out from piles of debris. Moving like high-wire aerialists, they were attempting to keep their balance as they extracted pieces of jagged metal and other objects from the dangling mass of debris and tangled wires, which hung like a lace curtain above their heads. Once they had a firm grip on the objects they had grabbed, they would carefully hand them to their fellow agents standing just below them. Others were painstakingly picking through massive piles of metal and concrete like archaeologists searching for remnants of past civilizations. I saw one agent examining what appeared to be a wheel from a car or truck. I later found out that this was one of the wheels from the vehicle that had carried the bomb into the basement parking area.

As I prepared my camera, Bob yelled down to the team that we were in position and that they should begin sending the bucket up. Each time the bucket reached us, we would carefully remove its contents and place each piece of evidence onto the frozen ground. Bob aimed his flashlight downward so that I could see the piece of paper that I had to fill out with each photo I took. Each of these postcard-size papers contained spaces for recording the name of the photographer, the case file number, the date, location where the evidence was found, and the number of the roll of film on which the shot would appear. Printed at the bottom of each card was a miniature ruler. I would position one of these little signs at the bottom of each shot, making sure that the ruler could be seen next to the evidence. This provided a sense of scale so that anyone viewing the photo would know the size of the item in the picture.

Although the frigid air was beginning to penetrate the layers of clothing beneath my parker and my hands were beginning to slow down because of the cold, I knew that I had to remain focused on the task at hand so as to ensure accuracy in photographing each piece of evidence. I placed so many of those identification cards next to recovered objects that by the end of our evening's work I had used at least twenty rolls of film.

As our shift drew to a close, I realized that we were now totally engulfed in darkness. The blast had had its effect on the electricity in the area. None of the lights which normally bathe the plaza in the evening were functioning. That meant that we would have to shimmy down the escalator in the dark. Frozen to the bone, I packed my gear and readied my nerves for the descent. Before beginning the treacherous downward climb we joked a bit about how the Bureau had turned us into members of some elite mountain-climbing team. Not knowing anything about my goals and dreams of being an entertainer, Bob looked at me as if I were nuts when I casually remarked that at this point in my life I had really planned on being in a Broadway show. We both laughed as he pointed to the space between the buildings reminding me that the street that we were looking at through that space was indeed Broadway. He reminded me that in order to get to our cars, we would have to walk down Broadway. I snickered at the prospect that in just a few minutes I would be able to scream out, "Hey, look at me, I'm on Broadway!"

Feet first, we slowly crept our way down the escalator's slippery metal handrails. Unlike the large gray case that I usually carried, this time I had brought my small canvas camera bag, since I was shooting with my 35-mm Nikon. In order to free up my hands I had the bag's strap slung over my left shoulder. At least once on the way down the damn strap wrapped itself around my neck causing a slight inconvenience as my carotid artery became constricted. I'm glad that I didn't strangle, as this would have caused the Bureau a great deal of embarrassment. At one point I considered throwing the bag to the street below, but then reconsidered after imagining what shape the expensive Nikon would be in after meeting the concrete down there. Every so often I would lose my grip, then quickly regain it. Maybe all that playing on the monkey bars in the park when I was a kid had prepared me for this night. As we inched or way to the bottom, we could see our breath turn into vapor as it hit the frigid night air.

Sliding down the last few feet of the heavily iced handrails, we breathed a sigh of relief. We now began the trek toward our cars. Walking down Broadway we laughed again about my debut here on New York's famous White Way. I pried open the frozen car door and placed the camera bag carefully onto the backseat, making sure that none of the valuable rolls of film fell out onto the floor. Shivering from my arctic experience, I collapsed into my seat, my oversized parka fighting with me as I forced it underneath the steering wheel. As I turned the key the engine protested loudly with a sound familiar to those of us living in the Northeast: "Don't waannna start, don't waannna start." It finally cranked itself to life. I quickly turned the knob on the heater into the red zone, knowing that I'd be through the Holland Tunnel and well on my way to Jersey by the time it became comfortably warm in the car. At that point it hardly mattered. All I cared about was getting home.

The following day I reported back to the scene, but this time it was to document the devastation in the interior of the Trade Center. Having heard that there were fatalities, I asked one of the agents if he knew how many people had been killed. He said that at this point five or six deaths had been documented. As I photographed the remains of offices and hallways, I stopped to look at photos on debris-covered desks: photos of little kids at birthday parties and family gatherings around wooden picnic tables. How it angered me to think that some of the folks who once worked at these desks were taken from their loved ones by a terrorist whose sole motivation was to disrupt and destroy democracy and the American way of life.

I distinctly remember entering one hallway and spotting the remains of a steel girder lying diagonally across the floor. Somebody told me that when the bomb went off, this girder flew through the air like a flying sword and was believed to have caused the death of at least one of the workers sitting at his desk. As I stared at the twisted shard of metal, I felt a shiver run through my body.

I worked my way through the rubble-strewn corridors over to the pit that had yielded so many buckets of evidence for me to photograph. As I looked skyward through the gaping hole in the ceiling two floors above, I could see one of the twin towers, a glimmering blue steel spike piercing the icy gray New York sky. "These must be really strong buildings to have survived a blast of this magnitude," I thought. "If they're still standing, I guess they can survive anything."

My photos turned out fine and as I later found out, proved to be a valuable aid in the investigation. The announcement that the terrorist had been apprehended was, of course, good publicity for the FBI and welcome news for the public, but by no means did this news bring closure to the issue of terrorism. The Bureau embarked upon new initiatives designed to thwart the threat. However, as we witnessed less than a decade later, the war was not over by any means.

WHO AM I?

A Baby Boomer. That's me. Born in 1946. Old enough to have grown up watching *Howdy Doody* on our little black and white TV in the living room. A creative kid who was always drawing, singing, making things. Sometimes they were little things that I would make out of wooden ice cream pop sticks, you know, the discarded ones left on the ground by some kid after a summer outing in the park. Most of them had a smudge of chocolate ingrained in the part just above the words "Good Humor." Sometimes I fancied myself an artist and set out to duplicate, down to the last detail, a scene that Norman Rockwell had painted years before for a cover on the *Saturday Evening Post*: maybe a Boy Scout whose olive-colored sash hung heavy with circular splashes of gold, each a merit badge declaring to the world that this scout was competent at doing just about anything he tackled.

As I created my masterpieces of wood or on canvas I would sing to myself. The tunes were those that had been made famous by artists like Tony Bennett, Frank Sinatra, or Doris Day. I'd memorize and mimic any song that came out of that dark brown plastic Admiral radio on top of the mahogany table in our living room. But the real excitement would well up in me when I'd hear a Broadway show tune. I just had to sing along. These were the songs of a generation screaming to the world that the war was over and it was time to let the fun begin. They were the tunes that echoed from the walls of theaters up and down New York's Great White Way—the blockbusters whose lyrics were belted out by Ethel Merman, whose syllables were stretched to the breaking point by Judy Garland, Rex Harrison, Julie Andrews, and Carol Channing. These were the sounds that were melted and molded into black plastic disks, which would carry the wonder of the Broadway stage into our living rooms. These were the beloved Broadway tunes from shows that I had never seen—shows familiar to me only from a picture on a record album cover. I remember how I would gaze intently at those colorful covers. To me, each one was a painting—a piece of art that was proudly displayed, not in a museum but on a gold metal rack in my friend Gary's living room.

I can recall quite vividly the times I spent in Gary's house, waiting for him to gather his baseball mitt and other stuff together so we could start out on our day's activities, or how on a rainy day we would play a board game just to pass the time until the rain stopped. As I flicked the metal spinner to see how many spaces I would move my little yellow figure, I could hear his mom Judy singing those glorious songs as she slowly dusted the blond wood end tables that flanked the couch, every inch of which was clad in clear vinyl. Gary's mom was a pretty good singer and like me, she considered music a treasure. She would pick an album, then begin the slow process of removing the record from its cardboard cover taking care to hold it by its edge so as not to scratch the grooves. She elevated the process of removing a record from its jacket to an art form. She would place the album cover down on the table ever so carefully, then gently position the record on the spindle in the Magnavox record player sitting in the living room. I would pick up the album cover and become lost in the picture as the record began to play. I would not just hear the music. I would absorb it, digesting every word like a morsel of food. To this day most of those words remain in my head.

As I'd sing along with the record I would stare intently at the picture on the album cover, imagining myself in the scene. I'd be magically transported onto the stage where I'd replace Yul Brynner, taking a commanding stance in the royal palace. I'd become the King of Siam about to dance with Anna. Sometimes I'd become Henry Higgins intent on teaching Eliza Doolittle how to speak proper English. I studied and memorized every detail on those album covers. In my head, I created a catalog consisting of album covers on the left and song titles on the right; a little jukebox of the mind, you might say. When the fancy struck I would summon up my catalog, pick out an album, match a song title to it, and begin to sing the song in my head. Having the ability to do this was not always an advantage. I distinctly remember playing the score from "My Fair Lady" in my head during a math test. When the problem came up dealing with the two trains, one traveling twice as fast as the other, I couldn't figure out what time the first train arrived at its destination because all I heard in my head was Eliza Doolittle saying, "The rine in Spine falls mainly on the pline." On some occasions, I actually sang the songs out loud, but this was only when I was alone. I guess I simply lacked the confidence to sing in the presence of others. I relegated myself to becoming the world's most famous shower singer. Only the square beige tiles on the shower wall would be witnesses to my talent. In those days I harbored two secret wishes. The first was to actually see a show and experience the magic of live theater on Broadway. The second was to become a performer and bathe in the glow of an audience applauding with wild abandon as I belted out the final words of a song. Just a dream, I figured—just a dream.

Two chances to actually perform occurred during my pre-high school years. The first one was a fluke. Being too shy to actually audition for a role in the sixth-grade play, I decided instead to "perform" behind the scenes. I tried out for the role of curtain opener. I figured that by opening and closing the curtain, I would be on stage but could avoid the problem of stage fright since I didn't have to actually face the audience. On the day of the first rehearsal, I was exploding with confidence. I had memorized the note the school orchestra would play which would serve as my cue to slowly begin opening the traveler curtain. The orchestra was, to say the least, horrific. The strings sounded like a dentist's drill at high speed. The horns were blasting out an explosion of sound reminiscent of a fleet of New York taxis honking their way through rush hour traffic. Then there were the drums, the underpinning of the orchestra. If only the sixth graders knew the power they wielded with those drumsticks in their little hands. The sounds they produced from the taut skins of those drums could have summoned a tribe of hungry cannibals. They were not, however, suitable for setting the musical beat for a school play. The teacher in charge held up her hand, signaling all the actors and production people to quiet down. As the chattering among cast members subsided, the musicians began to play a cacophony of sound which vaguely resembled some classical melody. Just as the music reached that certain note which was my cue, I heard a voice from the wings. "Richard, don't open the curtain. I've made a change." It was Mrs. Moon, my teacher and director of the play. "I've decided that you and Jeffrey should change places. He will pull the curtain open in this scene. I want you to play the role of the boy on his first day of school." "Oh, my God. She wants me to act!" was my first thought. As I felt my breakfast heading upward from my stomach, I turned to her and said meekly, "Okay Mrs. Moon, but I don't know the lines." "Oh they're very easy," she said. "You'll do fine." As the day of the performance drew near, I became more and more nervous. "My debut! My big break! I hope I remember my lines." Actually, the whole affair consisted of walking onto the stage carrying a notebook and saying, "Oh boy it's the first day of school!"

The day of the show arrived. That morning, my mom checked my costume, a clean white shirt with a red tie and navy blue pants. My "costume" was actually what I wore every Friday, which was assembly day. Walking down the school bus steps, I recited my lines over and over, "Oh boy, it's the first day of school! Oh boy, it's the first day of school!"

As the auditorium filled with kids, I stood in the wings wishing that it was the end of the day and I was home having a snack and doing my homework. I nervously practiced my lines, pronouncing each and every syllable carefully, just as Mrs. Moon had instructed. The kids were all seated now. The orchestra was starting to play. I saw Jeffrey begin to pull down on the long gray rope that opened the main traveler. I gulped as I heard Mrs. Moon say, "Richard, you're on." When I heard those words, beads of perspiration suddenly began to pour down my face. I could feel the salty sweat accumulating on my upper lip as I stepped forward and into the spotlight. As I reached the center of the stage, I turned toward the audience, just as I had during the three hundred rehearsals we had had over the past few months. In a barely audible voice, I spoke. "Oh boy, it's the . . ." In a fit of pure panic and desperation, I turned toward the wing where I saw Mrs. Moon. I repeated the words she was saying in a hushed tone, "First day of school." Practically choking on the word "school," I made a mad dash for the opposite side of the stage. I heard the rush of a crowd following me into the tiny space behind the curtain. It was the actors who were portraying the rest of the kids on the first day of school. An involuntary sigh of relief escaped from my mouth as my breakfast began its downward descent. I had completed the first step in my quest to become an entertainer. I had made my debut—and to think, since my school was located in New York City, I guess I had actually made my debut on the New York stage! Might as well start at the top!

My next foray into the world of entertainment took place in the ninth grade. Once a year our school put on a major production. The show chosen was always a current or recent Broadway hit. To my delight, that year's production was my all-time favorite, *The King And I*. I could sense the excitement as the school year progressed. Sets were being built, costumes sewn together, and auditions were soon to take place. Knowing inwardly that I could play the lead role, the King of Siam, yet once again not having the guts to audition for the part, I tried out for the role of one of the four Siamese temple priests. The part consisted of stepping out onto the stage near the edge and then bending down in unison with one of the other priests, our knees on the stage and heads bowed as if we were kissing the ground. At this point the curtain would close behind us as the scene ended. We were to remain in place for about thirty seconds like statues guarding the temple. We would then stand up and exit stage right while the other two priests on the opposite end of the stage exited stage left. With two stark white spotlights aimed at each pair of priests this was to have been an effective and dramatic conclusion of the scene.

Some of the costumes were purchased or rented. However, the priests' outfits were to be made by a few of the parents who were talented seamstresses. These moms decided that through the magic of needle and thread they would turn ordinary white bedsheets into exotic priestly robes. Each robe would resemble a Roman toga, but each would have a hood, giving it the solemn appearance of a monk's robe. The hood was to remain on the actor's head throughout the scene. Several times during rehearsal, the director reminded us to make sure that the hood never obscured our vision, since we would be positioned within inches of the edge of the stage. Now I know what you're thinking: the hood covered my eyes and I fell off the stage. No, that didn't happen. But here's what did occur.

The poignant ending of the temple scene went off without a hitch with the four priests remaining on the corners of the stage, each bathed in stark white light. We knelt in prayer as the curtain closed, leaving us in front of it as planned. Following the director's instructions we counted silently to ten, then began to slowly stand up, ready to exit. As I rose I felt a tug on my costume. I looked down and could see the problem. The top portion of the robe had gotten caught in the rope belt around my waist. I tried to free the cloth from the belt's grip but it just wouldn't give. I knew that time was running out. I had no choice but to stand up. As I rose, I could see the top portion of the robe clinging to the belt. A chill hit my bare shoulders. I looked down and saw the robe's upper portion wrapped around my waist. It no longer had the appearance of a priest's robe. Rather, it resembled exactly what it was—a bed sheet. With the stark white spotlight focused on me and me alone, since the others had already left the stage, I stood there in my sleeveless undershirt, the sheet draped around my legs in a shapeless lump. From the sound of the audience's laughter I must have looked like a circus clown wearing an oversized skirt designed for a portly woman. In order to avoid further embarrassment by tripping over the now-defunct costume, I began to pull the twisted sheet up above my ankles. With this graceful move, the audience caught a bird's-eye view of my white Keds high-top sneakers and my crew socks with the red and blue stripes adorning the ankle portion. As the shock of the moment turned into sheer panic, I made a beeline for the wing. I heard the laughter escalate and then die down as I realized that I had created a moment of comic relief at exactly the wrong time in the play.

One of the things I remember most about the show besides my costume malfunction was how all of my senses were affected and became attuned to the goings-on: the assault on my ears as the orchestra would hit a real clunker of a note while warming up, the rustle of costumes backstage, the actors' eyes all exaggerated with an overabundance of eyeliner so as to make them more visible to the audience. But most of all I remember the smells, the scent of makeup mingled with the acrid aroma of hairspray, the pungent odor of a thousand different deodorants, all blending into one enormous sensory experience.

Since I perform alone nowadays I rarely experience this sensory sensation anymore. However, once in a while when Audrey and I attend a Broadway production, as intermission begins I sneak up to the edge of the stage right near the wings. I lean in over the edge of the stage listening carefully, trying to catch a little bit of conversation between the actors. I breathe deeply in the hopes of capturing even just a small bit of that special smell that reminds me of the excitement of acting in live theater. As the lights flicker, indicating that the show is about to resume, the noise from the crowd escalates in anticipation then fades into quiet stillness. I take my seat savoring the wonderful experience. Nothing quite compares to the smell of the greasepaint and the roar of the crowd.

My overwhelming desire to be a part of show business continued throughout my high school years. No matter what I did it had to be a show. My desire to dance manifested itself in my becoming a member of the fencing team. Since the school offered no formal dance training I figured that the next best way to develop grace would be through the sport of fencing. This was, of course, a most unlikely choice of sports for a Jewish kid from New York, but I gave it a shot. As it turned out I loved to fence. I liked the look and feel of the foil in my hand, the fit of the bleached white uniform, the dancelike moves I made when I executed a lunge. When I fenced I envisioned myself as Errol Flynn, the daring swordsman of movie fame. However, I couldn't score a damn point. I really sucked at fencing. But man did I look good in that uniform! At one team victory dinner after everyone was cited for scoring remarkably well in competition, I received honors for my abilities and was voted "the worst fencer with the best form." Years later, while dancing in some regional theater productions, I would include some fencing moves as a part of my preshow stretching routine. I would mentally transport myself back to the school gym where I had executed those fencing moves with grace and agility. I remembered how the team coach had told me that I should pursue a career as a dancer since there was no way in hell that I would ever make it as an Olympic fencer.

A LOVE OF ART

As a kid I had a love affair with pencils. I could spend hours at a clip with a number 2 pencil in hand. Remember those yellow number 2 pencils—the ones with the little black letters that spelled out T-i-c-o-n-d-e-r-o-g-a or D-i-x-o-n on one side of the wooden hexagon? Remember how you'd chew on that pencil during the spelling test? Think back to a day that occurred every September. This was the first day of school. On that special day all of your pencils were new and sharpened to perfection. I remember the burst of anger and disappointment I felt when I'd break one of those new points as it hit the paper. I recall the little pink eraser sitting atop the brass ring on the pencil's end. By the second day of school that eraser had started to lose its perfect shape. By midweek half of it was gone.

I made good use of pencils in those days. For me they were more than just an instrument for writing down a math problem. They were artistic tools. You see, I just loved to draw. As I'd sketch away, those number 2 pencils would grow smaller and smaller and images of sturdy trees, bungalows by the sea, and train tracks traveling into infinity would magically appear. As I drew I sang. The more I drew the more I sang. The more I sang the more I drew. For me it was a vicious cycle of creativity.

I remember how on one occasion I was about to begin a drawing which I was going to enter into an art contest. As I stared at the blank white page in my sketchbook an image began to appear. As forms, shapes, and colors began to take their places on the page I began to recognize what appeared to be a photo from a record album cover I had seen. Within a minute or so, it was clear to me that I was gazing down at a scene from my favorite musical, *The King And I*. There on my pad in all his royal baldness was Yul Brynner, the King of Siam, facing Deborah Kerr, Anna the schoolteacher who had traveled to Siam to educate his children! In total amazement I dropped my pencil. I found myself unable to begin drawing. The image of the king and his lady in the royal palace remained on the page for what must have been the better part of two minutes. Gradually it began to fade, eventually disappearing, leaving the page blank once again. I was now free to begin my drawing.

As I began to draw an ancient barn covered with snow I found myself singing, "Shall we dance? On a bright cloud of music shall we fly, shall we dance?" The powerful music evoked images of faraway Siam. "What a magical place it must be. If only I could see it in person someday," I mused. As I drew I thought, "How wonderful—to make art with my hands and music with my voice, all at the same time. Oh well, I don't think anybody will ever hear me sing, and the chance of me visiting Siam is about as good as me someday writing a book. But maybe, just maybe, someone will see my artwork and applaud. I'll be a professional artist, creating wonderful images on paper—and get paid to do it!" But somewhere back in some recess of my brain was a tugging feeling and the nagging question, "Wouldn't I really rather be on the stage, an actor and singer? Lose that thought. It'll never happen," echoed my brain. But the tug of war continued. "Maybe I can be on the stage someday." We'll see. We'll see.

Yep here I was, a legend in my own mind, yet too embarrassed to let my parents into my world. Feeling threatened by the thought that they might hear me singing and think that I was crazy, I kept my voice down, always singing to myself. There was, and is to this day, a constant stream of music flowing through my brain. If only I had let them in on my secret, perhaps they would have signed me up for music lessons like so many other kids in the neighborhood. I bet I would have excelled in music. After all I knew I had the spark in me, but I stifled it. It was like holding in a sneeze. It was frustration to the max. Why didn't I just tell them? This, I believe, is one of those questions that we ponder as we grow older, and when we finally find the answer it's too late to remedy the situation.

"Boy," I thought, "would I like to see a show, a real Broadway show someday but I probably never will." Even though we lived just a short distance outside of New York City, my folks rarely went to see any of the popular musicals playing in theaters up and down one of New York's most famous streets. It always baffled me to think of all the thousands of visitors who travel from the farthest reaches of the globe to see these productions, and here we were within a stone's throw of them and my parents rarely allowed themselves to experience the wonder that was Broadway. This, I surmise, was due in part to my mom's theory which stated that Broadway musicals were simply ridiculous. More than once I asked her what she meant by this. Her answer was always the same. "Nobody walks down the block and suddenly starts singing." I could never get her to understand that this "ridiculous" behavior was an aspect of theater which enriched our lives by permitting us to escape, if only for a brief period, from real life, and to enter a place where people do break out into song when they're happy or in love or whatever even when they're walking down the street. I know that my dad, who was always quite musical and a bit of a philosopher himself, completely understood. But to prevent World War Three from breaking out in our house, he went along with the program.

When I was not creating some masterpiece of art that all the world would someday clamor for, I would engage in that great American pastime— watching TV.

I hardly ever watched cop shows. They just didn't interest me. I figured I already knew the ending; the bad guys get caught. So why waste a half hour? Now you already know that one of my passions was art. Man, did I love to draw! I was pretty good at it, so one of my favorite shows was the *Jon Gnagy Learn to Draw* program.

Jon Gnagy was the first TV artist. His method was simple. He would draw a scene, usually some trees and mountains, using pencil or charcoal, then demonstrate to the audience how they could draw the same picture using his simple method. Sometimes it was frustrating as hell because my drawing just didn't come out looking exactly like his did. I'm convinced that this show frustrated many folks when they realized that they were not going to be the next Picasso.

I was one of those kids that conned his parents into buying stuff we saw on TV. First I convinced them that I had to have the Jon Gnagy Learn To Draw Kit, which was nothing more than a box which contained every type of art pencil known to man. Then there was the Howdy Doody magic kit with the disappearing rabbit that popped up from the magic hat if you released the rubber band just right. I got the Winky Dink set too. Winky Dink, for those of you too young to know, was a little cartoon guy who kind of bounced all around the television screen. What made this show unique was that if you stuck the magic Wink Dink screen onto your own TV screen, you could draw along with Winky right on your parents' television. Of course you had to send away for the plastic screen which, as I later found out as an adult, was nothing more than a piece of clear acetate tinted green—a precursor to Saran Wrap. It clung to the picture tube by static electricity. How cool was it to draw right on your parents' TV? Real cool until the inevitable day when you couldn't find the stupid magic screen in your bedroom, so you simply drew directly on the picture tube. How many of us shuddered with fright as our parents turned into screaming madmen as they realized that, using our official Winky Dink crayons, we had drawn a circus scene directly onto the screen of their new thirteen-inch TV?

THE BURNING LADY

"Help! I'm a burning lady!" I cried in my highest falsetto voice. "I'm dangling upside down from this building and I'm on fire!" "What are you, crazy?" shouted the kids. "You're gonna fall off those monkey bars and break your head! Hey Gary, look at Richie! He's hanging upside down like a monkey on a swing!"

"Hey man, you're gonna break your ass!" "But I'm a burning person, a toasting marshmallow, a crispy critter!" I shouted. "He's nuts!" they screamed. The crazier I acted, the more attention I got—and I liked it!

"So this is showbiz," I thought. Act like a fool and they'll applaud. I had just learned the secret—and I was only eight. Just do things the others were too embarrassed to do and they'll yell for more. As the song says, "Give 'em the old razzle dazzle, razzle dazzle 'em."

I slowly lowered myself to the ground, heeding their warnings. Determined to make a perfect four-point landing, I executed my version of a gymnast's trampoline dismount. As I hit the ground I was greeted with applause! What a feeling! So this is show business!

Growing up in the Rockaways, the tiny peninsula adjacent to JFK International Airport, was different from the way in which other New York City kids grew up. It was an area that was totally isolated from the rest of the city. My entire childhood was spent just one block away from the chilly waters of the Atlantic Ocean. I used to marvel at the thought that there were actually kids around the country who had never seen an ocean. Yet here I was living with it, during my entire childhood, right at the end of my block!

Shorelines have always symbolized romance. Whitecaps lapping against sand crystals evoke images—thoughts that relax us, easing the tensions of living at our staggering American pace. Time spent by the sea both cleanses and soothes us inside and out. It was like that in Rockaway. None of us seemed to possess the intensity and anxiety of the kids who lived in the other New York boroughs.

My little slice of paradise known as Arverne was located at the midway point of the peninsula. This put our houses and schools directly under the flight path of the giant jetliners departing JFK International Airport. With no thought about noise abatement during those years, no one seemed concerned about the effect this would have on our ears or education. I grew up rarely hearing a teacher complete a sentence. Lessons were all learned as sound bytes, short bursts of language broken by the thunder of an airplane engine. A typical sentence during a lesson sounded something like, "Several species . . . [imagine here the teacher coming to a dead stop midsentence to allow for the rumble of a jet engine just a couple of hundred feet above your head] of this type of monkey [more rumbling] . . . were found on both continents." All of this while your desk and chair were vibrating like a scalp massager with a short circuit.

Living one block from the beach we Rockaway kids prided ourselves on being the first ones in New York City to have a suntan each year. We were the East Coast version of California's surf dudes. What we lacked in sunshine during most of the year, we more than made up for in the summertime. We spent practically every waking minute outdoors. Basketball, handball, swimming, bike riding, hanging out and of course, making out were all-consuming activities for us. We rarely spent any time indoors. And needless to say, a good deal of our time was spent on the beach. We literally baked ourselves out there—every single day.

However, some of my fondest moments occurred during the winter months. I remember many winter pilgrimages to the beach during which I would savor the serenity and surrealism of a beach scene without sunbathers. It was strange not to smell the suntan lotion as concerned mothers smothered their kids in gobs of Coppertone. It was fun to imagine the humming undercurrent of noise as hundreds worshipped the sun, rock and roll music blaring from their little transistor radios. I remember days where the thermometer hovered in the teens as translucent icicles clung stubbornly to the eaves on the little bungalows. On those bitterly cold days, the little gingerbread homes all boarded up against the elements seemed so forlorn, their many layers of paint peeling away, revealing colors from years gone by. I spent hours taking photographs of the stark contrasts that winter brought to these scenes. The dangling icicles glistening in the sun, the seagulls clinging to the frozen piers like medieval gargoyles guarding their perches—a black-and-white still life which remains in the museum of my mind. Photography was an important part of my life during those years. It provided an outlet for creative expression and a thoughtful time during which I could explore my own insights and emotions.

The sand in the winter seemed coarser than it did during the summer months when we raced to the water's edge to cool our parched feet. I enjoyed kicking up remnants of last summer's good times: Coke bottles, the shapely left leg of a Barbie doll, a red plastic shovel long since separated from its pail and five-year-old owner.

Did we ever escape from our peninsula of paradise? Sure. Even natives need a respite from Shangri-La. Each summer my folks would take my brother and me to a not-so-famous resort in the very famous Catskill Mountains in upstate New York. I remember one blistering hot day when my father decided that it might be fun to go on what he referred to as the "adventure trail." This could consist of anything from a two-mile hike through the woods to a trip to the deli counter in the local supermarket. As long as it took us away from our home base, he billed it as an adventure. On this particular day we set out to explore the hotel grounds and its buildings. As we approached the back of one building, my nose discovered a secret. We had stumbled upon the cooks' entrance to the kitchen. Located right behind the main dining room, this was the mystical kingdom that produced one of the highlights of all vacations—the food! The smell of warm muffins and small dinner rolls of varied shapes wafted through the air signaling that it would soon be lunchtime. Lunch? We just finished breakfast! "Dad, how come they're cooking stuff for lunch already?" "It takes a long time to get ready for each meal, so as soon as one's finished they start preparing the next one," he said in an authoritative tone. I, the eight-year-old, was pretty impressed. I figured that my dad knew something about everything. Now that I think back, I believe that he did. (I recently told him this and he agreed!) Hard as it was to leave those enticing aromas, we continued on our safari and soon came upon a large one-level, stucco-clad white building. On the front door, emblazoned on a foot-long brass plaque was the word "Casino." I knew that this was the place that the grown-ups went to each night to see a show while most of us kids were playing some kind of game organized by the counselors or were watching TV until our babysitter forced us to go to bed. I remember the distant sounds of a band and people laughing as I drifted off to sleep, wondering what I was missing and imagining how it would be when I was old enough to go see a show at the casino.

As we approached the door, my father said, "Rich, this is the casino, where all the shows are." "Can we go in?" I asked, with anticipation. "The door's probably locked but let's see." As he raised his arm to reach for the door, my hand shot out and grabbed the doorknob. I quickly turned it and pulled open the massive door. The lights were off but shafts of sun filtering through the screened windows lit up the dance floor like so many klieg lights aimed at a darkened stage. Surrounding the parquet squares in the center of the floor was a carpet whose design was made up of tropical flowers in various shades of blue. I looked at all the empty tables, imagining how the room would look tonight with all the guests sitting there clinking glasses and talking about grown-up stuff.

As I looked toward the front of the room I could see the stage. The curtains on either side were gold. Peeking out from behind them was a second set of curtains in a dark shade of blue. Thousands of glittery specks gave the cloth the appearance of a clear midnight sky strewn with flickering stars. I felt a tingle of excitement as I walked forward. My father followed me up the aisle between the tables and as I approached the stage I could see that the music stands had been set in place for that night's show. Center stage, sitting like a giant monolith, was the drum set. I had seen drums like this on TV but never in person. Not being the gutsy type of kid who would just run up there and sit down behind the drums, I asked if I could go up and try them out. To my dismay, my dad said that he thought this was a bad idea since they were probably all set for the show and that I could mess up the drummer if I moved anything. As we left the casino I looked back at the drums, the cymbals catching the rays of sunlight. "Maybe someday," I thought, "when I'm in a show, the drummer in the band will let me try out his drums—maybe someday."

I remember a "brush with greatness" that had a major impact on my desire to be a part of the entertainment world. It occurred shortly after returning home from our vacation in the Catskills. As Cub Scouts we were taken on several field trips, all designed to mold us into more well-rounded individuals. On one occasion we were taken to Rockaway's Playland, a seaside mini-Disneyland located right in our own backyard. Its clattering old wooden roller coaster had gained fame in a forgettable 1950's movie with a title which I vaguely recall was *So, This Is Cinerama*, or something like that. We were told that at the amusement park we would get to personally meet a child radio star.

Arriving at the park in our freshly pressed blue and gold uniforms the scouts eagerly scrambled out of the bus, anxious to get this annoying star-meeting process over with so they could hop onto some rides. Frankly, I was more excited about meeting the radio kid.

I asked one of the den mothers who the star was. She said that she was not sure of his real name but that on the radio he played a kid named "Jeet." I remember thinking, "What kind of a name is Jeet?" "Okay, I want the whole pack lined up right here!" shouted Mr. Young, the cub master.

As he guided us around a hot dog stand we saw a kid in a Cub Scout uniform standing with two adults whom I guessed were his parents. In the shadow of the cap's bill were two blue eyes which were scanning the crowd as we approached. "Okay, everybody, come on over and meet Jeet," shouted the cub master. We stepped forward and listened politely as Mr. Young told us that Jeet was the star of the radio show called *Meet Jeet*. Turning toward us he asked, "We all listen to the show, don't we?" Not one of us responded. I distinctly remember how bad I felt for the kid. I wanted to lie and yell out, "Oh yeah! What a great show! I listen every week!" but as scouts we were taught never to tell a lie. So like the rest of them, I just stood there. After the embarrassing silence died down a few of the kids stepped forward and shook his hand eager to complete this charade and get over to the rides, where the real action awaited us. I waited until I was last. I stepped up and shook hands. Being shy, it took all the guts I could muster to utter the words, "What's it like to be on the radio?" "It's fun," said Jeet. That's all there was to it. My first personal brush with a real live show business personality and it was over in three seconds. The length of time didn't matter. The experience has lasted a lifetime. As I shook Jeet's hand, I knew that someday someone would shake my hand and ask what it's like to be in show business.

So there I was, Mr. Showbiz, the next Milton Berle, a legend in my own mind living on this little peninsula, waiting for my big break, yet never facing the realization that big breaks don't just show up on your doorstep. It's up to you to make them happen or at least to nudge them along. After all, life is not a dress rehearsal.

Were there other budding stars in Rockaway? Sure—there was Reggie who was a star of New York radio, a child actress who was heard each week on a broadcast that reached all the kids in the New York City schools. She was known as the "Science Girl." Once a week our teacher would tell us to close our books and get ready for a real treat. She'd turn on the big black radio in the corner of the room. When the tubes had warmed up we'd hear a crackling noise followed by the deep baritone of an announcer who would welcome us to this week's science program with our host Reggie Rowe. The next voice we'd hear would be Reggie's. The simple thrill of hearing a fellow classmate on the air was, to us, a miracle. The program's lesson made little difference to us. More important was that our class had a star on the radio. As I listened I envisioned myself being listened to by an audience and longed for the day that like Reggie, I too would be a star.

THE TIMES, THEY WERE A-CHANGIN'

Rev up the time machine. It's the '60's—a time for peace, love, flower power, and hair (lots of it). Exclamations of "Oh wow, man!" were heard in conversations between everyone from age sixteen to twenty-nine. We were told never to trust anyone over thirty. In an obvious drug reference, they say that if you remember the sixties you weren't there.

I do remember the sixties and I was there. Vietnam was beginning to heat up. There I was, Joe College, or should I say Joe Half College. You see, I had this two-year degree, an associate in applied science degree they called it. I called it half a degree. When graduation day arrived they handed me a diploma with the words "applied science" on it. "Science?" I thought to myself. I didn't know one end of a Bunsen burner from the other! What I had learned was how to draw ads for magazines, books, record album covers, and just about anything else that needed artwork. They had taught me what they called commercial art—how to do magazine layouts and choose lettering styles. Nobody in my class ever pictured himself lying on his back painting the ceiling of some chapel in Italy or doing a portrait of some lady with a half smile. What we learned to produce was art designed to convince someone to purchase a product. Why they called that applied science, I'll never understand. Anyway my AAS (not ASS) degree was really one-half of a bachelor's degree in disguise. I figured it would serve the purpose of getting me a job in the art field, since at job interviews all they really wanted to see was your art portfolio. After nervously applying to virtually every ad agency in New York, something finally clicked. I landed my first job as a commercial artist. Imagine that! Me, a real artist working in New York City, the pulse of the nation's advertising heart. I guess the Jon Gnagy kit worked. I had learned how to draw and now I was a commercial artist!

The ad agency gave me my own little studio space with a draftsman's desk, the slanted kind that all the pros used. This, I declared, would be the desk on which I would produce the greatest and most creative advertisements known to man. Throw the product at me and I'll design an ad that will sell millions of those widgets, stereos, or slow-cooking electric Crock-Pots. My little haven in the studio was located in a corner with not one but two windows, one in front of me and one on the side. Natural daylight, an artist's dream! And to add icing to the cake this little kingdom looked out on New York's most famous and prestigious advertising alley, Madison Avenue.

The building I worked in was not one of those giants for which New York is famous. Rather, it was a six-story blue building, probably the only all-blue office building in New York. My studio was on the fifth floor. If I looked down I could see the New York advertising types walk by sporting their Beatle haircuts and mod fashions right out of London's Carnaby Street shops. Their form-fitting sports jackets accented by broad white stripes announced to the world that they were a part of the advertising elite. I am embarrassed to say that I still have one of those jackets. I now wear it during some of my shows, the ones with a carnival theme. The kids in the audience laugh at it calling it a clown coat.

Yeah I was a hotshot New York artist—or so I thought. My first day on the job the art director approached me with a sheet of letters that had some sticky stuff on the back. He told me that I had to paste them onto a layout in the little squares on the bottom of the page, making sure that they were all lined up properly for the printer. I wondered if this was how Michelangelo got his start. Well folks, it never got any better. I quickly realized that to make it in this field and actually get to draw an ad, I would have to spend months, perhaps years, pasting these stupid little letters onto a layout that had been created by someone else. I sat back at my thoroughly professional drawing desk and began to softly hum some Broadway show tunes.

I pasted up hundreds of letters over the next few months, all the while formulating a plan, a method of escape. As I pasted my days away, the anxiety about leaving created a great deal of stress. I knew that I had to take action, to leave the world of advertising or I'd explode. It was now the mid-1960's. The TV and newspapers seemed to be covering one and only one story—the war in Vietnam. As we ate dinner the nightly news force-fed us body counts and detailed descriptions of battles fought in places whose names became part of the English lexicon. The sounds of DaNang, ChuLai, and Hanoi became familiar to our ears. Through the glass eye of the camera we witnessed the destruction of objects, enemies, and friends. We prayed that the uniformed body in the newsreel was not that of our former school chum, neighbor, or cousin. There was no flower power here. Because of my age and nonstudent status I was ripe for the pickin'—a perfect candidate for the draft. I knew that before long Uncle Sam would snatch me away from my drafting table and replace my pencil with an M-16.

There were three types of young Americans in those days. There were the Protesters. There were the Participants. And there were the members of the "I don't know what the hell we're doing in some place I never heard of until Walter Cronkite mentioned it on the evening news" group. The Protestors voiced their feelings about U.S. involvement in Vietnam by either waving banners and screaming a lot or running away to some country just north of ours where no one ever heard of the word war. The Participants got involved in the war by either getting drafted or joining the military. The third bunch seemed to be professional students racking up degrees by the handful, suddenly switching their majors to education since the government was not drafting anyone studying to be a teacher. I was not a Protestor. I knew that I wasn't destined to be a perennial student and had no desire to become a teacher. Furthermore, I naively figured that if my government got us involved in a war it was the right thing to do. After all, I reasoned, they must know what they're doing—running the country was their full-time job.

UP, UP, AND AWAY!

One thing I knew for sure. I didn't want to get drafted. I would become a Participant, but on my own terms. I would join the air force. Why the air force? Because I liked airplanes. I had always enjoyed building those little plastic model airplanes as a kid, so getting to actually fly in the real ones might be even more fun. They wished me luck at the ad agency and even threw me a little going-away party, calling me Fly Boy.

Since there were no air force bases in the New York City area for the new recruits to report to prior to basic training, I was told to report to an army base, Fort Hamilton in Brooklyn as my point of departure. From there I would be shuttled to a New York airport where I would be flown to Lackland Air Force Base in San Antonio, Texas. There I would be molded into an airman, the official designation of a person serving in the U.S. Air Force. On the day I reported to Fort Hamilton I was one of the few not facing the trauma of losing his Beatle-like locks. The reason for this was that even though I was an artist, I never really looked like one. I was just too conservative. Oh I guess my clothes fit in with the New York advertising scene, but I never sported the long hair an artist was expected to wear. As a matter of fact, I still had Gus, my barber from Queens, give me a crew cut just as he had since I was nine.

We were truly a ragtag army of "rainbows" as they called the new recruits. Just imagine a group of thirty brash young New Yorkers in a dazzling array of multicolored psychedelic outfits. As we assembled, one guy with extremely long blond locks pointed toward his foot, bragging loudly about his custom-made Beatle boots. I couldn't help but glance down at what was probably the ugliest pair of red leather boots I had seen in my life. What a motley, disheveled crew of rainbows we were!

We all knew that just a plane ride away, the red boots and tie dyed tee shirts would be replaced by the latest fashions that Uncle Sam had to offer

41

in his spring collection. We were told by the sergeant in charge of our little ragamuffin squadron that we should all be seated and that within a few minutes we would be boarding the plane that would whisk us off to Lackland Air Force Base in San Antonio for basic training. It was then that I had my first exposure to the military's "hurry up and wait" policy. After about an hour and a half of sitting in chairs which felt like vinyl-covered stone I closed my eyes and yawned. My four-second reverie was broken by the piercing sound of a powerful voice shouting, "You, airman. Get up here!" I glanced around then looked at the front of the room. Pointing directly at me was the sergeant who had given us our instructions. I quietly performed the old school routine, looking around and saying, "Who me?" "Yes you." He motioned for me to come forward. All eyes in the room were on me as I quickly approached the sergeant. Pulling me aside he read me the official U.S. Air Force riot act ending with, "And if you're too tired or bored with this whole procedure maybe you don't belong in the air force. Perhaps we should call your recruiter and have him cancel your enlistment." At that moment all I could think of was the alternative. I'd go home, get drafted and end up in a trench in Southeast Asia. After apologizing profusely for my indiscretion I sheepishly returned to my stone and vinyl seat, sat down and remained motionless for the next forty-five minutes. Finally there was an announcement over the loudspeaker directing us to board our bus to the airport. I hopped onto the bus glad to escape the wrath of Sergeant Terror. As we pulled away from the curb I could see him gazing out of the large glass window. He seemed to be staring straight at me. Upon arriving at the airport we were directed to take seats in the terminal to wait for the call to board our plane. With that boarding call, I embarked on the four-year adventure of a lifetime.

As our plane taxied into Dallas Love Airport on that hot May evening, I thought of the old saying "Everything's big in Texas." No sooner had we entered the airport when I spotted not more than a foot in front of my shoe, the biggest and ugliest bug I had ever seen. Now we New Yorkers often enjoy bragging about the indestructibility of our world-famous cockroaches and the enormity of our water bugs, but this baby had them all beat. Just slightly shorter than the tail section of the plane we had just arrived in, this monster must have sensed my trepidation as he slowly began his journey toward my left foot. With the grace and agility of a member of the Alvin Ailey Dance Company, I quickly performed a step that is used by the Radio City Rockettes precision dance team during their Christmas show. My move must have scared the hell out of that insect. I last saw him exiting the terminal at the speed of light. Welcome to Texas. Everything here is big.

As I sat scrunched against the wall of the large blue military bus which drove us out to the base, I mulled over how the recruiting process works. First of all I had read the recruiting pamphlets. With their slick glossy covers they were hard to ignore and they were designed to entice. They promised worldwide travel, adventure, career choices, and education at the expense of the U.S. government. What a deal. They even listed a career field called "photographer!" Just pass the exam and off you go into the wild blue yonder!

Doubts crossed my mind. Could I pass the exam? I knew that if I did, the next four years would be an adventure. I would train to become an official air force photographer. After all, hadn't my recruiter practically guaranteed that with my art background I'd get that job with no problem? I reasoned that if I could draw something I certainly could photograph it. It would be a snap. (Sorry about the pun.)

One way or another I survived basic training. This included a heat rash in an area no self-respecting airman would attempt to scratch while standing at attention. By the final week of training I had been molded into a true-blue airman. I then received my first assignment and learned a lesson: Never believe a military recruiter. He's a used-car salesman in uniform. I remember my recruiter saying, "With your artistic skills, they'll put you right into the air force photojournalism school in Denver." Yeah. Right. Two months later, I landed at Dover Air Force Base, Delaware. Sure Dover and Denver both begin with the letter "D," but as I soon found out there was a vast difference between the two places.

"Welcome to the Supply Squadron. These white index cards here are marked AWP. That means 'awaiting parts.' These blue ones are marked NIS. That means 'not in stock.' The white ones get placed in this bin. The blue ones go over there. That's your job—for the next four years. Welcome to the U.S. Air Force."

My immediate reaction was, "NO WAY, JOSE!" I was not going to spend four years doing this. My next thought was to devise a plan to get a job as a photographer as quickly as I could before going either insane or AWOL.

My first stop was at the office of the base chaplain. I told him that I was extremely unhappy and that for some unknown reason both the air force and God had refused to answer my prayers about becoming a photographer. I guess the part about how God had disappointed me really got to him. Great! So far the plan was working. I had little trouble convincing him that my desperation was real. He listened and recognizing the anxiety and despair in my voice, he called the photo lab on the base and informed the sergeant in charge of the lab that sitting with him was the world's greatest photographer!

I didn't know and really didn't care where that came from, but thanks to the chaplain's divine intervention, I was soon reassigned to the base photo lab.

I immediately began shooting pictures, developing film, and having a ball. Apparently the air force liked my work. Within a few months, I began receiving assignments to shoot major news-making events on the base. Whenever anything newsworthy happened, I was there, posing and photographing generals, heads of state, and just about anybody else of interest who visited the base. Of course I didn't get every choice assignment. On one occasion, after taking some pictures of a damaged runway, I returned to the photo lab to be told that one of the guys had covered an assignment I probably would have enjoyed. They said that a ventriloquist named Jimmy Nelson, who was famous for his work on TV, had performed in the base theater. His dog puppet Farfel was the one that sang the Nestlé's chocolate commercial on television. Jimmy's son, Lee, who was stationed on the base, had made arrangements for his dad to do a little show for the guys. I was sorry I missed that assignment. Little did I know that more than three decades later I would meet Jimmy Nelson who, each year at the ventriloquist's convention, would offer me encouragement and advice regarding my own career as a performer.

The majority of photo assignments were not at all glamorous. I shot pictures of barracks windows that had been jarred open during a midnight break-in, close-ups of faulty nuts and bolts on an airplane wing, and other mundane objects. However, some assignments were much more interesting. I even got to do some medical photography. I remember the first time I took some close-ups of an airman's intestines during an operation. That pretty well convinced me that medical photography would be better left to someone who did not mind blood spurting up onto his new Nikon lens.

The assignment to photograph a crime scene involving a suicide provided my introduction to forensic photography. I was escorted to the scene by an air policeman. As I approached the room, carrying my official air force Speed Graphic camera (remember those big press cameras you see in the old movies?) and a pocketful of giant M5 flashbulbs, I saw people scurrying around, each with some sort of gas mask covering his or her mouth. Within seconds the acrid stink hit me. "Here, put this on before you go in there," a woman said as she handed me one of the masks. I turned to my police escort and asked him who she was. "The state pathologist," he answered, putting on a mask as he spoke. I approached the room knowing that death hung heavy in the air, yet not knowing quite what to expect or what I would be photographing. I told myself that no matter what the subject is these pictures had better turn out okay. They were evidence and this was a crime scene which could not be photographed again. I braced myself, entered the room and began to photograph the scene. I started shooting from my immediate left then continued, focusing in on each new shot as I panned to the right. My goal was to create a panorama of what lay before me. By overlapping adjoining areas, I would be sure to get full coverage of the entire room. Never removing my eye from the camera's viewfinder, I witnessed the horror unfold. It was a scene of sadness, reflecting the tragic end of a young man's life. As I aimed farther to the right, I could see the edge of a pornographic montage come into view. Tacked on each wall were magazine photos of nude women in seductive poses. The edges of the magazine pages had been carefully trimmed as if they were destined for use in a magazine layout. Their precise placement on the walls indicated that the airman had given careful consideration to creating this museumlike display. Once again shifting my camera ever so slightly to the right, the end of the gray metal air force bed came into view. I held my breath as my camera continued its journey. A shoeless foot came into view. In an attempt to look like a professional crime scene photographer I fought off the urge to shudder. But I could barely stop from shaking as I saw the body on that bed come into view. Even through the mask which clung tightly to my nose and mouth, I could smell an intense odor that grew stronger each minute.

Unable to resist the urge to view the entire scene, I lowered the camera. No Hollywood set portraying a drug-induced suicide could be more accurate in detail than what was before me. No training film for forensic photographers could more realistically depict the depravity of what I witnessed. On the bed were several pharmaceutical bottles containing pills of various shapes and sizes. Three or four sexually explicit magazines lay strewn on the bedsheets. In the midst of these glossy publications lay the partially clothed body of the young airman. The most striking thing was that his pants could barely contain his body. The corpse looked like an overinflated balloon on the verge of exploding. I turned to the cop next to me and asked what had happened. He said that the airman's roommate had returned from a two-week leave and found that he was unable to open the door. Since the room was on the ground floor, he figured that he could gain entry through the window on the other side of the barracks. He went around to the back side of the building, pushed the window up, and crawled into the room. Shock and horror had assaulted his senses as he turned the light on.

Having completed a series of general shots of the whole room, it was time to begin shooting close-ups. I moved closer to the bed and began to photograph the upper torso. It was at this point that I could see movement in the face. I jumped back when I realized that what I was viewing were maggots eating their way through the body. According to the police officer, this was an indication that the body had been laying here for some time—perhaps, a good portion of the time that the roommate was away. Secure in the knowledge that I had photographed every conceivable aspect of the crime scene, I packed up my equipment and headed for the door, anxious to rid myself of the uncomfortable mask and escape the pervasive stink. I exited the room thinking, "Man, this is photography from hell."

Although certain assignments were heartbreaking or even gut-wrenching experiences, I thoroughly enjoyed serving as an air force photographer. While others were tied to their daily tasks of boiling potatoes or filing index cards I bounced around all over the base from assignment to assignment creating images of others at work—images which later that week would appear in the base newspaper with a caption proclaiming that these airman were the best at boiling potatoes or filing index cards for the air force. I had one of the coolest jobs in the air force—outside of being a pilot that is. After shooting an assignment, I took great pleasure in rushing back to the base photo lab to complete the process. Here in the lab with its familiar pungent smells, I would stare into a metal tray filled to the brim with chemicals. I would place an eight-by-ten-inch sheet of light-sensitive paper into the tray and within a few seconds the wizardry would begin. As I gently shook the tray creating miniature waves, the very image that I had photographed just hours before would appear on the paper. Anticipation mounted as I envisioned my photo, later that week appearing on the front page of the base newspaper with the little byline just below and to the right saying, "Photo by Air Force Sergeant Richard Berger." This was one cool job!

Delaware was an okay place in which to be stationed. It was a state whose fortune and fame stemmed from the Dupont family's leadership in the chemical industry. During my two years at Dover Air Force Base, I, too, was involved with chemicals: photo chemicals. I spent hours and hours sloshing my hands through acidic baths all in the name of producing photos for the air force. I remember the countless hours spent alone in the dark, just me and the music on my transistor radio as I agitated containers filled with rolls of film immersed in the liquids that turned the little strips of acetate into negatives. The sound of the moving liquid seemed to blend with the tunes on the radio until they became one. I would envision myself standing on a darkened stage, lit only by a single spotlight as I sang to the accompanying melody. As the waves of liquid washed over the film I could hear the thunderous roar of the audience. I would raise my arms in a gesture of gratitude.

The large black timer on the wall with its glowing radium dial buzzed loudly. The spell was broken. The signal had been given that the film was now fully developed and should be removed from the chemical bath.

During those days I often felt a void, a need for more recognition, more action. Sometimes I would make things—craftlike items which filled my need to create something with my hands. It was at one of those moments that Ralphie was born.

At the end of each day we would air out the darkroom to rid it of the chemical odors that permeated the air. The one main problem here was that the door would not stay open by itself. I decided that I could rectify this situation by building the best doorstop known to man. The solution was simple. I grabbed a roll of the world's most indestructible material, duct tape, and began the lengthy process of ripping off pieces and sticking them to each other. Each day I'd spend a few minutes adding layer upon layer of tape onto the lump that would someday become the official Dover Air Force Base Photo Lab doorstop. After a few weeks, my creation was large enough to hold the door open. However, being an artist, I felt that it needed some final touches. As I stared at the gray blob before me I noticed that it resembled a rat. Using a marker, I drew eyes, a nose, and a large mouth on the rodent. It seemed to be crying out for a name. "Ralphie the Rodent" seemed appropriate. "Okay Ralphie do your job," I said, as I gently placed my little friend against the bottom corner of the darkroom door. The door stayed firmly in place. My invention worked and I was pleased. I was the last one out of the lab that night. I walked back to the barracks believing that I had created a masterpiece of industrial design. What I had created, in essence, was a puppet. Little did I realize that Ralphie was a part of my life's puzzle.

The following morning all of the photographers arrived at the lab, said the usual good-morning greetings and then approached the bulletin board where our boss, Sergeant Douglas, had posted the day's assignments. A couple of the guys grabbed some rolls of film to be processed and headed for the darkroom. As they approached the door I heard a cry of, "Holy crap. There's a goddamned rat holding the door open!" I saw the sarge whiz by with a broom in his hand as he headed toward the screaming. Then there was dead silence. It didn't take them long to figure out who was the creator of our newest member of the photo lab gang. As the realization hit, the guys started to laugh and then, of course, turned toward me. "Berger, did you make that f—n' thing?" "Man you are out of your mind," said one of the guys. That was an understatement.

After that Ralphie became a regular member of the lab's crew. He celebrated birthdays with us and when some lieutenant would show up to inspect the lab, we stood him on end so he'd stand at attention with the rest of us.

For the most part, my assignment as an air force photographer was eventful and exciting, but as in any job there were days that failed to raise my spirits. I recall one of those days when I felt sort of empty. Boredom had set in, and I just couldn't shake it. On that day I was facing a full eight hours of working in the darkroom. I was especially annoyed, knowing that I was stuck inside becoming paler by the minute instead of being outside getting a glowing tan in the hot Delaware sun. I got to work "souping" (which means developing) my film, a group of shots that I had taken the previous day. The photos showed a damaged aircraft engine, which had been rendered inoperable due to a bent bolt.

I had just removed the negatives from their chemical bath and was busily occupying myself singing a Beach Boys tune about surfing in Hawaii when the phone rang. It was Jerry, the editor of the base newspaper. He sounded a little excited as he described his latest foray into the world of news journalism. Paying more attention to the song in my head than to Jerry, I half-listened as he blurted out something about a really cool assignment. He said that he had considered all of the photo guys on the base and that I was the one photographer whom he knew could do the job, so he wanted me to take all the pictures for his article. Receiving that compliment provided just the little jolt that I needed to brighten the day, rekindle my enthusiasm, and pull me out of my state of boredom. I listened carefully as Jerry described the assignment being offered to me.

His emphasis on the words "cool assignment" had peaked my curiosity. I soon found out what that was all about. The story had something to do with a group of meteorologists who provided weather forecasts for the air force. "Oh boy," I mused, "just slightly more exciting than the airplane engine photos." But things changed as he spoke of how we would be documenting the lives and work of a small group of Danish weathermen who lived far up north, tracking weather patterns for half of the globe. It wasn't so much the weather part that interested me but the fact that these guys were able to survive in one of the coldest and most barren pieces of real estate on the entire planet. The air force based a good deal of its flight patterns and times on their information. Nord, the little outpost from which they dispatched the weather information was located in of all places Thule, Greenland. Now I got the "cool" reference he had made. He said that we'd stay in Greenland for about a week and would be living with these guys and reporting on how they survived in a place that was starkly barren and as he described it, "freeze your ass off" cold. Do you remember from geography class that Greenland is referred to as the "Land of the Midnight Sun?" That's because it's light there for six months of the year, all day and all night! No break. All the time! Then for six months it's dark there, all day and all night! No break. All the time.

I knew that this would probably be the only time in my life I'd get to see that part of the world. I had one question for Jerry, "Would we be there during the all-day or the all-night period?" "All sun, all the time," said Jerry. I told him that the idea sounded "cool." He laughed. I said that I'd pack my snowshoes and that he should count me in.

The morning of our departure arrived. I had packed my heavy air force parka, the one with the fur around the hood. That jacket weighed more than I did. As we walked toward the giant cargo-carrying C-141, I could see its albatrosslike wings dipping until they almost touched the ground. I always loved that airplane. It was one of the most dignified and aesthetically pleasing aircraft ever flown. Every time I got on board I felt so proud to be a part of America's air team.

As we flew through the clouds I reveled in the thought that I was traveling to a part of the world few people would ever see. We flew over glaciers as tall as some of Manhattan's skyscrapers. At one point I called the pilot's attention to a glittering piece of silver on the very top of one of the glaciers. Could it be that I had discovered the lost airplane of Amelia Earhart? I asked if we could circle around and fly lower so that I could get some shots. He agreed and began circling as we descended. Then, just as we leveled off, he completely deflated my ego by calmly announcing that I was viewing a World War II aircraft that had crashed here during the war and had never been removed from the glacier. It had become sort of a pilot's buoy, a marker that all of the flyers in this area used as a landmark to determine their location. It might not have been Amelia Earhart's plane but to me it was an exciting discovery, the likes of which I would probably never see again. I was totally enthralled with the tundralike landscape of Greenland. It truly was a living Ansel Adams still life.

During most of the day at the base station there was deafening silence. Suddenly the silence would be broken by a distant sound cutting through the frigid air. You could sense the excitement growing as the sound grew louder. A tiny speck would appear on the horizon. As the noise intensified it began to resemble the barking of dogs. The tiny speck would evolve into a shadowy mass. Within minutes we could spot several teams of sleds being pulled by very large dogs. I would raise my camera, which during that two-week period never left my hand. There's nothing quite like photographing a galloping team of gigantic huskies racing toward you at breakneck speed pulling a sled full of supplies through snow so pure and white that the camera's lens demands to squint just as I do from the glare. The dogs, although frighteningly large, were some of the friendliest animals I had ever encountered. They had a playful sense of humor and willingly engaged in a game of tag with us. When it came to taking pictures of them they were absolute hams. The minute I raised my camera they would stop and pose right on cue.

Of course, the subzero weather did bring with it several photographic challenges. There was the time my camera completely froze up and refused to go "click," giving me a ready excuse to go inside and, while waiting for it to defrost, have some hot chocolate and Danish. This, of course, provided an endless source of jokes about eating Danish, since the base camp and weather station was run by a group of Danes. And then there was the problem that would not go away. During my weeklong stay, the sun shined brightly twenty-four hours a day. I often found myself waking up at two in the morning with the sun glaring through my window. One sunlit evening, using some brilliant military strategy, I remedied this situation by simply placing my pillow on the windowsill so that the pillow covered the window. However, this creative move resulted in my not having a pillow on my bed. After searching every closet in the weather station, I was told that there was a shortage of pillows. Since I could not find a replacement, I varied my sleeping situation, sometimes enjoying the luxury of the pillow beneath my head and squinting through the night. At other times, I suffered through a pillowless night but savored the delicious darkness.

Somehow I survived. Did I really mind this small inconvenience? Of course not. This was a unique experience in my life, and I treated it as such, treasuring every minute. All too quickly, the assignment came to end and I was flying back to Delaware, rolls and rolls of undeveloped film packed securely in my photo bag. I had documented the essence of Nord, the mystical weather station at the top of the world, and I had the photos to prove it. The trip had been a unique experience, but I was kind of glad to be returning to a place where I was able to tell day from night and pillows were not in short supply.

Greenland wasn't the only exciting place that I visited. Come with me on my next adventure.

"Hey Jack, let's go to Japan!" With that sentence an odyssey began. Jack was a fellow photographer in the base photo lab. Like me, he had a sense of adventure. We agreed that we should take advantage of every minute of our four years in the air force, seeing, doing, and photographing everything we could. We both viewed our years in the service as an opportunity to experience things we might never have a second shot at. Jack agreed with me that Japan would be a great destination, but practically impossible to get to since we were not members of a flight crew. However, one option did exist. That was the possibility of catching a "hop" with one of the crews. This was the sky version of hitchhiking. Just about once a day a flight crew would arrive at the photo lab requesting photos of themselves for identification purposes in case their plane went down during a mission. Whenever I asked them where they flew to besides Vietnam, they'd always say, "Japan." They'd proudly show me the new Seiko watches on their wrists or talk about the great shots they got with their Nikon cameras, never failing to comment on how inexpensive those items are in Japan since that's where they're made.

We decided to approach one of the pilots and tell him that we were willing to use some of our leave time for the trip and were more than willing to share some of our photos with them once we had returned. We invited a few of them to bring their families to the photo lab during off hours so we could take family portraits. Once they started to arrive in droves we were a little sorry we had made the offer, but nevertheless we followed through with the project. One of the pilots agreed to let us come along with him and the crew on their next R and R (rest and relaxation) trip to Japan. Within a couple of weeks we were heading skyward on a C-141 Starlifter cargo plane bound for Japan.

From the moment we landed we realized that this trip was going to be one of the highlights of our careers as air force photographers. Never without our cameras, we photographed what seemed like every person, statue, monument, and reflecting pool in the country.

Our week in Japan flew by in a flash, and we knew we had better get back to the States or we'd be declared AWOL. Assuming that catching a military hop back to Dover Air Force Base would be as easy as getting one to Japan had been, we packed our stuff, checked out of the small Hotel Utage in downtown Tokyo, and bussed our way to the airport. Looking up at the board listing military departures, we thought that getting home would be no problem. There were plenty of flights bound for the East Coast, with several leaving within the next few hours. In fact, many of them were headed right for our base in Delaware. Carefully seating ourselves right up front in the terminal so that all departing flight crews could see us in our best dress blue uniforms, we embarked upon what turned out to be a nightmare. After four or five hours of politely asking pilots bound for Dover if they had any room for two military photographers who wanted to return to the States, it became painfully obvious that getting a hop back might be more difficult than we had bargained for. In fact, after a full day of trying, we realized that we were in trouble.

Day turned into night, which turned into day again. As each new day began, we were feeling weaker and weaker, dirtier and dirtier. With no showers in the terminal, we resorted to quick washups at the sinks in the restrooms. It had now been four days of confinement in the airport, hour after hour spent in search of a flight crew willing to take us home. By this point, we were really sick of airport food, but having no other choice, we just kept slugging it down to keep from starving. On the evening of the fourth day, a pilot we recognized walked by our seats. Before we could get up to approach him with our sad tale, he suddenly stopped dead in his tracks. Executing a perfect military about-face, he returned to where we were sitting. With what little strength and stamina we had left in us, we jumped to our feet, standing at attention. Before we could utter the word "sir," he said, "Hey, aren't you guys from Dover?" With eyes glazed from lack of sleep, we answered, "Yes, we are, sir. And can you please take us back to the base?" We even promised to shoot eight-by-ten glossies of him, his crew, family, his dog—anyone—if he could just get us back to our base before the air force declared us AWOL. "Sure, I'll take you back, but we don't have any extra seats. You see, this is a flight from Vietnam, and we're bringing home some of the fellas killed in the war. You know, the East Coast morgue is at Dover, so that's our destination. If you don't mind, you'll have to sleep on the floor between the coffins. Is that okay?" At this point, a couple of things crossed my mind. I could hear my superstitious mother going nuts over the prospect of me sleeping between the coffins. And second, one of my childhood friends had been killed during his first week of army duty over there. Could he perhaps be in one of those coffins? At this point, it didn't seem to matter. We had to get back home.

We said that we were more than glad to accept his offer. It was a long flight and quite different from any that I had ever taken. Sleep came easy to us after our ordeal, but every so often I'd wake up and glance around at the coffins, wondering if I knew any of the guys lying in them. I thought of the possibility that God had, for some reason, chosen us to be their escorts on their last journey home. After flying for nineteen hours, we touched down in Delaware. Luckily, the air force officials allowed us to claim a few extra days of leave, so we never were charged with being AWOL.

Dover Air Force Base fell under the auspices of the Military Airlift Command, which the air force referred to as MAC. As the principal MAC base for the East Coast, all supplies and personnel bound for the war in Southeast

Asia flew out of Dover. In addition, because the base was home to the East Coast morgue, all military personnel who had been killed in the war were returned to the morgue at Dover prior to their bodies being turned over to their families. About a week after fellow photographer Jack and I returned from Japan, I was assigned to photograph the morgue for a story the air force was running about its role in returning the bodies of military personnel to their loved ones. As I photographed the vast array of coffins, each placed precisely in line with the next one, I realized how lucky I was to be serving stateside and how Jack and I were the only two passengers in the cargo portion of the mighty C-141 aircraft that were alive that day.

My military experiences were vast and varied. There was the near-death experience flying through a monsoon in Taipei on a decrepit, shaky old C-130, an airplane that had no right to be in the sky. Then there was the weekend spent in one of the nation's most strategic locations, Miami Beach, courtesy of the Air National Guard. For the members of the guard, it was to be a training mission. However, for an air force photo buddy and me, it was all fun, since we had merely caught a hop with the crew to Miami. At the airport, we met the entertainer Wayne Newton. Seeing us in uniform, he thanked us for serving our country. I mumbled something to him about my desire to enter show business when I got out of the service. He offered me a few kind words of encouragement, but no offers to join his act. Miami was terrific, but before we knew it, we were back on the plane heading up the coast and back to the daily grind on the airbase.

One hot Delaware day, as I walked along the narrow sidewalks on the base, I spotted a small sign posted on a bulletin board just outside the dining hall. It offered an off-duty job to help build a model railroad. It paid two bucks an hour and refreshments during breaks. Such a deal! I took the number down and called the guy. A Mr. Bowman answered in a resoundingly deep voice, reminiscent of an old-time radio announcer. He said that his dad needed some help in setting up a miniature railroad on his farm, a kind of postretirement project. "Well," I thought, "that sounds like fun, putting all the little bridges and buildings in place." Mr. Bowman explained that the railroad was not as small as I had envisioned. In fact, each of the cars would be large enough to hold a kid or two. He planned on laying out about two and half miles of track so the ride would encircle a part of their farm. The idea sounded flaky to me, but if this guy was going to build the next Disneyland, I wanted in on the deal. Besides, I could use the extra spending money. After all, the air force salary was not quite placing me in the status of the Rockefellers. Since I had no car on base, there was no way for me to get out to the farm. This part was easy. I simply announced to some of my fellow photo buddies (the ones with cars) that I had a tip on the biggest employment opportunity of the decade. They all applied for the job and were hired. That Saturday morning the four of us began our Tom Sawyer adventure.

The farm was just a couple of miles from the base. To me, a kid from New York, it looked immense. With acreage as far as the eye could see, it offered the kind of view that is fast disappearing from the American landscape in favor of shopping malls and condominium complexes.

Once we got the lay of the land, summer evenings and weekends were dedicated to "workin' on the railroad." Although the project was, in essence, the creation of an amusement park ride, the tracks were full scale and pretty heavy to move into place. The ties were monsters too. In order to weatherproof them, each and every one had to be soaked in creosote, just as regular railroad ties are. Then each one had to be carefully placed on the bed of sand and soil we had built up, so that the sections of track could then be nailed onto them. John, Mr. Bowman's son, was our boss. A tall, sinewy heavily tanned guy in his late twenties, sporting an Elvis hairdo, he was the epitome of the word stickler. We soon learned that his mission was to make sure that each of us laid every tie in perfect unison with the previous one, ensuring that the track would sit firmly in place. This would prevent derailments, which could result in lawsuits launched by some kid's parents. This railroad was as much his baby as his father's.

One morning, I spent four hours driving the farm tractor around dropping off ties every few feet so that later that day we could begin nailing the ties onto the track we had laid the day before. Imagine that! Me driving a tractor! I got pretty good at driving that old John Deere. That is until the day I came too close to a ditch and nearly ended up another farm accident statistic. That afternoon, with the hot sun beating down on us, we pounded hundreds of four-inch-long spikes into the ties. Needing a break after two hours under the scorching sun, with my arm feeling as if it were about to fall out of its socket, I approached John and asked him what his father had done prior to undertaking this bold endeavor. John's answer surprised me. He told me that his dad had retired after years as a high-ranking executive with AT&T. He said that he had always harbored the dream of someday building a railroad for kids. When he retired, he bought the farm and plotted out just where his dream would materialize. He had located an amusement park that was going out of business and bought the cars, track, and ties from them. He then purchased whatever else he needed to bring his dream to life, brought it all to the farm, hired us, and the rest is history. I truly admired this guy.

He took a dream, turned it into a goal and persued it. He understood that life is not a dress rehearsal.

As the summer drew to a steamy close, we sped up our pace in order to accomplish as much as we could before packing away our tools. We anxiously anticipated next year when we would aim for completion of the project. Our year on the base whizzed by, and in a flash, spring flowers began to cover the surrounding fields. On my calendar, I noticed a note I had penciled in, a reminder to call John about setting up a work schedule to continue building the greatest little railroad of the twentieth century.

John received my call with eager anticipation in his voice. We agreed that as soon as the days grew long enough for us to spend a couple of hours working on the farm at the end of each workday on the base, we would resume our railroad project. Within a few weeks, we returned to the farm. As the days grew longer, we found ourselves working harder and harder to beat our self-imposed deadline, which was to complete the railroad by summer's end. By working ourselves into a lather each day, plus a few weekends, we were able to achieve our goal. By mid-August, we completed the final loop of railroad tracks, which by that time fully encircled the farm. We had even added in a few fancy figure eights, which gave some variety to the little journey the train would travel as it made its trip around the farm and through the shady woods which dotted portions of the landscape. When the last railroad tie was laid down and the final spike driven into the wood, a celebration took place to honor our hard work and commitment to the project. Mr. Bowman gathered us around his swimming pool and served enough food and drink to satisfy a hungry army. It had been a couple of summers to remember and quite an experience for a city kid whose only experience with farms had been to read about them in school.

The following year, the air force sent me overseas to play my part in the Vietnam War. During my year overseas, and even during my fourth and final year stateside, I often thought about my experience helping Mr. Bowman—a guy who set a goal, laid out a plan, and followed his dream.

Years later, I heard that the little railroad had been just the beginning of what later became a full-size amusement park. I'm proud to have been a part of Mr. Bowman's dream. My participation in his adventure helped to spur me on to pursue my own dream, as I'm doing today.

The pursuit of goals takes on many different faces, depending on the individual and the way in which he or she goes about reaching them. I knew one guy on the base in Delaware, a fellow photographer, who was truly unique, an entity unto himself. He was one of those people who not only marched to the beat of a different drum; he was in fact the drummer who marched in the opposite direction from where the band was heading. He was an artist who refused to give up his identity even when in uniform. His talent was evident in his photographs, paintings, and his thinking. A quirky guy, Bob was like one of those people who are written about in the *Reader's Digest* section called "My Most Unforgettable Character." He was a nut, a whacko par excellence, but a loveable crackpot.

When Bob was in your midst, something unpredictable always happened. For instance, there was the time we ran out of film in the photo lab. Although the supply sergeant made every effort to ensure that there was constantly a full supply in the lab, for some reason, we always seemed to be running short. We all knew that each weekend Bob would "borrow" a few rolls of film to go out and shoot artsy photos of flowers and stuff like that, but it never occurred to anyone that he could be the source of the problem. The sergeant, knowing about Bob's propensity to procure a few extra rolls of film a week, usually looked the other way, rationalizing that the activity was actually "extra training" and was therefore permissible. When the shortage was discovered, the sergeant immediately called Bob into his office. "Bob, have you got any film in your locker or back in the barracks?" "Sure, Sarge," replied Bob nonchalantly, adding, "what kind do you need, black-and-white or color?"

Bob was not only a photographer, he was also an artist, and he was not afraid to let everyone know it. He felt that one of the biggest failures of the air force was how it housed its personnel. He believed that the service should have taken a more creative approach to this program. In this vein, he proposed to those in charge of housing that the barracks, and in fact all of the buildings on base, be repainted in lively shades of blue, green, and even pastel pink—colors reminiscent of the cars in the 1950's. Needless to say, the suggestion was immediately laughed at and then relegated to the circular file. Not the type to give up easily, Bob persisted. He presented his case to anyone who would listen. "Pink barracks? What is this, some kind of sissy organization?" was the usual reply. He tried to convince the higher-ups that coloring the buildings would have a really positive effect on moral around the base. His theory was simple: happy colors = happy surroundings = happy personnel. Unfortunately, this fell on deaf ears. The buildings remained unchanged until a new captain arrived on the base. He was a young guy who, according to the latest rumors, was forward-thinking and unlike his predecessor, not opposed to change. When the captain heard about Bob's plan, he agreed that it was an interesting concept and agreed to give it a try. He sent out orders for gallons of new paint to be procured, in shades of blue, coral, and even a shade of pink! He agreed that a boost in morale would result in a more productive workforce.

Within a week, the painters began to spray the barracks bright blue. Initially, there was a great deal of laughter about what it was going to be like to work in Wonderland under Captain Alice. However, within a matter of days, the attitude changed to one of pleasant acceptance. Most of the people on base, including the civilians, thought the whole thing was pretty cool. Some compared it to working on a colorful giant game board—Candy Land to be exact.

Without flying any rescue missions or taking part in a war, Bob became an air force hero! Here was another tale of a dream followed through to fruition. Had Bob said, "One of these days they should paint the buildings in bright colors," chances are, nothing would have happened. However, Bob took action. He understood the meaning of "one of these days is none of these days."

"Are you guys ready?" "Yeah, let's go." It was another Friday evening. At five in the afternoon each Friday, I was a part of the Great Escape. Each of us reveled in the knowledge that for the next two days there'd be no uniforms, no salutes. We were the New York contingent, a lucky group of guys who got assigned to a base located just a few hours away from home. Every Friday, like clockwork, we would gather outside the barracks to form up our carpool, hop into Sonny's gray Buick Skylark, and head up the New Jersey Turnpike to the world's greatest city, New York.

As the Delaware highways disappeared beneath the tires, our anticipation of getting home for the weekend began to grow. There were movies to be seen, girlfriends to make out with, friends and families to greet, and real food to be eaten. As we traveled through northern Delaware and southern Jersey, the Philadelphia radio station faded and was replaced by the New York stations so familiar to our ears. The crackle of Philly's WIBG and WFIL would fade into the tones of New York's WABC with Cousin Brucie screaming "Eeee . . . ee, cousins" at us, as Dion and the Belmonts sang of teenage love. When we heard those sounds, we knew that we were nearing home.

Another thing that confirmed that we were getting closer to our destination was the smell of the portion of New Jersey which we affectionately dubbed the Mile-Long Fart. This was a stretch along the New Jersey Turnpike, which consisted of what is probably the greatest conglomeration of petroleum storage facilities and refineries on the East Coast. As we'd drive past the massive tanks bearing enormous logos such as Esso and Shell, the acrid fumes barreling out of their smokestacks would assault our senses. So putrid were these odors that even with the car windows closed, the stench would invade our noses, making the hair in our nostrils bristle in defense.

The weekends would pass far too quickly. In the blink of an eye, it would be Sunday evening, time to reassemble our little carpool of air force escapees and begin the trek back to Delaware. A whole different attitude prevailed on the Sunday return trip. A sense of maudlin anticipation of the return to the base permeated the group. We tried to overcome this by telling jokes or comparing tales of the weekend's adventures. Each week as we climbed into the car, Hal would ask Sonny, the driver, if he had the bread. The answer was always a firm, "Yeah, how could I forget it?" The first time I heard this conversation, I asked what bread they were talking about. I was told that each week, one of the guys would go to the local Jewish bakery and pick up a corn bread. Now, if you're not from New York, you probably think of corn bread as that yellow stuff that's kind of like a muffin. Well, let me explain. Jewish bakeries in New York make a type of bread that is very much like rye bread. However, this bread is made with corn meal. This results in a loaf that looks very much like rye; but it is much heavier and denser. There's nothing like it anywhere, and New Yorkers love the stuff.

Each week I heard the same conversation confirming the pickup and transportation of the corn bread back to the air force base. The bread, said Hal, was destined for a couple of guys back on the base who were stationed far from their homes and remained on base all weekend. The delicious bread, apparently, brought an extra little spark into their otherwise uneventful weekends on the base. One day, during our typical Sunday journey back to air force life, I raised a question. "Don't these guys who eat the bread ever get tired of the stuff?" I asked. Raucous laughter rang out through the car. "Was there some kind of joke that I'm not been privy to?" I wondered. "Oh, they never get tired of the bread, or, actually, what's in it," said Hal. "What do you mean?" I asked, with the innocence of a five-year-old. "You know, Berger, the stuff inside the loaf of bread." "What the hell are you talking about, Hal?" I asked, feeling like an outsider. "Look, man, when the guys use the stuff hidden inside that bread, life is good!" Now I got it. "Oh my God," I thought, "I'm in a carpool of guys transporting pot, or something worse, back to the base in a hollowed out loaf of bread! Holy crap! If the cops pull this car over, these guys are dead—and so am I, the innocent bystander!" I never asked them exactly what was in that bread. I guess I really didn't want to know.

Luckily, by the time I found out about the great bread caper, I had only a few trips left with these guys before my reassignment to a base overseas. However, during each Sunday-night journey, I'd sit in the back of the car, my stomach tied tightly in a knot as I listened to the words, "Did you bring the bread?" Who would have ever thought that within a few years, I would be a law enforcement officer, a member of an elite organization, with a mandate from the attorney general of the United States, to investigate activities involving the illegal interstate transportation of drugs!

THE SIAMESE SECRET

One day, while taking routine photos of the damage an airman had inflicted on a building while backing up his car, I got a call to report to the Personnel Office on the base. As I opened the door, I was greeted by the sound of someone barking out the words, "Here to get your orders?" "What orders?" I replied in a nervous voice, which began to crack like it did when I was eleven. "What's your name?" "Berger, sir." I instantly became angry with myself, thinking, "Why the hell did I call him 'sir'? He's no officer. He's an enlisted jerk just like me." "Burger, Burger, like in hamburger, huh?" "Oh, there's a crisp new one," I thought, having heard this joke about a trillion times since second grade. "No, like in cheeseburger," I replied, playing into his stupid sense of humor. The self-professed King of Comedy grinned, then began mumbling as he scanned a list of names on a long sheet before him. "That's with an *e*," I said. "You know, B-E-R-G-E-R," I said, emphasizing the *e*. "Oh, here it is. Let's see where the good ole air force is sending you," he said. "Oh, lucky you. You're going to Thailand. I think they used to call it Siam."

The words rang like magic in my ears: "Thailand," "Siam." My thoughts raced back to my favorite show, *The King And I*, the ninth-grade school play that I had performed in. I recalled the sketchpad on which the scene with Yul Brenner, the King of Siam, had appeared. I knew all the songs from the show—by heart. I was going to Thailand! Now I was the king! "They're not sending me to Vietnam," I mumbled. No spending endless hours worrying that some little guy in black pajamas was out to get me. No, I was going to fight the war from Thailand, the R and R capital of the world, where all the military sent its troops for rest and relaxation. Man, did I luck out. If Yul Brenner was the King of Siam, I was the king of the world!

Weeks later, my parents tearfully said good-bye, advising me to be careful. I was on my way! Jammed into a C-141 military transport aircraft, the same type that I had flown on during my Japan odyssey, only this time there were no coffins, just a bunch of GIs excited about the prospect of spending a year away from home. This was considered, by most, to be the true military experience. It was going to be a long trip, maybe nineteen hours or so, with a stop in Japan, but this time, with a guaranteed seat for the return flight. The engines roared as the monstrous craft lumbered skyward. I drifted off, humming to myself, "Shall we dance, on a bright cloud of music, shall we fly?" I was, for that brief moment, on Broadway. I was the King of Siam.

Upon arriving in Thailand, I was immediately struck by the beauty of the tropical jungle surrounding the base. The year was 1968. I was not much of a philosopher in those days. It did not strike me at the time, as it later did, that regardless of all the natural beauty surrounding the base, the reason for its very existence was a far cry from anything beautiful.

The base at U-Tapao was large. It housed a hoard of B-52 bombers, all neatly parked in angled parking spaces, revetments, they called them, adjacent to the runway. The scene reminded me of the parking lot on a Sunday at the mall at home. But these were not Chevys. These were the Trojan Horses of the U.S. Air Force, a phalanx of old war heroes, each finely tuned to gently taxi out to the runway, heavily laden with bombs destined for some target in Vietnam. I figured that if I had to be a part of one of the most unpopular wars in U.S. history, this was not a bad vantage point. No foxholes here and no Vietcong chasing us through rice paddies. We were the elite fly guys; we could view the war at a distance.

When we first arrived on base, we received a lecture from the top brass. "This base and its mission are classified 'Secret.' Under no circumstances," said the colonel, "are you to send home information about this base or its mission." "No problem," I said to myself. "I'll just keep my mouth shut."

During my first weeks on the base, I sent home a letter each day. Most of what I wrote was general talk. I described the *hootch* we lived in, how the smell of the canals, known as *klongs*, mixed with the aroma of JP-4 jet fuel to form an ever-present odor which to this day over four decades later, still fills my nostrils if I close my eyes and picture the airbase. I told of how the air force made every effort to ensure that we had good food at each meal (no kidding!). It was during my second week there that my folks sent me a copy of the *New York Times*. Right on the front page was a feature article about U-Tapao Air Base. The piece included a detailed aerial photo of the base, my home away from home, the super-secret haven of the US B-52 fleet. Reading the article about the base and its role in the war, I questioned one of the fundamental principles of our system. Was this how freedom of the press worked? Does this make sense? What the hell is going on? Here I am, keeping the nation's secret, just as the colonel had told us to, and the whole world now knows every last detail about our military presence here in Thailand.

During my year there, first and foremost in my mind was that I had a job to do for the air force. And that job was to document the U.S. war effort through the lens of my camera. But I also knew that I would not allow this special year in my life to pass by without having fun—a lot of it. I made sure that every day I spent in Thailand was an adventure. Whether I was shooting pictures, working in the darkroom, exploring ancient Buddhist temples, or just lying on Pataya Beach on Thailand's fabulous gulf. (I did get some days off, you know.) I made sure that I would accumulate enough memories and photos to last a lifetime. To this day, I cherish both. One of my extracurricular activities was my radio broadcast on AFTN, the Armed Forces Thailand Network. This gig came about in a rather strange way. You see, by now I had made my folks aware of my interest in all things about showbiz, so they would mail me copies of *Variety*, the showbiz trade paper. Variety was a goldmine of juicy gossip about everyone and everything in entertainment. One day, the thought came to me that perhaps the guys and gals on base would be interested in hearing some showbiz news from the States. I knew a few disc jockeys at the station, so I approached them and the station manager with my idea of taping an entertainment news show. Fearing rejection for voicing a really dumb idea, I braced myself for a barrage of laughter. They didn't laugh. They liked the idea! Anything, they said, that would take the troops' minds off the war for even a short time was a good idea. All I had to do was find a name and a musical theme for my show and hit the airwaves!

I was ecstatic! Imagine, me on the radio! At about that time, the British rock group, the Dave Clark Five, had a hit song called "Bits and Pieces." Taking this name as the musical theme and title of my broadcast, I launched *Bits and Pieces*, a peek into what was happening on the entertainment front back in the States. As the group singing "I'm in pieces, bits and pieces" faded, I'd come on and say, "Hi! This is Air Force Sergeant Richie Berger, and this is *Bits and Pieces*." I'd then go on telling about what group was coming out with a new single, who's starring in what show, etc. I was full of confidence being a radio broadcaster, as long as my program was pre-taped. But, one day, fellow disc jockey Paul Dolan suggested that I do the piece live. "Live? Who me? Are you crazy?" I was scared to death. "It's just radio," Paul said. "No one will see you." "But they'll hear me, when I fall off the chair as I faint from fright!" I said. Anyway, I did a couple of live broadcasts before totally chickening out. I then went back to airing my pretaped show. I began to enjoy the celebrity aspect of the deal. People around the base started asking if I was the *Bits and Pieces* guy on the radio. Sometimes they'd ask how come I have two jobs, one taking pictures and the other on the radio. "Just lucky I guess," was my usual reply, but I knew the truth. I made this happen. I believe that, to a great extent, we have control over what takes place in our lives. I know someone who, when hearing that something good happened to somebody, says, "It should happen to me." Well, it won't happen to you, unless you make it happen. Sure, some good things can happen to you—like winning the lottery. But even that takes some action on your part. You have to go out and buy the ticket!

My stint on the radio took place during the late sixties, a tumultuous time during which many people voiced their opinions about our society and the things that affect it. We heard these statements in songs from singers such as Bob Dylan. Even FBI Director J. Edgar Hoover had something to say. His statement about rock and roll music hangs today on the walls of the Rock and Roll Hall of Fame in Cleveland. It reads, "Rock and roll is repulsive to right-thinking people and can have serious effects on our young people." How ironic to think that when he said that in 1968, I was broadcasting on a rock and roll radio station, then just two years later ended up working for the man who regarded this music as "repulsive." Perhaps even more ironic is that today, as part of my act, both my puppets and I sing several songs which audiences seem to love. And they're all rock and roll tunes!

"What the hell was that?" The ground was shaking. Bottles of photographic chemicals crashed to the floor as the walls of the photo lab shook uncontrollably. Ear-shattering explosions permeated the steamy jungle air. "Oh, shit, we're under attack!" cried the sergeant. We dove for cover as the shaking continued, subsided, and finally ceased. A silent stillness enveloped the base. I crawled out from under the darkroom sink and looked out the window. I could see personnel running across the runway. Grabbing my camera, I headed out to the runway. "What's going on?" I screamed to a guy running in my direction, his uniform soaked with sweat. A B-52 just blew up on the runway! It was fully laden with bombs. "Did the crew get out?" I asked, worrying that someone I knew may have been killed. "Yeah, there was a fire, but they all got out in time." "Thank God," I replied. I knew that my job was to begin documenting the incident. That meant photographing everything in sight from every conceivable angle. As I began to take pictures from a distance, I realized that since the camera had no capability for telephoto shooting, I would have to get in closer if I were to capture the details in the scene. I knew that this could be dangerous. "What if all of the bombs on board had not detonated?" I thought. I knew that I'd have to wait. It was too early to run up to the remains of the aircraft based on some hearsay that no more live bombs were out there. I ran to the nearest air policeman and requested permission to approach the aircraft, or what was left of it, as soon as it was deemed to be safe. Within a few minutes I received the okay. He verified that there was no live ammunition left at the site. At first I began to run, then I realized that with all the debris strewn in my path, I could easily trip on something. I slowed down and began to carefully walk toward the wreckage of what had been a B-52 aircraft. As I walked, I shot pictures. There was a surreal feel to the scene. The carcass of the aircraft was just sitting there looking like the remains of a Thanksgiving turkey. The shell of the huge behemoth was completely surrounded by thousands of pieces of shrapnel, each piece blackened by the intense fire. Smoke was rising from virtually every piece of metal and rubber lying on the ground for as far as the eye could see.

I made my way through the eerie haze which blanketed the runway. I remember thinking, "So this is what happens when these bombs strike in Vietnam." My thoughts raced on, "I hope this is as close to the war as I get. When these babies go off, there's no escape. If you're in the area, there's little chance for survival." I guess we were just lucky that the photo lab had not been any closer to the runway and how fortunate for the crew that the fire system on the aircraft had sent out its signal in time for them to escape.

After I had shot hundreds of pictures that clearly documented the scene, I began to amuse myself by getting a little artsy. To this day, I cherish the one shot I got of the charred aircraft tire standing—yes, actually standing, by itself, a monolith in the hazy mist on that field of debris and destruction.

A far less devastating, yet nonetheless colorful incident occurred a few days later as I was driving around the perimeter of the base. The vehicle assigned to the photo lab was a Metro step van, a large dark blue clunker that should have been left back in the States to haul broken aircraft parts around. As if it weren't difficult enough to learn to drive on the opposite side of the road, I had to learn how to drive a truck. To make matters more complicated, it had a stick shift. I quickly discovered how a pianist feels holding a pedal down while doing other things with his hands. The delicate balance between the clutch and brake became evident the first time I attempted to stop at the top of a hill and found myself rolling backward toward the car behind me.

As I drove the beast of a truck toward the area which housed the B-52s that were waiting to take off, the sky began to darken. Rolling up the window to prevent getting soaked from the approaching monsoon, I heard a rumbling sound which seemed to be growing steadily louder. Within seconds, I could barely see out of the large windshield in front of me. The sound began to resemble that of hailstones striking the van, pounding against the windows and doors. The truck was now totally enveloped in darkness, yet there was not a sign of a raindrop on the windshield. Suddenly, a dull glow appeared as the darkness retreated. On the road in front of me, I could see three or four Thai people in their large straw hats, bending down and picking something up off the roadway. Each of them was carrying a brown paper bag. I slowly drove the van forward to get a better glimpse of the bizarre scene. As one of the Thais walked toward the truck, I rolled down the window to ask him what was going on. "Sawadee!" I shouted, loudly calling out the Thai greeting. "What are you doing?" "Picking up rice bugs!" he shouted back. He walked toward the van holding up the brown bag, which appeared to be bursting with its treasure of wiggling insects. I glanced down into the bag and saw that its contents were rapidly moving around in an attempt to escape. I could see that each insect was at least three or four inches long, resembling a giant grasshopper. "What are you going to do with those?" I asked. "We eat. Very good to eat." He then proceeded to remove one of the bugs from the bag. He waved it in the air and then placed the head in his mouth. I could hear a crunching sound as he bit the bug's head off and began to chew forcefully, all the while smiling as if he were an eight-year-old eating a chocolate ice cream cone. At the risk of interrupting his culinary journey, I asked him if he were going to eat the whole bug. He grinned broadly as he told me that the shell was too tough, but that the next step was to suck out the body from the shell and eat that since it was the tastiest part.

In the rearview mirror, I could see the cloud of flying insects vanish into the distance, spreading a wave of darkness over another area of the base. To this day, I can hardly look at an insect without thinking of that scene in Thailand, and whenever I hear the sound of hail pounding against my car's windshield, I am reminded of the day the sky darkened and of an experience that has remained with me for more than forty years.

Unforgettable incidents seemed to occur on a daily basis in this strange and wonderful land. Take the time I walked into a Buddhist temple, its spiraled orange dome gleaming in the sizzling midday Thai heat. I respectfully tiptoed in, then stopped and stood still, noticing that the robed priests up front were kneeling in prayer. Within a few minutes they got up and began to file out of the temple. One of them beckoned for me to come forward. He greeted me with a smile, but upon noticing my camera, quickly said in excellent English, "Welcome, but no pictures please." He spoke in a pleasant but stern and slightly threatening tone. He smiled again, then proceeded to leave, running quickly to catch up with the others. After he had gone, I walked around the temple observing the small stone carvings sitting on a shelf near the raised platform at the front of the room. With a photographer's eye, I was struck by the beauty of a delicate shaft of light shining streaming into the room from one of the large windows. I knew that this would make a great photo, but I remembered the priest's order that I not take any pictures. I remembered, too, the slightly threatening way in which he had said it. Not willing to give up the opportunity for a picture-perfect Kodak moment, I rationalized by thinking, "There's no one in here. All the priests are gone. Besides, what could they do to me if they caught me taking one little picture?" I quickly raised my camera, composed the shot, and clicked. "Just one more from a slightly different angle," I thought. *Click.* "There, that's it. I'm outta' here," I mumbled. As I strode down the front steps, the guilt and fear combined into one wave of emotional self-doubt. "Did I really do something that bad?" I said to myself. "Well, the important thing was that I got the shot." Feeling pretty secure that since Buddha had not struck me down with a lightening bolt, I was free to head back to the base where I could develop the film and take a look at my latest photographic triumph. I walked from the temple and headed toward the street where I would catch one of the rickety miniature taxis heading toward U-Tapao Air Base. As I stepped from the rocky ground surrounding the temple onto the poorly paved street, my clunky military boot got wedged between two jagged stones. In an effort to extract myself from this booby trap, I turned quickly to the left. As I did so the extra lens case that was hanging on a cord around my neck dipped forward. I looked down in time to see my expensive new 200-mm Nikon lens do a perfect half gainer onto the steaming asphalt. As I picked up the lens I could hear the jingling of pieces of metal and glass. Buddha had taken his revenge. I placed the broken lens back into the case. As the tiny taxi drove me back to the base, I reflected on high-level philosophical and religious things, like why the hell I hadn't heeded the priest's warning. Walking into the photo lab, I had strange thoughts. For instance, "What if I develop the film and the two frames of the temple shots are blank?" Well, that didn't happen. The photos turned out fine, but every so often when I think about the incident, a cold shiver runs down my spine. Perhaps we're not totally in charge of everything.

I had a lot of fun with the Thai people. They were friendly and possessed a great sense of humor. Many of them, including several that were employed on the air base, came from rural farm areas and were quite unsophisticated and unworldly, to say the least. I would often see them, during breaks or when they were off duty, gathered around the TV in one of the recreation rooms on the base, staring with rapt attention at old movies, particularly Westerns or gangster flicks. On one occasion, one of them told me that he'd love to live in Wyoming with all the cowboys and Indians shooting at each other as they rode across the plains. He refused to accept my explanation that this was history and that the cowboy and Indian days had long since died out. Another fellow said that he had hopes of one day visiting Chicago and witnessing Al Capone and his fellow mobsters in action. I just couldn't convince them that the United States had changed slightly since those times. I think the crowning glory was the day that Neil Armstrong set foot on the moon. On that day, as I approached the TV room I heard the sound of raucous laughter. There gathered around the TV, were some twenty Thais, poking each other in the ribs. The mood was beyond festive. It was more like *Animal House* meets Mardi Gras. I immediately asked one of them what was so funny. He said, "Cartoon funny." "What cartoon?" I asked. "Cartoon on TV," he replied. "That's not a cartoon. That's an American walking on the moon!" Through his laughter, he blurted out, "No! Cartoon! Man can't walk on moon!"

I didn't even try to explain. They seemed to be having such a good time that I decided that I didn't want to be a party pooper and spoil things. I walked back to the hootch we lived in where I met some of my fellow airmen. I told them the story. They reacted to the Thais' shenanigans with as much laughter as the Thais had shown toward the TV coverage. Fun is fun wherever you are in the world.

No matter what religion you are, being away from home during the holidays is a real downer. When holiday time arrived in December, everybody on base overreacted. An overabundance of decorations was hung in every nook and cranny. Even the airplanes were draped with garland, tinsel, and just about everything associated with the holidays at home. Christmas music resounded through the hallways. There was, however, one thing lacking—snow. To create the wintery feeling here in the tropics, we let our American ingenuity take charge. We crushed up pieces of white Styrofoam. The hand-size pieces became our snowballs while the smaller chunks were used to represent tiny snowflakes. The Thais found these antics extremely amusing.

On the day before Christmas, I had just completed crushing up a huge piece of Styrofoam that had been used as packing around a refrigerator that had been transported from the States. I was standing in a mound of the white stuff in a dirty deserted corner of a warehouse when one of the Thai cleaning people approached. He knew about the snowmaking effort going on around the base. When he saw what I was doing, he told me that he'd let me in on a little-known secret. He went on to say that even here in the heat of Thailand, they have snow. As I shot a puzzled glance in his direction, he motioned for me to come over to a dark corner of the warehouse. Hidden in the shadows was a small and, I might add, filthy table. He proceeded to wipe the tabletop with his hand. Then, holding his dirty palm toward me, he gleefully shouted, "See this dust? This is Thai snow!" In every culture, in every corner of the world, there's a comedian.

THE SHOWBIZ CONNECTION

One of the highlights of my year overseas was the USO show visit to our base. The USO, United Service Organizations, did a wonderful job brightening the lives of service personnel stationed overseas during each war in which the United States was involved. They did this by bringing top flight entertainment to the troops, even to those in the most remote areas of the globe. For just about every occasion in which the United States had troops overseas, the USO troupe was led by an American hero, Mr. Bob Hope. Accompanying him were singers, dancers, musicians, jugglers, and other acts which would make the troops forget that they were a million miles from home and their loved ones. The cast always included a bevy of beauties from the world of film, theater, beauty contests, and any other arena in which good looks counted. Although the majority of the audiences were men, Mr. Hope never forgot that women also served in our military. For this reason, there were always a few hunky-looking guys in the troupe as well.

Through my radio and photo connections with the public relations people on base, I received early notification that the Bob Hope USO Show would be coming to our base at U-Tapao. Once the word got out, everyone became pretty excited. Spirits rose. Guys began loading bombs onto the planes faster. Perhaps they were trying to get rid of as many as possible so that they wouldn't get stuck loading bombs on the big day. Either way, anticipation mounted. The base bulletin boards began to get flooded with posters showing the performers who would be arriving. There was the sultry Ann-Margret, her husband, actor Roger Smith, Miss World, sexy Penelope Plummer, ex-football-star-turned-actor Rosie Greer, Les Brown and His Band of the Renown, the singing groups the Gold Diggers and Honey Unlimited and on and on. The show was to be our Christmas present from Bob Hope, the USO, and the U.S. government. The year was 1968. The Beatles had landed on U.S. soil four years before.

That was rock music's British Invasion. The Bob Hope Show was to be an all-American invasion, and we welcomed it with open arms.

The day arrived and I was ready with my camera in hand. How lucky I was to have been assigned the job of photographing the show! I had found out the day before where Mr. Hope's tent was located. It was now two hours to showtime. With camera and press pass in hand, I carefully worked my way through a chain of military cops, promising to get them all some eight-by-tens of the show. I had now found my way to the "Emerald City," Bob Hope's tent, which served as his dressing room. Now, to meet the Wizard. I began thinking of a plan—an excuse to meet Bob Hope. As I approached the tent, my plan not yet completely formulated, the tent flap flew open and there, standing in khaki pants and a sleeveless undershirt was the king of the entertainment world. Looking at my nametag, he cheerfully said, "Hi, Airman Berger, come on in." "Okay, sir," I calmly replied, as my lunch turned fully upside down in my stomach. "Here for an interview?" "Uh, yes, sir, and some photos if that's okay with you." "Sure is. By the way, what's your first name?" I had to think a second about that one. My parents called me "Rich," but on the radio I was "Richie." "Richie," I replied. "Okay, Airman Richie, as soon as we're ready for the photos, I'll put my shirt on." "Great idea, sir." ("Oh, my God, he's even agreeing to a photo shoot!") The lyrics from the Broadway show "Sweet Charity" started to play in my head, "If they could see me now, that little gang of mine . . ."

Well, the dream of meeting Bob Hope in person lasted for a scant five minutes, but it was the experience of a lifetime. To think, a private audience with Bob Hope! He seemed to take a real interest in what I was doing. He asked about the radio show, my photography, my family, and a million other things. What a talent and what a genuine human being. I just knew that someday I would be in the same business as he was in.

The show went off just as planned. The lights lit up the giant amphitheater. The music echoed through the jungle surrounding the base. I remember wondering if the tigers and snakes were peering through the dense foliage to catch a glimpse of Ann-Margret.

On several occasions, as I raised my large Speed Graphic camera to my eye, Mr. Hope turned toward me, always holding a pose until he saw my flashbulb light up the night sky. Then he'd wink, and I'd wink back, a little signal, acknowledging that I had gotten the shot. As I carefully composed each shot of the performers, I found myself dancing along with the dancers, singing with the singers. My mind and body felt perfectly in synch with all that was going on. I envisioned myself not in a uniform, but rather in a costume. Instead of taking pictures, I was a performer in the show. My flashbulbs would go off in time with the rhythm of the music. As I inserted a new bulb into the oversized flash attachment, I did so in perfect time with each melody. I was totally in harmony with the sights and sounds emanating from the stage. I was truly a part of the production.

"We can't say Saigon is Hollywood California, or Chu Lai is anything like Duluth. No matter how hard we try, we gotta tell you just why, we all are in love with you!" Though the melody was recognizable, the lyrics were not the original ones. Bob's writers had changed them so that they became a personal message to the troops. His shows were just that, an individual message, tailored to fit each of us—a message designed to convey the thought that our loved ones were home rooting for us and our safe return.

It's a few decades later now, and Mr. Hope is no longer with us, but whenever I look at the photos I took of Bob Hope and the show, I can't help but remember the immense amount of joy that he and his troupe brought to us. Thanks for the memories, Mr. Hope.

CALIFORNIA, HERE I COME!

My year in Thailand whizzed by. I accomplished a lot. For my efforts in photographing the war effort there, I won worldwide acclaim and was voted Military Photographer of the Year in the Black-and-White category. It was, as Sinatra had once proclaimed, "a very good year."

It was now 1969 and time for me to be reassigned to the States, where I would spend my last year in the service. As the plane took off and I saw the now-not-so-supersecret base disappear beneath the clouds, the newsreel in my head cranked through all the year's scenes. Some were happy, some tragic, yet all were filled with vibrant colors and the excitement of the adventure of a lifetime.

My last assignment was at the flight test center at Edwards Air Force Base. Cool. Well, not literally. Actually hot. You see, Edwards is located right in the heart of the Mojave Desert. Not exactly the garden spot of California. But it was the home of the SR-71, the latest spy plane. Being a photo guy put me in a great position. They always needed shots of this highly sophisticated military marvel, a secret the air force was determined to protect. Armed with my security clearance, I was privileged to shoot the pictures of this aviation marvel. Oh, how I enjoyed being escorted into the hangar, where the Black Bird lived. I felt important as hell. Times have certainly changed. The secret's out. Now, any of you can see this mysterious stranger of the skies by visiting her in New York City as she quietly reposes on the deck of the USS Intrepid, where she is one of the stars of the Air and Space Museum.

The adventures continued even during the final phase of my air force career. The photo lab at Edwards Air Force Base was not what you'd call a hotbed of photographic excitement. However, one day does stand out as being kind of unique. This was the day that one of the photographers hatched a plan to steal a camera, case and all, and hide it out in the Mojave Desert. Then, just prior to his discharge, he would retrieve it and sell the thing in downtown

LA—a master plan of thievery if ever there was one. The Air Police investigated the missing camera, recovered it and arrested the thief, who had confessed to the crime and led them to the camera. This misadventure resulted in the arrest and conviction of the photographer, who served time and received a dishonorable discharge.

"Hi, Brian. Whoa, what are those?" I said. "Hi, Rick. Oh, they're just some rejects. The good prints are over there on the finishing table." Brian was the chief photographer in the color lab at the Flight Test Center at Edwards Air Force Base, a separate photo unit from the base photo lab where I worked. I stared at the large eleven-by-fourteen-inch prints. "Rejects?" I thought to myself. "They look pretty good to me." I walked over to the finishing table and stared intently at the photos. On the top print, there, in full color, was Neil Armstrong, taking his famous "small step for man" which he described as "one giant leap for mankind." The remaining shots showed other facets of the moon mission. These were the photos we had all became familiar with after seeing them so many times on the cover of *Life* magazine, in newspapers, and on TV. "Why are you throwing these out, Brian? They look pretty good to me." "Compare them to the others," he said. "The color is a little off. They're a little too red, and these prints have to be perfect. You know, someday, these could be in the White House or the Smithsonian."

Here, in the color lab, they produced the beautiful full-color shots of the test firings of missiles, fighters in flight, and all the other dramatic photos of aircraft which make great calendar shots. He really knew his stuff. "Boy, I'd sure like to bring these prints of the moon mission home." "No problem. There's nothing classified in any of those shots," he said. "Take the discarded ones. I'm just gonna throw 'em out anyway." I felt like a little kid getting a holiday gift. I was hardly able to contain my excitement. I knew that these were historical items—especially since they were originals, which had been made from the negatives that were exposed on the surface of the moon. I thanked Brian, took the group of prints, and headed out of the lab and back to my official air force blue Chevy pickup truck, the one assigned to the base photo lab where I worked. Back at my lab, the guys went nuts. "Where'd you get those?" they all asked. "Up at the color lab. They're rejects, but aren't they cool?" I knew I had opened a Pandora's box. I imagined poor Brian getting requests from all the photographers on base as well as their buddies for sets of the prints. Well, luckily that never happened. I spoke to Brian later that week. He assured me that no other prints of the moon mission were being handed out.

So here I was, in California, in 1970. It had been six years since the arrival of the Beatles. Six years since, disguised as a reporter for my school newspaper,

I had snuck into the terminal at New York's JFK Airport and photographed George, Paul, John, and Ringo. I wonder if the Beatles remember me—the kid with the Yashica camera raised high in the air, yelling, "Ringo, look over here, now smile." Probably not.

I was just ninety miles away from LA and riding the tail end of the psychedelic '60's. Just about everyone was sporting long hair but me. First of all, I was still in the military. Second, I was too damn conservative. Why wasn't I a wild and crazy guy? I thought all creative people were way out and a bit off the wall. To this day, I can't fully figure it out. I guess that just wasn't me.

The shocking musical *Hair* was playing at the Aquarius Theater in LA. It echoed the sentiments of American youth, with their hair down to their rear ends, a far cry from the mop tops sported by the Beatles during the years that Americans considered that to be long hair. Imagine a musical in which the cast members took their places downstage at the end of the first act costumed solely in their birthday suits. How shocking it was then! How not so shocking it would be now.

California was very different, a difficult to describe kind of different—especially for a kid from New York. Visitors to New York sometimes find it an insane place, fast paced, open for business day and night. But visit LA, and you're on another planet. I guess it's a combination of the California weather, the car culture, and a general feeling of permissible flakiness. Either way, it was a great year. I even took the typical tourist tour of Universal Studios and got to see how movies are made. "I should be in one of these movies," I thought to myself as I lifted a prop, a foam rubber boulder, high above my head. "Damndest things, these props. They look authentic, feel like the genuine thing, yet they're not real. Sort of like me in an air force uniform, apocryphal, a charade." There's that gnawing feeling again. "I belong on this movie lot. I'm a performer. I know it. Go back to the base," I thought. "The feeling will pass." It never did.

The phone rang. I grabbed the roll of film out of the chemical bath and threw it into the wash tank. "Photo lab, Sergeant Berger speaking." "Hey, Berger, it's Airman Gates down at Personnel. I need you to come over to see us." "You need some photos of something?" "Nah, it's something else." "Now what could they want from me at Personnel? I wonder if I'm in trouble or something." I knew that this was my last year in the military, so I wasn't going to be reassigned, not with just months to go. As I entered the Personnel section, I heard a bunch of guys talking about getting an early out. I knew that the air force was trying to save some money by cutting down its numbers and that the early out program was one method they used to accomplish this.

I approached the front desk and told the airman that I was directed to report there. He handed me some papers and said that I should read them and then come back to his desk. I sat down and read about the opportunity that was being afforded me to leave the air force in March instead of May. Under this early-release program, my four-year obligation would be considered completed, and I would receive an honorable discharge.

"Mmm, get out in March instead of May." It took me about a third of a second to go back to the guy's desk and accept the air force's generous offer. I signed the papers and began the two-month countdown to the beginning of the rest of my life.

I was going home in March instead of May! But did I really want to go back to New York? I loved California. Sun, surf, girls, cars, acting, movies. I formulated a plan. I would go back to New York for a little while, just to kind of readjust my head, you know, rid myself of that "military feeling," then return to California. "Good plan," I repeated to myself, "good plan."

I flew back to New York that March and quickly settled back comfortably into the New York lifestyle—too fast, too much to do, lots of stress. I was home. Ah, the joys of being a New Yorker. "Maybe I'll just stay for a while, but what the hell should I do while I'm here?"

Since I was a pretty good photographer, I had no trouble getting work in the New York advertising photography studios. The life of a studio photographer was harried, to say the least. Each day consisted of creating illusions. There were the long-legged models reclining on the pure white sands of Caribbean beaches. Of course, there were no beaches—just sand on the studio floor and a background so convincing you'd swear you'd get a sunburn. There were shots of food—savory eggs, just cooked, sunny-side up, their yolks glistening for the camera lens. Of course they glistened. They were coated with glycerin. In fact, they weren't yolks at all. They were peach halves! But they sure were convincing to the eye of the camera and when they appeared in the food section of a ladies magazine!

LOOKS AREN'T EVERYTHING

By now, I had become a jack of many trades, but one occupation I had not considered was modeling. I didn't look much like a model. (For that matter, when I was in the Bureau I didn't look much like an FBI agent.) However, in spite of my lack of the classic model look, at one point I found myself thrown into the modeling business.

The posing gig came about quite unintentionally. It occurred during my stint as a photographer's assistant in one of the advertising studios. If I learned little else working in these photo factories, it was that the field of advertising photography was geared to accomplishing one goal: making money. It had nothing to do with the lofty pursuit of photographic excellence or the desire to produce fine art with a camera. Big Bucks was the name of the game and cutting corners was an essential part of the process. If a studio could find a cheaper way to do something, they would move heaven and earth to do it that way—as long as it would save them some money. One way they accomplished this was to use in-house personnel to take the role of models. If they could avoid paying a modeling agency a fee, they'd do it. (Of course, they'd still bill the client for the fee, using the rationale "what they don't know won't hurt 'em.")

The studio that I was working in at the time was shooting a men's clothing ad for a large department store. The ad was to depict a young man posed against a wall in a house. The idea was to keep the background simple, so as to draw attention to the clothing.

One of my jobs as studio assistant was to paint the flats. Each flat consisted of a frame which was the size of a typical piece of wallboard, four feet wide and eight feet high. A piece of heavy canvas was stapled onto the frame, just as it would be for an artist's canvas. Butted up against each other, these structures formed a wall. With a framed picture or two hung on them, they created the illusion of a wall in a home. When painted a bright white, the flats could be used to bounce light off of and into a shot.

It might surprise you to learn that painting flats and building walls are a part of a photo studio apprenticeship, but I guess everyone begins at the bottom rung on the ladder to success. In one studio in which I worked, the chief photographer, Marty, was a boating enthusiast. Many of the flats were cut in half or thirds, then hinged together so that they could be opened or closed like a giant book. By varying the boards' positions, we could bounce light into the photo at several different angles. Marty referred to these large flat boards as "sails." A day spent in that studio left me feeling as if I had just completed an outing on a schooner. While setting up the shot, Marty would scream out, "Pull up the mainsail!" At this command, I would have to yank on the thick rope attached to the flat, causing it to unfold. When the two-hinged sections were in just the right position to bounce the light onto the objects in the photo at a certain angle, he'd yell, "Secure the sail!" I'd then have to tie the rope down, locking the contraption into the proper position.

"Rick, are the sails secured?" he'd yell out. Most of the time I'd just say, "Yeah, Marty." However, on some of my more goofy days, I'd scream at the top of my lungs, "Aye, aye, sir!" or some other seafaring exclamation. On one particular occasion, just after I had secured the "rigging," Marty said, "Okay, now go change."

"Change into what?" I responded. "Your outfit for the first shot," said Marty. It didn't take me long to figure out what was going on. Instead of paying an agency a modeling fee, I was going to be used as the model. All I could think was, "I don't look like a model. How're we gonna pull this one off?"

I entered the dressing room, saw an outfit hanging on the back of the door, got out of my jeans, and reached for the cream-colored dress pants. As I pulled them up, it became apparent that the waist was going to be far too tight. I yanked them up over my hips, struggled with the zipper, and then, holding my breath, forced the button on the waistband closed. I completed the tortuous ritual by closing the belt. By this point, I could barely breathe.

Struggling my way onto the set, I asked Marty if we could make this quick since I was beginning to hyperventilate. As I took my position, I glanced around at the newly painted flats with the watercolor paintings hanging on them. Damn if this didn't look like a real room in a house! I had done a good job! Marty began to swing the big view camera into place. The stylist, Lisa, a supposed expert in setting up photo shoots, was a serious-looking woman who appeared to be in her thirties. As soon as I stood still, she approached me, grabbed my belt, and yanked sharply upward. I screamed as the crotch of the pants cut sharply into an area of great importance. "Sorry," she proclaimed, "but the cuffs were hanging too low on your shoes."

"Now, fling the sports jacket over your left shoulder and look back as if you had just heard your name being called." "In which direction—toward the camera or away?" I asked. "I don't give a shit. Just look back." "Very sweet. My kind of woman," I mumbled.

Click, flash, turn to the right. *Click*, flash, turn to the left. "Okay, Rick, go change into the other outfit." "Okay, Marty, I hope the pants are not as tight as these." By the time I had changed into the next outfit, I had decided that the life of a fashion model was not for me. Thankfully, the next waistline was not as tight, so I was able to breathe through the next series of shots.

I reentered the dressing room and began to change back into my jeans. Just then, one of the real models arrived. Extending his hand, he said, "Hi, I'm Gregg," sounding like a radio announcer. "Nice to meet you, Gregg. I'm Rick." Seeing Lisa on the set, Gregg immediately said to me, "I've worked with her before. She's a real bitch." With my crotch still burning from her delicate move to adjust my pants, I told him that I knew exactly what he meant. "You been modeling a long time, Rick?" "No, as a matter of fact, I just had my first job about a half hour ago. See, I work here in the studio." "Well, you seem like a pretty bright guy. Someday you'll probably own your own studio." "I hope so," I replied.

I left Gregg in the dressing room and walked back into the studio. "Grab the rigging and tilt the jib!" screamed Marty. "What am I, in the goddam navy?" I shouted back. Marty, a rotund little guy in a yellow Mickey Mouse tee shirt just grinned as he pulled the other "sail" into place.

Just then, the dressing room door opened and Gregg strolled out wearing nothing but a pair of briefs. They had that glowing white, never-been-worn-before look. He took his place slightly to the left of the cheap landscape picture hanging on the flat. It was one of the three that I had found lying against the wall in the prop room earlier that morning.

As Gregg struck a pose for the underwear ad, Lisa stepped forward. "Fix yourself!" she barked out. "What?" said Gregg defiantly. "You know what I mean. Adjust yourself." By now the look on Gregg's face clearly indicated that he was purposely egging her on. "Adjust what?" said Gregg in a tone reminiscent of a third grader teasing a fellow classmate. You could feel the tension as Lisa strode forward onto the set. Looking him straight in the eye, she slowly said, "Your thing. It's hanging too far to the left." "Oh, that," remarked Gregg in a flippant manner. Reaching down to make the necessary adjustment, Gregg just stared at the woman he had referred to as a bitch. I knew that his assessment was correct. "Okay, can we get on with the shoot?" said Marty, who by now, had entered his "time is money" mode.

The remainder of the shoot went off without a hitch. Marty got some good shots. Lisa had lived up to her reputation, and Gregg got to keep the sample underwear. I got a lesson in human behavior—once a bitch, always a bitch.

The following day, I was given another assignment in front of the camera. By now, I considered myself a seasoned professional model and was beginning to resent the fact that I wasn't being paid a salary commensurate with my two jobs in the studio. We were shooting an ad for a lock company, and I was to play the role of a burglar who was picking the lock on the front door of a house. The wool ski mask ruined my big chance at having a facial close-up. Besides, it was hot and itched like hell. It was a night scene and I was to hold up a lit match to illuminate the lock. We must have lit fifteen matches before we got one to stay lit long enough to get the shot. With each match, Marty would refocus and reangle the camera. Each time, I could feel the heat from the flame as it began to lick at my thumb. Just before each match would inflict a severe burn, Marty would yell, "Perfect! Hold it!" I'd hear the click, see the flash, and drop the match just in the nick of time. Except on the last try. Marty was just a millisecond too slow. I spent the next two hours with ice on my thumb, which by now looked like an overcooked Oscar Mayer wiener. After a couple of days of ice and first aid cream, my thumb returned to normal, and I was once again able to hoist the rigging.

Well, as much fun as it was being a photo assistant, part-time model, and indoor sailor, I felt that it was time to set sail for a port with a more promising future—one that did not include lit matches and men's underwear.

THE FORK IN THE ROAD

A quote attributed to baseball player and great philosopher of our times, Mr. Yogi Berra, states: "When you come to a fork in the road, take it." I came to that fork, and I took it. After working in an advertising agency for a few months, I received a call from a friend of mine, a guy named Jeff, who had served with me as a fellow military photographer. Jeff was a colorful guy who hailed from Ogden, Utah. When I received his phone call, what surprised me was that he had not returned to the West, but rather was still living on the East Coast. He said that he was working once again as a photographer, but this time for the FBI. He went on to say that he was FBI Director J. Edgar Hoover's personal picture taker and that he was really happy to be employed by the Bureau. I told him that I, too, was a photographer and worked in New York. He thought that what I was doing, shooting models for magazine covers and layouts, sounded exciting. I mentioned my part-time modeling assignments, but I told him that my plans for the future revolved around my work behind, not in front, of the camera. I said that the job of a photographer in New York was exciting but that his position in the FBI sounded even more enticing.

According to Jeff, the Bureau was always looking for good photographers, so he suggested that I apply for the job. I told him that the problem was that I really didn't want to work in Washington DC. I explained that I was a native New Yorker and that I thrived on the sights, sounds, smells, and excitement of New York. So Jeff suggested that I contact the FBI's New York office and see if they needed some help in their photography section. I followed through on his suggestion, and the rest is history. After a lengthy background investigation, the Bureau welcomed me on board as their newest photographer.

Now, everyone, to this day, asks me, "But after you were a photographer, how did you become an agent? Didn't you have to be a lawyer or accountant?"

The answer is a resounding *no*. Here's how it worked. Back in 1976, when I was appointed a special agent, the rules for getting into this "club" were a lot different. First of all, J. Edgar Hoover was the big boss at the time. In those days, he was the Director, and I mean *The* Director. To those of us on the inside, it appeared that he had been the Director since the Bureau's inception and would remain so—forever. There was never any doubt as to who was in charge. His words and portrait were everywhere.

Under Mr. Hoover (as he was known to all Bureau employees), a program existed through which the FBI obtained a great many of its agents. We insiders knew it as "The Clerical Program." To fully understand this novel approach to hiring new FBI agents, I think I'd better explain the use of the word "clerk" in the FBI. In the '70's, and for several decades prior, the FBI categorized its employees as either agents or clerks. The division was clear and simple. A clerk was any employee that wasn't an agent. Some clerks were actually just that in the true sense of the word. They handled purely clerical tasks such as sorting mail and typing. Other folks performed more complex jobs such as analyzing and classifying fingerprints, taking photographs to be used in court presentations, or even serving as one of the FBI nurses, a job which also called for one to act as a psychologist, nutritionist, and often, retirement party planner.

Many of the Bureau's employees, including me, resented the title "clerk." We regarded ourselves as an integral part of the organization, folks who, by performing our "clerical" duties, were supporting the investigative mission of the FBI. My resentment, in particular, came from the fact that when I joined the Bureau, in 1970, I was already a trained professional photographer who had an associate in applied science degree. That didn't matter to the Bureau. I wasn't an agent. Therefore, I was a clerk. Not a great way to build self-esteem and morale. And then there was the salary. When I was hired, the Bureau initially offered me $85 a week, but after I convinced them that with my training, skills, and college degree, I was worth much more, they saw fit to allow my salary to skyrocket to the staggering amount of $110 a week. Since one cannot put a price on prestige, I tried not to think about the low salary and instead reveled in the glory of serving in the world's premier investigative agency. However, when I went to pay my bills, I could not help but realize that I was pulling down a salary which placed me just slightly above eligibility for food stamps. Ah, the sacrifices we make for God and country!

In today's FBI, the term clerk is no longer used. Employees other than agents are referred to as support personnel. These include investigative assistants, analysts, translators, and a wide variety of other talented and well-trained individuals.

Now that you're well versed in at least one area of FBI terminology, let's take a glimpse into the world of an FBI clerk, circa 1970. Imagine me, a legend in my own mind, the FBI's best clerk, I mean photographer. With my fabulous salary, I was ready to make the biggest purchase of my life, a car. I had found the perfect vehicle, a 1971 Dodge Dart Swinger. I think I was in love with the name as much as the car itself. Didn't it just reek of coolness? Was I going to be James Bond or what? I'd be an ultracool FBI guy cruising the neighborhood in my shiny new Bergermobile! All I needed now was a car loan. In those years, the FBI office was located on Manhattan's posh Upper East Side, a suitable setting for a legendary organization. Directly across the street was a branch of one of New York's largest banks. All of the tellers there knew all the Bureau people by name. Everyone from our office banked there. On Fridays, when the Bureau paychecks were issued (no such thing as direct deposit in those days) the bank became a mini-FBI office. Within minutes of the checks being handed out, the bank was filled with more FBI personnel than were left in the FBI building safeguarding our nation. The unspoken rule among bank robbers in the know was "never rob the bank across the street from the FBI building on a Friday." Believe it or not, on at least one occasion, some dope wearing a ski mask tried it anyway. The bank's surveillance cameras captured some wonderfully revealing moments showing a lone bank robber handing a note to a teller. In the next frame, you could see the line of patrons suddenly becoming a squad of gun-bearing FBI agents approaching the jerk from behind. The final frames show the startled ski-masked knucklehead being removed from the bank by a whole squad of agents as tellers grin from behind the windows in their booths.

In order to avoid the Friday banking rush, I picked a Wednesday morning to apply for my car loan. Dodging a phalanx of yellow New York taxis, I made my way to the bank's main entrance, strode in with my head high and chest out; after all, I was an FBI photographer. As I approached the desks of the bank officers, all wearing their official bankers' faces, I began to wonder what these people looked like at home. At day's end did they greet their spouse's with these looks of officialism, or were they real people, whose hair is a mess before their morning coffee?

The robotic bank officer at the first desk peered at me over the top of her glasses and, in her most commanding banker's voice said, "May I help you?" Feeling as if I had just been spoken to by a drill sergeant, I replied, in my best FBI voice, "Hi, I'm Rick Berger with the FBI." On her wood-grained Formica desktop sat a distinctively dull nameplate bearing the name Miss Crane. Looking up over her glasses, she shot a piercing glance at me reminiscent of the look I once received from my fifth-grade teacher, Miss Hess. In precisely enunciated tones punctuated with an air of utter condescension, Crane said, "And what may I help you with?" Right from the get-go I didn't like her, but determined to stay the course, I said, "I'm here to see about getting a car loan." "Fine, Mr. Berger," she replied, getting more officious as the seconds ticked by. "I'll need to see your FBI identification." Reaching into my left breast pocket, I carefully withdrew my FBI credentials. The credentials are the official identification documents carried by all FBI agents and certain support personnel including photographers. They are two small placards about the size of index cards and are carried in a leather case. They bear the agent's photo and a paragraph stating that he or she is charged with investigating violations of the laws of the United States. I held my credentials up for her to read them just as I was trained to do, never surrendering them to anyone. Crane obviously could not have cared less about FBI training, rules, or anything else. She immediately grabbed the credentials from my hand and began to scrutinize the hell out of them, attempting to ascertain whether I was a fraud. She looked at the one-inch photo, looked up at me, looked again at the photo, then, as if ready to announce that I would not be permitted to see the great and all-powerful Wizard of Oz, she handed them back to me, motioning for me to sit down. "I see from your credentials that you're not an agent—you're a . . . clerk," drawing out the word, treating each letter as a dagger being twisted in the heart of a despicable enemy. "Photographer," I shot back. "If you're not an agent, Mr. Berger, you're a clerk." "Crane," I thought, "I may be a clerk, but you, my dear queen of banking, are an asshole." "Very well, Mr. Berger, I'll give you a loan application, but since you're a clerk, you'll have to have your parents cosign, for the loan."

I was devastated. I was twenty-five years old, had served overseas in the Vietnam War, had an associate degree, had been recognized as an award-winning photojournalist, was employed by the most prestigious law enforcement agency in the world, and had just been told that my mommy had to sign my report card. From the first day of my FBI employment, I had been told to always obey the unofficial credo of the FBI, "Don't embarrass the Bureau." "Okay, I'll go along with that," I thought. I took the sheaf of papers in my hand, thanked God's gift to the banking industry, and left the bank, forcing a weak smile as I offered Crane a firm handshake. With the paperwork signed by my parents, within a week, I the clerk, was driving my new 1971 Dodge Swinger, despite the humiliation of dealing with New York's original Queen of Mean.

By now, you've probably gotten the feel for what it meant to be a clerk in the FBI. And, as I said above, although most folks had heard that you have to be a lawyer or accountant to become an agent, the truth was that you could sneak in through the back door by beginning your career as an FBI clerk. To make the process an official one, J. Edgar, whom I often called Jedgar, created the "Three-Year Rule." Under this doctrine, anyone who served successfully in a non-agent capacity for a period of three years or more and possessed a four-year college degree (any major) was eligible to become a special agent of the FBI. He (no "she's" in those days) would then receive an interview, take the special agent exam, be given a physical and, if found qualified, would be sent to the FBI Academy for training. If the candidate successfully completed the training, he was appointed an FBI special agent. It was as simple as that.

Jedgar was big on loyalty. To his way of thinking, if somebody could survive three years as a clerk, earning a poverty-level salary, he must be a loyal employee and would therefore make a good agent. In most cases, this theory proved to be correct. However, there were those who slipped under the radar, were appointed agents, and, in the final analysis, turned out to be less-than-legendary investigators. Then there were the ones who just couldn't meet the qualifications to become an agent but wanted, nevertheless, to remain with the FBI. I recall one guy who was terribly frustrated over the fact that he had not become an agent. Rather than quitting, he appointed himself an agent in his own mind. He even went as far as carrying a stapler tucked into his belt. He'd cover the stapler with a sports jacket. This, he believed, gave him the agent look, the cool investigator with the slight bulge on his side, indicating that he was a force to be reckoned with since he was carrying a powerful "Hoover Heater." As they say, "It takes all kinds," and some of them were in the FBI. However, the majority of us that performed well as clerks typically turned out to be pretty damn good agents.

LESS-THAN-PERFECT PEOPLE

How many of you can think of a sentence that has both the words "FBI" and "fun" in it? Not many I bet. Off the top of my head, I can only think of one: "Hey, Jimmy, we just got back from Washington DC and did we have *fun* taking that tour of the *FBI*." Other than that, there aren't many FBI-fun combinations around. Well, we're going to explore this weird word combination as I guide you through a little tour of the FBI as seen through the eyes of an agent who did a "180" at the end of his career in order to pursue a lifelong dream.

I'm sure that all of you think of FBI people as ultra serious. What could be funny about the FBI you ask? After all, this is serious business, investigating violations of the laws of the United States. Well, of course it's serious. But let's face it, nobody can be serious all the time. Besides, get any group of people together, for any purpose, and there's bound to be some levity. It's in our nature to laugh and poke fun at the various aspects of life. Well, the FBI is no different. But I have to warn you. If you're looking to find out some real secret things about the inner workings of the FBI, look elsewhere. This is just not that kind of book, and, frankly, I'm not that kind of person. I pledged to the Bureau from the beginning, never to reveal things of a sensitive nature, the kind of information which could compromise the effectiveness of the organization or national security. Being a man of my word, I'm playing by the rules. However, here are some old Bureau tales, the likes of which have never been revealed to the general public. I hope you enjoy them.

Many, if not all of you who are reading this book, have heard of the most famous of all FBI Directors, J. Edgar Hoover. To some he was a threat; to others, a hero, a champion of the American cause. Still to a great many more, he was simply a legend. We all know that whenever a human being rises above his own mortality and is elevated to the stature of a legend, myths about his life begin to swirl around him like a silken veil caught in the updraft of an elevator. Allow me to present a small yet colorful example of the Hoover mystique that never quite reached the headlines. This is the tale of the Hoover Limousine.

Back in the early 1970's, all clerks were assigned duties that had absolutely nothing to do with our primary positions in the FBI. One of these oddball jobs was to guard the director's enormous black Cadillac limousine, which was housed in the FBI's not so secret parking garage located on New York's Upper East Side. Ask just about anyone living in New York City at that time where the FBI garage was and they would immediately identify not only the street, but also the building that housed the garage. The location was not exactly one of the nation's best-kept secrets. The FBI, like any good bureaucracy, did things in exact opposition to anything sensible, so it inconveniently placed this parking facility a good mile away from the FBI field office. This made it quite difficult, if not almost impossible, for an agent, in urgent need of a car, to get one from the garage. Anyone who lives in, or has even visited, New York will attest to the fact that getting uptown, downtown, across town, or anywhere in town in a hurry is attempting a feat much like climbing Mt. Everest wearing flip-flops. An agent who had to get somewhere in a rush might just as well have grabbed the nearest taxi, 'cause he sure as hell knew that he had better not depend on getting one of the bucars (note the clever abbreviation for Bureau cars) from that garage quickly.

Now that you're familiar with the FBI garage, here's the skinny on Mr. Hoover's fancy limousine. The exterior of this metal monster presented an imposing picture. It seemed to scream, "There's somebody very important in here." The inside was equally intimidating, with its rolled and pleated leather seats, burled wood dashboard, and carpeting thick enough to dampen the sound of honking New York taxi horns. It certainly was a suitable office on wheels for the director of the premier law enforcement agency in the world. The truth is that he hardly, if ever, used that car. It seemed that whenever Hoover came to New York, whatever car he arrived in was the one that was kept ready for him outside his hotel, and that was the vehicle used to whisk him off to his next destination which, rumor has it, was often the racetrack.

Whether the limo stayed in the garage till it rusted away from lack of use was not a consideration. What was important was that the car was guarded with the utmost security. And upon whom did that mighty task fall? Why, it was, of course, that sophisticated and highly trained group known as "The Clerks." After all, who could better guard this modern-day Trojan Horse than this poorly paid, yet dedicated workforce? Each of us assigned to this mammoth task got his chance to prove just how fearless he was. My turn came on a blustery winter night in February 1971.

It was one of those New York winter evenings where the wind whips through the vertical canyons of steel creating a sirenlike howling throughout the city. I had prepared myself for a night chock full of boredom. Here I was watching the Director's car, lest any Soviet spies attempt to implant listening devices under the dashboard, or some car thief attempts to steal the steering wheel. After a couple of hours of staring intently at every corner of the darkened garage, it dawned on me that should an intruder show up, I would be about as effective as a ninety-eight-pound bouncer at a bar frequented by professional wrestlers. You see, I had no gun. FBI clerks did not carry a weapon. Only agents had guns. Clerks carried pens. If an intruder were to enter the garage and attempt to steal the Director's car, what the hell could I do? Call 911? I can just see it now. "Is this an emergency?" "Uh, yes, sir, my name's Rick Berger, and I'm with the FBI. I'm at the FBI garage, and some guy is trying to hotwire the FBI Director's car, and I can't do anything about it." "Well, draw your goddamn gun!" the operator would say. "I'd love to," I'd reply, "but I don't have one. See, I'm a clerk. I have a pen!"

By two in the morning, I was getting pretty tired of standing next to the car. I decided to do what any insightful FBI employee would do. I opened the rear door of the monster and hopped in. The leather was soft to the touch, and though I would have much preferred to be home in bed, I thought, "This is not a bad way to finish my shift." Lying down, I drifted off, imagining that I was the Director or, better yet, a movie star, being whisked away in my shiny black limo to a day's shooting at the studio.

Morning seemed to arrive quickly. I glanced at my watch. "Six thirty! Already?" I knew that the auto mechanics would soon be arriving for their shift. I hopped out of the car and took my post, acting as if I had been standing just outside the driver's door all night. "Hey, Rick, how was your shift?" "Oh, hi, Bill," I said, as I looked up and saw the head mechanic arriving. "Uneventful. I'm glad the heat was on full blast in here last night. You know it can get pretty cold standing here guarding this Hoovermobile for all these, uh, hours." "Yeah right," said Bill, as he stared at the rear door of the limo, still open, since I had forgotten to close it after my quick exit from the car a few minutes before. I knew he was on to what I had done. We both laughed.

Shortly after I began working at the Bureau, I came to realize that it was run on one principle and one principle alone: FEAR. J. Edgar Hoover was, as we know, a legend in his own time. People who worked in government were deathly afraid of him. People in the private sector were also aware of his power. Even today, the rumor persists that he kept files on just about everyone. It was known throughout the Bureau that he kept rein on all FBI employees through his fearful management techniques. His dreaded inspections of the field offices often culminated in agents receiving admonishment, reprisals, letters of censure, and even demotions. The fear trickled down from the highest-ranking management types to the lowest level mailroom clerks. The way the inspection process worked was that a group of senior agents that had been "knighted" by Hoover with the title "Inspector" were sent out to the various field offices throughout the United States. Their length of stay in each office was determined by the size of the particular office they were assigned to inspect. Their job was to virtually tear the place apart, file by file, and case by case, in order to determine whether it was running efficiently, to cite any discrepancies in how the cases were being handled and to measure how effectively that particular field office was being run. The concept of self-inspection, whereby an organization checks on itself, as opposed to bringing in outsiders to scrutinize it, has some merits. It is designed to keep the organization running efficiently and effectively. However, inspections often take on a life of their own. Now, rumor has it that during one inspection, an overweight agent was told that if he did not lose a substantial amount of weight within a few weeks, his job was on the line. Since inspection of an office as large as the New York division took about a month, the agent was told to report back to the inspector in three weeks to demonstrate a sufficient weight loss. Not all agents possess the investigative acumen of a James Bond; however, most are clever enough to find ways to thwart the system. The agent, fearing that he would be fired, devised a plan by which he could continue to eat cheeseburgers and fries, yet appear to lose weight during the allotted amount of time. He simply bought a few suits in progressively larger sizes. Each week, he would put on a larger suit, giving the impression that he was rapidly losing inches off his waistline. By the end of the third week, it appeared to all of his coworkers that he had truly slimmed down, so much so that suggestions began to surface that he should invest in some clothes that were more suited to his new figure.

With the preciseness of a typical FBI operation, week three of the inspection arrived, and the agent was summoned to the desk of the inspector. The agent, wearing his biggest, baggiest suit, approached the desk of the almighty inspector with a great deal of trepidation. Quite taken aback by the agent's appearance, the inspector, after staring in utter disbelief, pronounced the agent fit for continued duty, adding that he would most certainly relate to

Mr. Hoover how seriously agents in the New York office took the "suggestions" voiced by the inspection staff. The agent is said to have thanked the inspector profusely for his interest in the agent's health and career; after which, he went back to his desk to continue typing a report, all the while, virtually swimming in his three-sizes-too-large outfit.

The following Friday, upon the departure of the inspection team, the agent promptly dumped his baggy clothes. Upon his return to work on Monday, his fellow agents noticed that he was, once again, sporting the same sack of lard hanging over his belt that he had carried prior to the inspection. In an effort to thank his fellow agents for not ratting on him and exposing the charade, he took his whole squad out to lunch during which they all celebrated by eating far too many cheeseburgers and fries in his honor.

Now, here's an FBI misadventure I call "Photo Farce." The FBI Photo Lab is an integral part of the Bureau's investigative network. Because a picture is worth a thousand words, in law enforcement, photos are used for evidentiary purposes, documentation, surveillance, etc. Since the New York Office of the FBI is its largest field office, its photo lab is one of the largest, most well-equipped, and busiest in the Bureau.

The year was 1970, and I was working in the FBI photo lab with a group of other young Vietnam War veterans. The lab was a different world from the rest of the offices in the FBI building. Picture a large photographic darkroom whose walls are lined with hundreds of boxes of the special light-sensitive paper on which photos are printed. Each box contained five hundred sheets of this paper which measures eight by ten inches. The boxes have a very distinctive look, since each one bears the familiar red and yellow Kodak colors and logo. Imagine this room in which four or five guys labor, all day, ethereal figures in gray wrap-around smocks. We looked like ghosts from a scene in a Fellini film or, perhaps, the subjects of a surrealistic painting by Salvador Dali. So there we were, working in this cavelike atmosphere bathed only in pale yellow light. Day after day, this was the scene, our little cast of characters producing high-quality photos, some of which would make their way into courtrooms and others which would turn up in newspapers. Still others would be seen on the nightly news as the news anchor alerts the public to be on the lookout for the sinister person in the photo.

While in the military, all of us had experienced the idiosyncrasies of working in a bureaucracy. Don, the photo lab supervisor, was an expert in these matters. He was the consummate bureaucratic government employee. He was the ultimate "yes man" in the FBI. Whatever his superiors told him to do, no matter how inane, he would follow orders and do it. His sense of humor ranked with that of a garden slug. He did, however, run an efficient operation, a paramilitary unit which operated on the previously mentioned Hoover Fear Doctrine. The method was simple—just fear everyone in authority. Fear the Director. Fear your supervisor. Fear the FBI. And you'll do just fine.

Most of us in the lab, being Vietnam War veterans, were able to function under the fear factor without it really affecting our performance. After all, we figured, how bad could anything be compared to bombs going off near your quarters or someone shooting at you in the middle of the night? So we carried on despite the circumstances. But we also complained, and did we complain! Not about the fear factor, mind you, but about working for Don and his ridiculous theory which was that FBI agents were born photographers. He believed that each agent possessed the skill and photojournalistic techniques of Mathew Brady, the famous Civil War photographer who poignantly documented the war while lugging around a camera about the size of a Volkswagen Beetle. So the agents were the photographers. We, the real photographers assigned to the FBI photo lab, were merely the agents' servants. It was our task to process film and produce prints which celebrated the photographic expertise of the investigators. We were there, according to Don, to make the agents look good when the photos were exhibited in court as evidence. It was our place to be unseen, the stagehands behind the scenes. He wanted us locked into the darkroom for our entire eight hour shift. We were allowed our two fifteen-minute breaks a day, as prescribed by Bureau rules, and a forty-five-minute lunch, which he personally timed on the big government clock on his office wall.

The work, to say the least, was tedious. There were no minilabs like you see in the stores today, where the photo technician simply presses a button and—voila! The machine processes the pictures. It was quite different in the '70's. In those days, the photographic processing took place in the dark. Some of us became quite capable of functioning without light and, in the process, gained some limited insight into what it's like to be blind. On most days, Don rarely came into the darkroom. Rather, he reminded us of his presence through the smell of his pipe smoke which filtered through the air ducts and into the darkroom. It was a deep scent of cherry wood, which was reminiscent of an ancient college professor in a British tweed suit, who, while pondering a point in English literature, would puff on some fine blend of English tobacco. These smells were always accompanied by the clanking of Don's pipe on a government-issued ashtray. These were sensory experiences which, to this day, I can clearly recall by closing my eyes and allowing myself to return to that darkroom.

On some days, it was actually quite comforting to be buried in one of those dark rooms, especially when the winds of a New York winter whipped around the corners of the FBI building. Yet we still believed that our place was out there in the field, at the crime scene taking the photographs. But this was not to be, because Don lived in fear—fear that one day, Mr. Hoover would arrive at our little smoke-filled sanctuary only to find that no personnel were there. Instead, we would be out doing what we were hired to do—take pictures. That, Don believed, was not our mission. He also made it quite clear that nowhere in our job description as FBI photographers was there a reference to our being allowed to experience or exhibit humor. We, the mighty warriors of the FBI photo lab were about to change that.

According to Don, humor was synonymous with laziness. After, all, how can you have fun and still get the job done? And, even more importantly, what if the almighty Jedgar Hoover were to show up and find us laughing as we produced photos of some guy robbing a bank? The truth, however, was simply that Hoover rarely, if ever, visited the New York office. Once comfortably ensconced in his suite at New York's landmark hotel, the Waldorf Astoria, he would conduct all of his business there. If he were to visit the office, the chances of him coming to the photo lab would be the proverbial slim to none.

Anyone who has ever worked in an office environment has either witnessed, or been a party to, an office prank. For the most part, these jokes are designed to brighten up what might be an otherwise boring day of shuffling papers and responding to e-mails. People may assume that since the FBI is such a serious organization, this type of behavior would never take place in an FBI office. Nothing could be farther from the truth. Perhaps, because of all the seriousness surrounding the work, Bureau folks need these little breaks even more than other office workers. I'll give you a couple of examples.

One day, during a period of complete disgust with our supervisor, a wave of mischief hung heavy in the air. We hatched a plan to get back at Don for some of his ludicrous bureaucratic rules and regulations. Our little band of pranksters, most of whom had spent time in the military, were well experienced at launching pranks designed to bust the chops of a superior.

Our plan was multidimensional. Part A, an operation known as the "The Doughnut Caper" was conjured up in response to one of the unwritten rules of the photo lab, which stated that no eating was to take place in the darkroom. Don's reasoning behind this was that Mr. Hoover might show up and catch FBI employees engaged in an activity that would prevent them from working.

We began our attack the following morning. Chris arrived early, carrying a box of freshly baked jelly doughnuts, the kind that make a morning smell like a great day is about to begin. Smuggling the box into the darkroom under his lab coat, Chris dashed quickly past Don's office. With Bill assigned as the lookout, we began to devour the savory feast, all the while dropping white powdered sugar onto the black rubber mats, which covered the darkroom floor. Within seconds, Bill gave the signal. Don was on the way. We quickly ditched the evidence—into our lab coat pockets. "Are you guys eating in here?" barked the bureaucrat. "Eating?" cried Bill, as he wiped the telltale red jelly from his lips. "Yes, eating", Don said. Chris, in his most mature voice, replied, "We know the rules. We never eat in here." "Well, it smells like a damn doughnut shop in here to me!", screamed Don. Noticing that Don was staring at the dusting of white powder covering the floor mat, Chris blurted out, "Oh, looks like we spilled some of the chemical powder on the floor. We better get that cleaned up!" As Don left the room, I heard him mumbling something about Mr. Hoover firing all of us for eating doughnuts in the darkroom.

With Plan A successfully executed, we discussed how, within a week or so, we would launch Offensive B, to which we assigned the code name "The Musical Darkroom." This plan was in response to Don's theory that listening to music in the darkroom would reduce productivity.

The plan was simple and virtually foolproof. We would remove one of the boxes of photographic paper from the shelves, take out the paper, and replace it with a radio. Don would enter the darkroom, hear the radio, and accuse us of listening to music. At this point, we'd pull the plug and deny the accusation. We knew that this would drive him crazy.

My job was to punch a group of tiny, practically invisible holes in the box so the music would ring out loud and clear. Knowing how Don hated rock and roll, we set the radio on one of our favorite rock stations, placed the box back among the others, and left for the day, eagerly anticipating tomorrow's coup.

The following morning, as we shuffled around the darkroom, I turned on the hidden radio, then rejoined my cohorts who were busy printing shots of some bank robbery suspect. As the pounding sound of Chubby Checker singing about "The Twist" pulsated the air, the familiar smell of pipe smoke began to drift under the darkroom door.

Within seconds, the heavy gray metal door began to open. As Don entered the room, he came to a dead stop. "Where's the radio?" he blurted out. Not a sound emerged from any of us. The silence was broken by Ike bravely asking, "What radio, Don?" The music continued to thrash through the room . . . "like we did last summer. Let's twist again, like we did last year. Do you remember when . . ." With a quick kick of my foot, I yanked the cord from the outlet. The music ceased. Chubby Checker had left the darkroom. Angrily shaking his pipe at us, Don repeated his original question, "Where's the radio?" We all stood in silent protest as he turned abruptly and left the darkroom. As he did so, I plugged the radio back in. The thumping beat of "The Twist" once again permeated the airwaves. Another successful coup had been completed!

I don't think that Don ever quite recovered from that one. To this day, when I tune my radio to an oldies station and hear Chubby Checker twisting away, I can't help but remember the day the music died in the darkroom, only to be reborn the moment that Don walked out the door. Let's twist again like we did last summer, let's twist again like we did last year . . .

Perhaps it never occurred to you, but the FBI is looked upon by many as a sanctuary, a safe haven, a place to call on a lonely Saturday evening. After all, everybody knows that the Bureau is on duty twenty-four seven. Because of this, the FBI, throughout the years, has always received phone calls that really should have gone elsewhere. Some of these calls are made by unstable individuals. Some come from lonely souls seeking solace in the sound of another human voice. Sometimes they are mental patients calling from public phones in the hallway of an institution. Here are a few incidents involving the FBI switchboard staff and the highly sophisticated methods which FBI personnel have employed in dealing with strange calls from even stranger people:

Let's call this first one "They Have Just Landed in Brooklyn." It was the onset of the midnight-to-8:00 a.m. shift. On this particular evening, I was assigned to the Complaint Desk, a less-than-glamorous position consisting of answering the phone. At the time, in addition to my FBI employment, I was a night student at the City University of New York, so that I could obtain my bachelor's degree. I had brought a small pile of textbooks with me in order to get in some studying between phone calls.

At about 1:00 am, while staring blankly at a book entitled *People in Quandaries*, I was jolted by the piercing ring of the black rotary dial phone in front of me. Answering in my most official FBI voice, I said, "FBI. May I help you?" A raspy male voice replied, "They just landed." "Who just landed, sir?" "The space guys," said Mr. Raspy. Mindful that the FBI must show respect to the public, I expressed genuine interest as I asked the caller for details. "Well, see I'm in this phone booth in Prospect Park in Brooklyn, and I just saw them land," he said in a quivering voice. "Who just landed, and what did they land

93

in?" I asked. "It was a spaceship, kind of round and flat, like a pancake. Real shiny looking and silver like tin foil. And it had lights all around the edge." "I guess they need those lights to see where they're landing," I commented. "Yep. And you should have seen the space guys that got out of that thing!" "I'm sorry that I wasn't there to see them," I remarked. "Were they wearing helmets?" "Of course!" he screamed, berating me for being so ignorant. "Were you able to you see what they looked like through their helmets?" I asked. "Oh yeah. They had bright green skin," he said without hesitation. His voice began to get shakier as he went on to describe the aliens as "typical space guys who land in Brooklyn." Having overheard the conversation, the other clerk who was on duty that night was itchy to get involved. I told the fellow on the line to hang on while I got an expert in these matters to handle the situation.

I handed the phone to Hank, a career FBI clerk who had handled just about every type of caller over the years. He proceeded to tell the guy that it was his civic duty to convince the aliens to return to their ship and head home. The guy agreed but said that he had no idea what to do. Hank told him that he should speak to them in a language that they would understand, perhaps the ancient language of Moshna Goshna. Listening in on the other line, I could hear the guy begin screaming into the night, shouting sounds which bore no resemblance to English, or any other language spoken on Earth. Suddenly the screaming stopped. A recording came on the line saying, "Please deposit another nickel to continue this call." There was a click, then dead silence. It was over. I guess the guy had successfully convinced the aliens to return to their home somewhere out in the galaxy. More likely, he ran out of change.

Some months later, I was told that the guys on night duty had received a similar call during which the caller said that the Russians were bombarding his brain with sound waves from space. In true FBI fashion, one of the guys on duty told the caller that the only way to defeat this was to place wads of tin foil in his ears in order to deflect the signals. It was reported that the following night the same guy called to report that the remedy had worked and that his brain waves were now clear.

Years later, as an agent working in the field of foreign counterintelligence, I interviewed a young lady who had contacted the Bureau to reveal some important information regarding Russian spies. The interview seemed productive at first, until she claimed that the Russians had implanted chemicals into her skin which were not only making her act strangely, but were also causing her breasts to get larger and larger. She was fearful that they would get too large and eventually explode. After thanking her for her patriotism in providing the information, I ushered her out of the office, all the while thinking that perhaps she was going home to Brooklyn to join her husband who was sitting on the couch watching *The Twilight Zone* with his ears filled with wads of tin foil.

Now, not every misadventure in the organization involved interaction with oddballs from the general public. Some revolved around FBI employees themselves. For instance, here's one I call "Divorced by Memo."

The mountain of mail on the SAC's (special agent in charge) secretary's desk had grown to the size of a small volcano. Looking at it with disdain, she mused in wonderment over how it had seemingly doubled in height since yesterday afternoon. "I'll just never get ahead," she mumbled under her breath. As she began to sort through the pile in an attempt to prioritize the stack of papers, she spotted one paper with the word "Deadline" near the top, next to the line that read, "To SAC." "I guess he'd better see this one first since it has a deadline," she continued to mumble. As she placed the memo on the top of the pile, her eye caught something familiar. It was her husband's name, SA (Special Agent) James Harney (not his real name). She began to read the short paragraph. In concise bureaucratic language, it read, "In compliance with FBI policy, I hereby notify the SAC of my divorce. Further details will follow." As her complexion changed to a mottled shade of gray, an intense burning began to swell within her stomach. "How could this be?" she questioned. Things had not been going so well lately, but she and Jim had agreed to try to work things out. "Was he this insensitive and afraid to confront me that he's divorcing me without telling me first?" She placed the memo on top of the stack of other priority papers that the SAC would read that morning, then she withdrew it. With the memo in her trembling hand and tears flowing down her cheeks, she quietly approached her boss's door and knocked politely. "Come in, Dorothy." She entered his office, quietly closing the door behind her. Seeing her condition, he immediately said, "Sit down. What's wrong?"

In a tiny quivering voice and in a manner not at all like her usual boisterous self, she told of her discovery of the memo. Her boss was as shocked as she was. In all of his years in a managerial position, he had never had to deal with a situation of this nature. Throughout the next half hour, Dorothy poured out her woeful tale of a marriage gone sour. The SAC was able to offer some comforting words followed by the suggestion that she take the rest of the day off to give herself time to sort things out. In fact, he offered that, perhaps, she should take a few days off, if she felt that this was necessary.

From what I heard, the divorce went through, and Dorothy eventually returned to work. Her former husband, at his own request, was transferred to another field office. As the years went by, the office gossip about the incident faded away. However, every so often, when a few of us would reminisce about "the good old days," someone would say, "Hey, remember when that secretary got divorced by memo?"

Here's a surprisingly shocking little tale from the FBI archives in my head. Back in the 1970's, the FBI office faced a swank apartment building which was so close that it was easy to see into the windows. One of these windows was located directly opposite my squad's area. On any given evening, there was always a handful of agents in the office diligently typing away in an attempt to catch up on some paperwork. Each evening, at about nine o'clock, a young woman would appear at one of the windows facing our desks. That, in itself, was of no great consequence. What made the event special was that each and every time she made her appearance, she was completely nude. At this point, all typing would cease. Lest you think of FBI agents as voyeurs, I will make no mention of the many pairs of binoculars which suddenly came out of several desk drawers during the course of these disgusting exhibitions.

Interesting folks, those FBI people. There was one young lady, a support employee, who, it was said, was married a total of five times—each time to a different FBI agent. I personally knew two of these lucky gentlemen. Being a native New Yorker who was enamored with the city, she refused to leave, except for vacations. It seems that every time the agent that she was married to received a transfer, rather than leave the Big Apple, she would simply divorce him. At last count, she remained married to the fifth guy, although there was one small problem. On weekends, she and her husband, an FBI supervisor, would drive the FBI car which was assigned to him to their weekend home in Pennsylvania's Pocono Mountains. This little infraction, a violation of FBI rules, had a major impact on both of their careers. The supervisor was not very well-liked by the agents on his squad, so one fine day, they mounted a surveillance and tracked the loving couple to their second home as they racked up tons of extra miles on the FBI car. They then presented the evidence, including photos of the couple enjoying their government transportation, to the Bureau. The whole sordid affair ended in both the husband and wife being fired. The FBI looks down a bit on employees who misuse government equipment.

There's nothing as serious as an FBI agent who takes his work seriously. Joe was just such an agent. Always busy investigating the hell out of some matter of interest to the FBI, he would sometimes forget to have lunch or make an important phone call. At other times, he would fail to attend a mandatory briefing or miss a scheduled date to attend firearms training because he had some pressing Bureau matter to attend to. Although his dedication is to be lauded, upon retiring, he discovered that the FBI is still in business and hasn't folded since his departure.

One of the Joe's greatest moments was his brief stint as a movie star. Picture this: Brad Pitt and Harrison Ford are in the street right in front of the entrance to the Federal Building in New York. They're filming an action-packed chase sequence complete with dodging cars and pedestrians. Upstairs, in the FBI office, droves of FBI employees are craning their necks to catch a glimpse of the action many stories below. At the time, having just returned from my lunchtime walk, I was right on the block where the filming was taking place. As the cameras began to roll, Brad Pitt crossed the street and then headed down the block. At this point, a female actor in a tan trench coat was directed to begin crossing the street. After stepping off the curb and taking a few steps, the director yelled, "Cut!" He called her over, spoke briefly with her, then ordered the cameras to begin rolling again. Once again, the woman began to cross the street, and the action was halted as she approached the opposite curb. After a few brief changes, the action again began. I could see that the director looked pleased with how the action was going. Then, suddenly, he yelled, "Cut!" What had happened was that just as the woman got halfway across the street, a man crossed directly in front of her path. Slightly brushing her coat and briefcase, he continued steadfastly on his way, looking down as if in deep thought. It was apparent that he was completely oblivious to the goings-on surrounding him. How this was possible I'll never know. With camera crews, lighting technicians, soundmen, makeup artists, and dozens of other movie folk scurrying around like so many rats on a feeding frenzy, how could he walk right onto the set as if he were crossing a normal New York City street? That was Joe. As always, deep in thought about some case he was working on—probably the Big One, the one case that would make FBI history that year.

Joe had been caught on film. He was now a part of moviemaking history. He, and he alone, had disrupted the filming of a major motion picture. Brad Pitt and Harrison Ford had nothing on him. For the next few weeks, Joe was considered the movie's true star—at least by us guys in the office. We couldn't stop laughing every time someone who had seen the incident recounted how the actress had stared in disbelief at Joe as he continued to cross that street, staring intently at the blacktop, completely unaware of what was going on around him. Yep, Joe was a star—an entity unto himself.

And now a word about FBI leadership. The Bureau has always prided itself on employing individuals considered to be the cream of the crop. This of course, extends itself into the management arena. For the most part, Bureau managers are truly capable leaders; however, even among the finest of managerial types, quirky behavior sometimes surfaces. Take the case of the head of the New York office during my early Bureau years, John F. Malone. My experiences with Mr. Malone were often more personal than others may have had due to the nature of my position as a photographer. As I told you earlier, my time was mostly relegated to darkroom duty. However, on rare and very special occasions, my skills in actually taking pictures were allowed to shine. During these unusual occurrences, I was assigned to photograph dignitaries visiting Mr. Malone in his office. Because of this, I got to speak with him on a different level than others in the organization. On one occasion, he thought that his pants were too high above his shoes. He called me into his office just before I was due to take some shots of him meeting with a governor. After telling me how he was going to have to find a different tailor, he said, "Do these 'high waters' really look too short?" He wanted truthful answers, and I gave them to him. After all, it was my job to make him look good. Few, if any, agents or clerks could say to him as I did, "Mr. Malone, I think the governor is going to wonder why you wore tennis shorts to work. If I were you, I'd pose behind my desk. No, better yet, I'll shoot you from the waist up." He laughed, agreed, and upon seeing the photos the next day called my boss exclaiming that I was one talented photographer.

A few times a year, Malone would be visited by an old childhood friend, bandleader Lawrence Welk. I shot many pictures of Mr. Welk with female FBI employees whom he referred to as his "Champagne Ladies," the same phrase he used with the women on his TV show.

John Malone was a fine man, but a little quirky and, I might add, quite hard of hearing. The guys around the office just loved to goof on him. On one occasion, Malone was driving his official FBI car, designated Unit 10. A call came in to the radio room from Malone's car. The dialogue went something like this: "This is Unit 10 calling the radio room." "Go ahead, Unit 10," said the operator. "Uh, this is Unit 10" "Yes, sir. What can we do for you?" "I'm, uh, Unit 10." "Yes, sir, we know that, sir. What's the problem?" "I'm not sure where I am." "Okay, sir, are you in the vicinity of the office?" "No, I'm on my way home to Pennsylvania." "Okay. Can you give us any landmarks?" "Yes, I'm approaching a big mountain. Wait a minute. Now I'm going around the mountain." Apparently, other Bureau cars had picked up this conversation on their radios. Within a few seconds, the personnel in the radio room could hear mics clicking on, followed by several agents singing almost in unison, "He'll be comin' round the mountain when he comes." We never found out whether Malone appreciated this or not. And to my recollection, he rarely relied on the radio room again for directions.

Another Malone story involved an embarrassing situation in an elevator. This tale centered around Cindy, a young FBI secretary who had had not one but two car accidents in one weekend. On Monday morning, Malone, who wanted to be kept apprised of any information regarding Bureau personnel, was told about Cindy's accidents. He then entered a crowded elevator car in the FBI building and was immediately greeted by several agents and the young secretary, all arriving for work. Seeing Cindy, he smiled, then turned to the agents, and said in his booming voice, "Do you fellas know Cindy here?" pointing to the young lady. "She got banged twice this weekend!" Perhaps incidents like this are the reason why, at times, Malone was referred to as Cement Head.

One last Cement Head story you might enjoy: About once a year, the FBI field office would hold an "All-Agents Conference." In essence, this was a staff meeting of all the agents assigned to the office. Although there were no female agents during those years, several secretaries and the FBI nurses were permitted to attend. Administrative matters and updates on what was happening in the FBI were discussed. This annual get-together was not exactly the most scintillating event on the FBI's yearly calendar. In fact, several agents managed to catch a few winks during the meeting. I'll never forget the one conference where, as the hush of the crowd became a low hum, a tapping on the microphone was heard. As silence enveloped the room, an aging Assistant Director Malone addressed the crowd, beginning with, "Good morning, boys and girls." Now, I will admit that he was old enough to have been my grandfather, but "boys and girls"? Give me a break! Reactions from the audience varied from insult to hilarity. While some of the burliest agents made motions of thumb sucking, others merely shook their heads in disbelief. Some found it impossible to control themselves and burst out into waves of raucous laughter. Once again, Mr. Malone, though meaning no harm, had truly lived up to his reputation as Cement Head.

Does anyone out there remember Martha Mitchell? For those who don't, Martha was the verbose wife of U.S. Attorney General John Mitchell during the 1970's. More than a few folks in Washington, and beyond, referred to her as "Martha the Mouth." Martha had an opinion on just about every subject and believed that everyone was entitled to it. She seemed to be on an endless publicity tour which, on one occasion, included a stop at the FBI's New

York office. On that day, I was happily devouring doughnuts in the photo lab darkroom. As I placed a group of prints classified as "Secret" into the tray of chemicals, the door slowly opened, and in walked our supervisor, Don, followed by a woman whom I immediately recognized from the newspapers and TV. Clothed in a luxurious camel-colored wool coat, in strode Martha Mitchell. With an air of authority, she walked straight toward me and, in doing so, completely ignored Don, just as he was about to begin an explanation of how the photo process works. It was quite obvious that her only interest was in the pictures I was producing. Peering down into the tray, she said, "Oh, I know that building. Isn't that the_____building? I understand that you fellas are interested in the spies in there." In a state of utter surprise and shock, I replied, "Well, uh, yes it is, and, uh, yes, we are." In a flash, she had identified a building that housed several individuals, whom the FBI suspected were spying on the United States! How the hell did she know this? This stuff was highly classified. You had to possess a Secret clearance to have knowledge of the FBI's interest in this building. Here I was printing pictures which could possibly lead to the conviction of spies attempting to pilfer U.S. technology, and Martha knew more about the case than most of the agents in the New York office! In addition, she was very personable, asking each of us how we enjoyed working for the Bureau, how our families were doing, and who was planning on becoming an agent someday. When she left the room, with Don in tow, like a puppy following his master, we all had a good laugh at how the boss had been tossed aside while we became the stars of the show. We turned the Kodak box radio back on, grabbed a doughnut, and went back to work, secure in the knowledge that the nation's secrets were being guarded by the wife of the attorney general.

Martha was not the only celebrity to visit the lab. On one occasion, I had the privilege of joining forces with another one of the photo guys in taking the official mug shots of organized crime boss, Joe Colombo. In an attempt to drum up business for his weekend job of shooting wedding photos, one of my fellow photographers, who was known for his outrageous behavior, handed Joe's wife his business card, announcing that he would be glad to shoot any weddings that the Mafia might have coming up. I damn near collapsed at the thought of Don coming into the room and hearing that offer. That would have been even worse than a radio in the darkroom!

One day, I received an assignment to photograph some valuable jewelry that the FBI had recovered from a jewel heist. After I finished taking the pictures, I brought the jewels back to the equipment storage room at the rear of the photo lab to hand them back to the agent handling the case. Sitting there with the agent was the victim of the crime. She was perched atop a dingy gray vintage World War ll government desk, her long legs draped over its edge. They looked like liquid flowing down to the tile floor. I could not help but stare at what must have been the longest and most shapely legs in the universe. Noticing my obvious interest, she began to laugh. I stammered a weak, "Oh, hi, Miss Loren!" as Sophia extended her hand and thanked me for taking the photos. I remember thinking, "Someday, I'll be in show business, just like you, Miss Loren—someday."

Another "star" that I met in the photo lab was an artist. Well, actually I didn't meet him, but rather, a piece of his work. El Greco, with whom I had become familiar from my art history classes in college, was a world-renowned painter who died several centuries ago. One of his most famous paintings had been stolen and was later recovered by the FBI. When the stolen work was found and brought to our office, it had to be photographed for evidentiary purposes. This task fell to me. Although it was simply a matter of taking a few shots of a famous painting, I got quite a thrill out of having a private audience with the masterpiece. I spent about an hour photographing it and studying the details which raised this piece to the highest level in the world of art, thus making it worth several million dollars. While taking the pictures, I became overwhelmed by the sense of awe over being alone in the presence of one of the great masters. Believe me, I ate no doughnuts in that room!

Here's one of the all-time classics: In the early 1970's the FBI employed what it called "The Char Force." This was a group of highly dedicated, yet minimally educated folks who cleaned the FBI building. All of them had gone through an extensive background investigation; after which they had been granted a security clearance to work in spaces within the office that handled sensitive documents. One of these folks was a lovely lady named Lilly. Lilly was a true Southerner, a large forty-ish-year-old woman with a heart of gold. To FBI employees, she was a psychotherapist. She would listen to your problems, then dole out a good dose of Southern philosophy combined with common sense and humor. It was guaranteed that you'd walk away feeling better about yourself and the world, after a therapy session with Lilly.

Lilly cleaned from morning till night, making sure that even the drabbest of the dull gray metal cabinets was dust free. One of her tasks was to clean the Interview Room. This was a room right out of the movies. On the far wall was a series of black horizontal lines with heights in inches marked on one side. At the opposite end of the room was a viewing booth with a large glass window. This booth also served as a projection booth when films were shown in the room. It was in this Interview Room that lineups were conducted.

Four or five people were lined up against the striped wall, each holding a numbered plaque. One was the suspect and the others were just fillers, or "extras." At times, agents were used as the "extras" along with the suspect. The witness was brought into the glass room accompanied by two or three agents. A bright light shone down on those in the lineup as the witness peered through the glass, seeking to identify the suspect. One of the agents would sit in the room next to the witness and issue orders through a microphone. These instructions, such as, "Everybody, turn to the left" or "Number three, turn to your right" could be heard loudly, echoing through the room where the individuals in the lineup stood. The Interview Room was located in close proximity to the photo lab, making it easy for those of us working in the lab to take one of our two daily fifteen-minute breaks in there, provided that the room was not being used.

One day, after escaping the tedium of a morning spent in the darkroom, a couple of the photographers decided to liven things up by playing a practical joke on Lilly. We all knew her greatest fears: God, death, and J. Edgar Hoover. About five minutes before she was to begin cleaning the Interview Room, my photo buddies hid themselves in the projection booth, while I witnessed the whole sordid affair from the hallway. Within a few minutes, Lilly—with her broom, mop, and pail—approached. All was silent as Lilly entered the room. She placed the mop and pail in a corner adjacent to the wall where the lineup gang stands, grabbed the broom, and began to sweep, all the while singing some rousing gospel melody about getting to heaven on time.

Through the microphone, one of the guys, in a deep voice, began to chant, "Lilly, Li . . . lly," drawing out each sound, "this is the voice of the dead agents." At this point, Lilly froze in place, the broom stopping in the middle of its arc across the floor. "Lilly, you better clean faster. Mr. Hoover is on his way up to this rooo . . . m."

As I peered through the doorway, I could see the broom fly across the room as Lilly spun around like a top. I felt a rush of wind as Lilly dashed out the door past me and down the hallway at breakneck speed, screaming something about the dead agents and Mr. Hoover.

As I walked back to the lab, I felt sorry for Lilly. But I have to admit, it was a good trick. That evening, before going home, the guys confessed, telling Lilly how sorry they were. Lilly laughed along with them. That's how she was, a forgiving soul.

I love urban legends—those implausible, yet tantalizing stories that people declare are true because they heard them from someone whose cousin actually knows the guy it happened to. Sure, he actually saw the alligator come out of the sewer in the street in New York! And of course he knew the lady that sold the vintage Chevy Corvette for $5 just to get it out of her garage. Well, here's an FBI urban legend that's true. I know because I was there. It's the legend of Special Agent Harold Carr.

Back in the early 1970's the FBI had on its payroll a quasi-agent named Harold. Here is his story:

On my first day in the Bureau, I was told to report to the basement in the FBI building and ask for Special Agent Harold Carr, who would administer my Bureau driving test. "What are they talking about?" I thought. First of all, I had been driving since I was seventeen and possessed a valid New York State license. Why would I need to take another test? Second, why would they have a Special Agent of the FBI spending his valuable time giving driving tests instead of investigating crimes? Knowing that it was not my place to question FBI procedures, I dutifully reported to the basement where I saw some guys loading boxes marked "Evidence" onto a cart. Upon asking them where I might find Mr. Carr, they immediately turned defensive and asked why I had to see him. I found the whole thing vaguely reminiscent of the scene in *The Wizard of Oz*, where the characters were trying to get to see the all-powerful Wizard and were told by the gatekeeper that nobody sees the Wizard, no way, no how. When I told them that I was reporting for my Bureau driver's test, they immediately changed their demeanor. Acting again like the Wizard's gatekeeper, one of them proclaimed, "Now that's a horse of a different color. You must be new here." Once they heard that it was my first day, with a knowing glance, they directed me to a desk in a dimly lit corner of the room. There sitting behind the desk, reading a copy of the *New York Post*, was an elderly-looking black fellow sporting a white shirt and a yellow polka dot bow tie. Unlike the Wizard in every way, he looked more like a character out of some early Hollywood movie. Perched precariously on the very front edge of his desk was a sign proclaiming that he was, in fact, "Special Agent Harold Carr."

He looked up and in a voice much like the grating of two sheets of sandpaper rubbing against each other, said, "I'm Harold, son. What are you here for?" He seemed a little disturbed that I had interrupted his reading. I sheepishly replied that I was here to take my driver's test. Straightening his bow tie, he got up slowly, saying, "Well, let's go get it over with so we're not late for lunch." He guided me back to the elevator, which carried us up to street level. Once outdoors, he pointed to a car, handed me the keys, and said, "Once around the block." I got in, let him in on the passenger side, and watched as he positioned himself in a protective driving instructor posture.

103

Raising his hand as if he were about to signal the start of the Indy 500, he simply said, "Go." So I went.

As I negotiated my way through snarled New York traffic, he turned to me and said, "Know how to park?" "Sure," I replied, "I'm from New York." "Good, let's go back. You passed." I remember thinking, "That's it? I passed?" I had barely driven around the block! My top speed never exceeded eleven miles per hour! How can this test prove that I am worthy of driving an FBI vehicle, particularly at high speed? Leaping back into reality, I realized that I was not yet an agent. I had been hired as a photographer. This wasn't the movies. I had as much of a chance of being called upon to drive a high-speed pursuit vehicle as Ronald Regan had at being president. When we returned to the FBI building, the parking spot I had left was still open. I was amazed. Nowhere in New York can you leave a parking spot and return to find it still unoccupied. I asked Harold how this could have happened. He simply said, "We're the FBI. Nobody takes that spot. Not nobody. Not no how." He truly was the Wizard.

When I returned to the office, I was taken to the photo lab to be introduced to my new coworkers. "So, Rick, do you have any questions?" one of them said. Without a moment's hesitation, I fired my questions on semiautomatic, blurting out without a breath, "Who is Harold Carr? How old is he? Why is he located in the basement? And why is an FBI agent giving driving tests to new employees?" Here's the legend as it was told to me:

Harold Carr was a "sort-of" Special Agent of the FBI. As you may know, one of the requirements to be an FBI agent is that you must have graduated with a four-year degree from an accredited college. Harold had never gone to college. Also, you must have completed the training course given at the FBI Academy, including firearms training. Harold had never attended the academy, nor did he carry, or even know how to use, a gun. So how did he become an agent? FBI Director J. Edgar Hoover had "knighted" him. He had appointed him an agent, and he did this for a particular reason. The story is told that Hoover, at some point, was in need of a chauffeur for his limousine. However, he insisted that the person be an agent. While searching the ranks for a loyal employee to fill this role, it was suggested to him that a fine young man named Harold Carr would be an excellent choice. However, it was pointed out to Hoover that Carr did not quite fit the bill since he was a clerk and not an agent. Despite his lack of qualifications for the special agent position, Mr. Hoover found Carr to be an outstanding candidate because of his years of service as a clerk and his loyalty to the Bureau. In order to satisfy the agent requirement, he simply waved his magic pen over some official document, instantly transforming Carr into an agent. In order for Harold to demonstrate to the world that he was a real FBI agent, Hoover authorized him to carry credentials, the official identification carried by every FBI agent.

As Harold got older and older, his duties went from giving driving tests to picking up theater tickets for visiting dignitaries. During the 1970's, when I went from being a photographer to an agent, I visited with Harold several times. I would find him crouched in his own little corner of the universe in the basement. With each visit, I could see that he was becoming more frail. His frame seemed to be shrinking, and he eventually walked with his head down, barely able to lift his eyes to greet me. Arthritis and age were taking a toll. He no longer had any real duties. The FBI knew this, but the Bureau had been his life, and no one even gave a thought to asking him to retire. So he just sat in the basement of the FBI building reading the newspaper and remembering the days when he served as the FBI Director's trusted driver. Officially, he was never a real agent, but to all of us, he was as special as any Special Agent could be.

And now a charming little tale known as "Tunnel Vision." The two cops sat staring at the traffic through the window of their cruiser, anticipating, and perhaps hoping for, an uneventful shift. The chatter on their radio was suddenly broken by the sound of a female voice announcing that all units on the Jersey side of the Holland Tunnel should be on the lookout for a vehicle expected to be exiting the tunnel shortly. In clearly enunciated tones, the voice said, "The suspect was spotted entering the tunnel carrying a concealed handgun. He is described as a white male in his forties, approximately six-foot-two. He's driving a red Plymouth Fury with New York plates. We don't have the plate numbers yet. We're checking the surveillance cameras in the tunnel for that info. He's wearing a light blue shirt with a navy blue tie. He's armed and considered dangerous. Once again, he's carrying a concealed handgun, probably on his hip. He's to be apprehended as soon as he exits the tunnel. He should be coming out on the Jersey side in about two minutes. Backup units and officers on foot will be on the scene to assist. I repeat, this suspect is armed and dangerous."

With his eyes steadily trained on the gaping tunnel exit, Juan, the younger of the two officers said, "Okay, Bill. Looks like we got some action." "Sounds like it," replied Bill, a twelve-year veteran on the force. Thinking that perhaps he had missed part of the alert, he questioned Juan, asking, "Did she say what this guy's status is? Is he a terrorist or something?" "No. She just gave his description," Juan replied. He then added, "Hold on, I'll ask." Before he could ask for additional details, the radio crackled. The female voice came back on.

"Our report is that a witness observed this guy getting into his car on the New York side of the tunnel at five fifteen, and as he took off his sports jacket, she observed a gun, in a holster, on his waist. We have no further information at this time." "Oh, great. Maybe the guy's a cop, undercover, or something. Well, I guess we'll find out when he comes out of the tunnel."

The traffic was horrendous that day, barely crawling out of the tunnel. This, of course, was not unusual for a New York rush hour commute to New Jersey, where many New York workers lived. As the Plymouth slowly pulled out of the tunnel, Jack, the driver, noticed a hubbub of police activity. Within thirty seconds, it became obvious to him that he was the center of that activity. The red lights on the roof of the police cruiser became a blinding blur of color as the voice on the PA system told Jack, in no uncertain terms, that he was to pull over and remain in the car. Not one to ignore the orders of law enforcement officers, Jack slowly brought the car to a halt at the curb just outside the mouth of the tunnel. Turning his head to the left as he rolled down the window, he was met square on by the business end of a shotgun barrel. In the background he could see several other cops, some with handguns drawn, others holding shotguns aimed in his direction. Jack knew that there had been some kind of misunderstanding. After all, Jack was certainly not a terrorist. He was, in fact, an FBI agent—and a firearms instructor at that!

"Take your hands off the wheel and slowly place them on the door," ordered the officer holding the shotgun. No sooner had he finished the sentence when the other cop yelled, "Don't move!"

Jack knew that he had to remain calm. He also knew that these cops didn't exactly have their act together. Leaving his hands resting on top of the steering wheel, he said, "I'm an FBI agent. One of you just told me to move my hands and the other said not to move. When you guys are in agreement as to what you want me to do, I'll gladly do it. First of all, the car is still in gear." With that, the second cop reached in, grabbed the gearshift, and jammed the car into the "Park" position. Still keeping his foot on the brake pedal as a precaution, Jack continued, "Now, if you reach into my shirt pocket, you'll find my FBI credentials." With that, the officer reached over and pulled the identification from Jack's shirt pocket. After scrutinizing the ID and noting the name, he said, "Looks authentic. Where's your gun, Agent Kammer?" "Holstered, on my right hip," said Jack. "Mind if I check?" said the cop. "No problem," Jack said. Jack felt the cop's hand slowly remove his gun from his holster. He resisted the urge to assist the officer, not daring to move. Both officers examined the gun, then reexamined his credentials. They then lowered their weapons. As the shotgun was removed from his face, Jack heard the officer mumble, in official police lingo, the words "oh shit." Signaling the officers in the distance to also lower their weapons, the cops then returned Jack's gun to him. Both then apologized for the incident, explaining that someone had seen Jack's gun as he got into his car and had called the precinct to report what they had seen.

Jack knew that the cops had reacted properly to the threat posed by someone carrying a weapon in one of New York's tunnels. After all, he could have been a terrorist, deranged individual, or who knows what else. But the conflicting orders given to him by the cops left him a bit disconcerted since one wrong move on his part could have resulted in him having his head blown off. The fact is that at the end of each workday, hundreds of FBI agents leave New York via the tunnels and bridges linking the city to New Jersey, Long Island, and other areas where the agents reside. Imagine the traffic jam that could be created by cops stopping every agent like they did in Jack's case!

As Jack pulled away from the curb and re-embarked on his trip home, he thought of how he'd answer when his wife would ask him how his day went. He figured that since he hadn't taken a shotgun blast to the head, and he'd arrived home in one piece, he'd merely respond with, "Oh, just another day at the office."

Here's a doozie that should be immortalized in the annals of FBI folklore. I call it "The Doctor Is In."

When somebody applies for FBI employment, he or she must submit several references on their resume. These are usually the names of friends, neighbors, former employers, and, in some cases, teachers. These folks are contacted by an agent on the Applicant Recruiting Squad and asked some brief questions regarding the applicant's background, reputation, honesty, loyalty, etc.

On this particular morning, the agent on the Applicant Recruiting Squad began his day's task of reviewing the applications that had been assigned to him by his supervisor. As he scanned the first one, he noted that in the space asking for references was the name of a person whom the applicant had identified as one of his college professors. The name was Professor Arglesbarger—Professor Charles Arglesbarger. The agent stared at the name for a second, realizing that this odd name was spelled exactly as was the name of an agent on one of the foreign counterintelligence squads. "What a coincidence!" he thought. "Another Arglesbarger? Must be some relative. How many people have that name?"

That morning, the agent contacted the applicant, seeking to set up an interview with the young man. On the phone, the agent mentioned the professor who was listed as a reference. "If you don't mind my asking," he said, "what course did you have him for?" "Psychology," said the young man, adding enthusiastically, "he's a really great teacher! As a matter of fact, besides teaching the subject, he has a private practice. There's nothing like having a teacher that actually works in the field that he's lecturing about." "I have to agree with that," said that agent. "Okay, I'll see you here at the office on Tuesday at ten for our interview. Nice talking to you." As he hung up, the agent knew that he had to follow up on this with his supervisor before going on to look at any other applications that day.

Although I hadn't worked on any cases with Special Agent Charles Arglesbarger, I was aware that his reputation was that of a competent agent who consistently put in a good day's work for the Bureau. His area of expertise was that of foreign counterintelligence. Like the other agents that handled these matters, on most days, he was barely able to stay afloat in the sea of paperwork that was generated by his investigations. However, just about every afternoon, he was out of the office, digging up some new information on some Russian spy—or so we thought.

Everything about Arglesbarger appeared to be quite average, with the exception of his name, which hardly anyone in the office could pronounce correctly. In reality, Charlie was way above average. He had a doctorate in clinical psychology, something which few other agents possessed. Perhaps this is what caused his downfall. Maybe he was just too smart for his own good.

The supervisor stared at the application and looked up at the agent. "Did you ask the young guy what course the professor teaches?" "Yeah, Joe. He said psychology." "Are you thinking what I'm thinking?" "Probably. Do you think that Charlie is moonlighting?" "Got me. But how can the name and the psychology both be a coincidence? I'm gonna call his supervisor."

Charlie Arglesbarger's supervisor was stunned by the possibility that an agent on his squad might be in violation of the Bureau's rule against agents having outside employment. Besides, he surmised, there aren't enough hours in the day to be a full-time FBI agent, teach college courses, and run a private practice as a psychotherapist.

A series of surveillances, combined with interviews at the college, and reviews of the agent's times in and out of the office confirmed the worst. Professor Arglesbarger, Dr. Arglesbarger, and FBI Special Agent Charles Arglesbarger were one in the same. It was an episode straight from a made-for-TV movie. The Bureau's investigation showed that Charlie had pulled it off successfully for quite some time—years, perhaps. He had simply divided the day up into segments. He was able to successfully investigate his cases, get in the necessary paperwork on time, teach in the afternoons (when he was out of the office, supposedly searching for foreign spies), and see patients in the evenings.

Needless to say, Arglesbarger was fired. His eighteen-year Bureau career went down the tubes, as did his pension.

Were other agents caught in the same web? Not many, but there were a few. There was the fellow who was paid for giving sailing lessons on weekends. I know, you're probably thinking—but weekends, isn't that an agent's own time? Well, it is, sort of. You see, officially, FBI agents are on duty twenty-four hours a day, seven days a week. So the "no outside employment rule" applies all the time. In this case, the Bureau chose not to fire him. Instead they merely reassigned him to another field office, leaving his wife, another FBI employee, assigned to her office, thus creating a gap of hundreds of miles between the two. This left them with quite a dilemma. I'm not sure of the outcome of that one, but the Bureau does have its own way of making a point.

Let's not forget Kevin. He was a good agent, but a little quirky. His moment of crowning glory occurred when he walked into a well-known New York deli and ordered a roast beef sandwich to go. As the clerk began to wrap it up, Kevin glanced at the sandwich and was not pleased with the amount of meat on the sandwich. He immediately whipped out his badge and in an authoritative and demanding tone said, "FBI. Heavy on the roast beef." Needless to say, when his supervisor heard about this indiscretion, he was not pleased. Kevin spent the next few weeks assigned to the complaint desk answering calls from every nut in New York that called the FBI just for the hell of it.

And finally, a quick "oops" story.

The surveillance had been as boring as any surveillance could be. The agents had been staring at the doorway for a full two hours, praying for some action. Then the announcement came over the FBI Motorola radio. "The subject is leaving his residence. He's wearing black pants, black shoes, and a yellow shirt. He looks like a bumblebee."

Suddenly the guy who had just exited his front door frantically began to look around him in all directions in an attempt to determine where the sound was coming from. The explanation was simple. One of the agents had inadvertently turned the car's radio to the PA (public address) setting. The lovely description comparing the target of the surveillance to a buzzing insect had just gone out, at full volume, into the street. The guy ran back into his house and wasn't seen for several days after that. Law enforcement professionalism at its peak.

Combat photographer, Thailand

B-52 explosion, U-Tapao, Thailand, 1968

Me photographing B-52 explosion, Thailand

Lonely tire—an aftermath of B-52 explosion

My prizewinning war photo

Bob Hope during USO show

Sebastian Cabot arriving at the U-Tapao for USO show

Singer Ann-Margret arriving at USO show

With actor Sebastian Cabot

With comedian Morey Amsterdam

With Gypsy Rose Lee

Taping my radio show Bits and Pieces

FBI Photographer, 1970

Recovered El Greco painting, 1971

Lawrence Welk visiting FBI New York Office, 1973

In the subway for Crayola case investigation

The Big Haul, weapons and cash, 1989

1993 World Trade Center bombing

Performing at 1993 FBI Christmas party

Performing with Jed, 1999

Ceil, Murray, and Nick

Audrey decorating a puppet's costume

Oh wow, man, it's Mercury Speedhead!

Ventriloquist Convention, 2002

At home with the "family", 2007

With Audrey at my daughter's wedding, 2008

Performing for the seniors, 2008

Singin' Sinatra

ME . . . AN FBI AGENT?

For most clerks, the process of becoming an agent was quite intimidating. In my case, the scenario went like this:

It was a quiet day in the FBI photo lab. There was nothing going on which would cause any of us to race around in a tizzy, except my assignment which consisted of turning out, in as little time as possible, four hundred copies of a poor-quality photo shot by a ceiling-mounted bank surveillance camera. Like most of these photos, it was a blurred black-and-white image of some nut, who, on a sweltering August day, had donned a heavy wool ski mask with the intent of convincing a teller to make him rich at gunpoint. My job was to produce photos which would accompany a MUM (maximum utilization memo) describing the bank robber, identifying the bank, etc. These would be handed out to agents in the field who would then get in their cars and comb New York in an attempt to locate this guy or obtain some information dealing with his whereabouts.

Producing four hundred of these photos was no easy task since in the early 1970's the whole process had to be done by hand. Every print had to be run through trays of chemicals until the image appeared on the paper. The prints then had to be rinsed and placed, one by one, on large heated, drum-shaped dryers. As they rolled off the dryer, they had to be neatly stacked and then sent to the bank robbery squad for distribution to the agents whose car engines were already running.

So there I was, racing to get those prints out, when my supervisor strode into the darkroom. I glanced up and then quickly back down at my work. I had a mission. Get these photos to the agents so they could catch the bank robber.

"Rick, the SAC (special agent in charge) wants to see you," Don said. I knew I still had another two hundred prints to produce, but this sounded important. I placed the group of fifty undeveloped prints in my hand into the developing solution. With my mind on why I was being called into the SAC's office, I stared at the prints, as they got darker and darker until they were so overdeveloped as to render them useless. I thought, "Oh shit, the SAC wants to see me. What did I do wrong? Why the hell was I getting fired?"

"Okay, Don, do you know why he wants to see me?" "I have an idea, and I think its okay. You're not in trouble. I'll have Paul come in and finish the prints." That's all he said, as he picked up his pipe, took a puff, and exited the room.

I raced to rip off my well-worn gray lab coat. Underneath I had my official FBI outfit, shirt and tie, neatly pressed polyester pants and well-shined shoes, a habit ingrained in me from my air force years.

As I approached the SAC's office, I took a deep breath, telling myself that its only a job and that if I got fired, I'd just become a famous photographer somewhere else in New York. There were photo studios on every block in the city. Or maybe I'd become an actor and singer. After all, isn't that what I really wanted to do?

"You're Rick Berger from the photo lab, and you have a one o'clock appointment with the SAC," said his secretary. "Yes, ma'am. That's correct." "Oh damn," I thought, "I'm still saying ma'am like I had to in the military." "Go right in." I knocked politely on the massive walnut door which was partially open. Upon hearing a booming voice say, "Come on in," I pushed the door open just wide enough to let myself into the room. The SAC, a large man, in stereotypical FBI attire sat before me at a desk which looked to be about the size of an aircraft carrier. He was wearing the standard well-pressed blue suit, white shirt and red tie. He looked every bit as threatening as he did in the photo on his desk which showed him during his college days, when he was a star football player. If he didn't look like an FBI agent, I didn't know who did. He motioned for me to come in and take a seat. I approached the burgundy-colored leather chair which was angled toward to his desk. I gracefully lowered myself onto the chair, attempting to avoid making the leather squeak, lest he think that I had farted in his presence. Before placing his pen down on his desk, he slowly twirled it between his fingers, giving me just enough time to wipe the beads of sweat off my upper lip. As if noticing that I had that "if I don't get off this roller coaster soon, I'm going to puke" look, he said, "Rick, I guess you're wondering why I called you in this morning. Well, relax, you're not in trouble." I think I mumbled, "Thank God" or something to that effect. He continued, "You've been with the Bureau for over five years now. I've looked at your records and spoken with Don, your supervisor in the photo lab. All indications are that you've done an outstanding job for the

FBI, and you have obtained your bachelor's degree by attending night school. Do you plan on staying in the Bureau and making this your career?" "Yes, sir," I replied. I felt my mind race ahead as fleeting thoughts darted through my brain, "Is this what I really wanted to do? Was I lying to the SAC? Was I lying to myself?" "Well, Rick, in light of your performance and career goals, we've decided to offer you the opportunity for further advancement in the Bureau to the position of Special Agent. Of course, you'll have to go through an interview with an agent from our applicant squad, just as anyone from the outside would do, and then there'll be the written test and, of course, a physical exam, but I'm sure you'll have no problem with any of these. You are in good health, I assume, aren't you?" "Oh yes, sir. I've been exercising since I was a teenager, and I rarely get sick." "And you do like girls, I assume." "Yes, sir. Love 'em." "Fine then, we'll schedule you for your interview within the next couple of weeks, and you'll be on your way to a great career here in the FBI." "Thank you, sir." He then held out a hand that resembled a huge side of beef. Making sure to shake hands with all the strength I had in my entire body, we shook hands in agreement, and I exited his office, slowly and quietly closing the door behind me. I walked briskly back to the photo lab, my head and heart racing. "Right now, there's only one thing to do. Finish getting those prints out. Those agents on the street are waiting for their photos."

When I returned to the lab, all I wanted to do was to go back into the darkroom where I could gather my thoughts. I never even made it past the front door. I heard the clanking of the pipe on the ashtray. "Rick, how did it go?" "Oh, hi, Don. Just great. The SAC asked me if I was interested in becoming an agent."

"What did you tell him?" "I told him yes, of course. He said he'd begin processing my paperwork soon." "We'll miss you here in the lab." "Well, I won't be leaving that quickly. There's the interview, the test, the physical. You know, all that official stuff." "Yeah, all that official stuff," he said. "Well, good luck. Now I guess you better go help Paul get out the rest of those prints. The agents have been screaming for them. There's a bank robber on the loose and he's A and D (armed and dangerous)."

The FBI has gone through an unprecedented evolution since those days back in the early '70's. For one thing, there are now female agents. And why not? Can they shoot as well, investigate as thoroughly, and solve crimes with as much competence as their male counterparts? Yes, they can. Not only are they skilled in what they do, but also in many cases, a woman is the more sensible choice to use in an investigation. Prior to the introduction of female agents into the Bureau, certain roles were filled by female "understudies" in cases where this was appropriate. For instance, when an investigation called for a surveillance to be conducted in a restaurant, the logical and most discreet approach would be to have a couple dining there, as opposed to using a single male agent, who, sitting by himself, would most likely draw the attention of any savvy bad guy on the lookout for law enforcement. Instead, an arrangement was made whereby a female clerk, usually a secretary, would accompany the agent. After all, a couple having dinner would look quite natural and certainly not attract the attention of anyone in the restaurant. Besides enhancing several investigations over the years, at least a few instances in which females were utilized resulted in some real-life relationships developing between agents and their official FBI "dates."

Many other changes have also occurred since I made my debut on the FBI stage. The pay is certainly better, and the focus in the training has shifted so as to better prepare agents to deal with current issues such as terrorism. Today's agents are more able to handle a wider variety of investigations than the Bureau has ever had to deal with in its history. There is a continued effort to train agents to be prepared to handle challenges never before encountered by the FBI.

LET'S GET PHYSICAL

What the hell was I thinking? My days in the military had ended ten years ago, in 1966. Here it is, a decade later, and once again, I'm suffering the effects of basic training, ripping the flesh off my hands as I act out some *Jack in the Beanstalk* fantasy. The thick, taut ropes dig into my palms as I climb toward the cloudless Virginia sky. As I look down, I can see the others, all nervously waiting their turn. Some had never been any higher than the lowest branch of the tree they attempted to shimmy up when they were nine. Others had only gained height by riding in elevators in bustling cities where they had worked.

"So this is the FBI," I thought to myself, as my biceps strained to pull me up that last twelve inches. This is the FBI Academy in Quantico, Virginia. Just like on TV, only without the commercials. What I learn here will make me an official government man, a "G-man" as they used to call FBI agents in those 1940's gangster movies. In the near distance, I can see my dormitory and the other buildings which comprise the campus at the academy. I can also see the glass tubelike structures which connect the buildings. These aboveground tunnels allow the students to pass from building to building without having to go outside and experience the myriad of weather changes common to Virginia. That's the plus side. The bad news is that these enclosures turn each agent-in-training into Harry the Hamster as he negotiates his way through the vast glass menagerie.

"Whoa, I made it to the top. Now for the quick trip down. Just straddle the rope and don't go down too fast. Keep your feet wrapped around the rope. Remember, your feet are your brakes. And no racing. Rope burns hurt." That's what the instructor had said. Ouch, he wasn't kidding. A little too fast on those last two feet. He's right. My palms are burning. "Okay, I'm down. Next sucker."

Next day, more ropes. I wonder, "What is the FBI's obsession with ropes? Does someone in the Training Unit have stock in a rope company?" Oh, now this is different. Today we'll be dangling on a rope draped over the side of a building. Now, wait a minute! Whose idea was this? Did you guys forget? I'm from New York! I don't go down the outside of buildings. I was trained, even as a kid, to make my way down from the fifth floor on the inside of the building. Now, where the hell is the elevator? "Okay, Agents, this is called rappelling," says the instructor in a booming voice. "Oh sure," I think to myself, "rappelling, now that's a pretty fancy name for trying not to break a leg while scaling a building like Spider-Man." "You know," I say to the instructor, "I have this great idea. I'm sure that all of us can do this retailing stuff, so why don't we go over to the firearms range and learn to shoot a gun instead?" "Okay, New York wiseass. In the first place, it's called rappelling, not retattling or whatever the hell you called it, and second, today's schedule does not call for firearms training till after lunch, so start rappelling." "Yes, sir" I reply, meekly.

"Now the trick here is to not look down," he counsels. I listen carefully to what he says because I trust him. That's one thing about the Bureau. You trust each other. So down I go, all the while hearing my mother's voice, sounding just like it did when I was a kid, "I don't care what the rest of them are doing. If they jumped off the Empire State Building, would you do the same thing?" (Just a little aside here, every New York kid has heard this phrase at some point during his childhood.) Bricks, nothing but bricks, staring at me, just six inches from my face. Is this any way to spend a beautiful Virginia afternoon? "Berger, let's go. What the hell are you doin' up there, daydreaming?" "Uh, yes, sir. I, uh, mean no, sir. I'm comin' down!" "Oh, man," I said, mumbling under my breath, "what they need here is an elevator, or an escalator for that matter! I wish I were home shopping at the mall." *Thump*, went my left heel on the hard ground. There, I'm down. Next victim.

Training at the FBI Academy runs the gamut from the physical to the mental. When they're not filling your brain to capacity with facts, figures, procedures, and the law, they're pulling your body every which way in an effort to train it and mold it into the stereotypical physique of an FBI agent. In most cases, the process works. However, the food in the cafeteria is so good that some trainees find that they are constantly fighting the battle of the bulge. But most are motivated to stay trim so that they'll look like FBI agents on graduation day. One of the most enjoyable parts of training is the challenge of surviving scenarios set out in Hogan's Alley, a Hollywood set laid out as if it were a real town.

Hogan's Alley is considered by some to be the crown jewel of the FBI Academy. It had a main street lined with stores, a bank, restaurant, and just about everything else you'd encounter in a small American town. To add an air of realism to the training, there were professional actors playing the roles of the folks in the scenarios. In their roles, they depicted restaurant patrons, bank tellers, people being held hostage, or whatever part they were given on a particular day.

As trainees, we were formed up into squads, just as we would be in an actual FBI field office. The squads had to respond to a variety of situations that were devised by the academy training staff. I was assigned to a squad that was to investigate a bank robbery. We were told that our actions would be videotaped and that later in the day we would review the tape and be critiqued on our performance.

This type of training is particularly effective. The fact that you're acting out an investigation in such a realistic setting causes you to react as if the scenario unfolding around you is real. For safety purposes, the gun each agent trainee is carrying is neither loaded nor operational. In fact, during many of the training exercises, a "red handle" weapon is used. This is either a wooden gun or a standard weapon (with the handle painted red) which has been rendered inoperable. This safety procedure, however, has little bearing on the aura of realism created by the surroundings and the feeling of holding a drawn weapon in your hand as you move about. As the scene is enacted by the members of your squad and the role players, the adrenaline begins to flow, and you become enmeshed in the action.

In this particular scenario, we were told that initial reports indicated that one of the tellers was being held hostage. In response to this, George, a burly former state trooper whom we had elected as our team leader, had given one agent the assignment of hostage negotiator. It came as no surprise that George had assigned this job to Mike, who in real life had been a prosecutor and, here in the academy, had the reputation for having the biggest and loudest mouth.

We knew that our primary goal was to ensure the safety of the bank patrons and the employees, including the hostage. Our hopes were that no shots would be fired and that the felon could be removed from the scene without incident.

As the signal to begin the action was given, we pulled up to the bank, exited our vehicles, and approached the door, guns drawn and ready for action. We had received notification that the bank robber was to be considered A and D (armed and dangerous). Hank, a hulk of humanity who had gained fame as a semipro football player, entered first. The rest of us followed, all eyes scanning the scene in every direction, checking for any associates the robber may have brought with him as cover or to provide assistance.

As the cameras rolled, we stepped around the bank patrons, lying on the floor on their stomachs, as they had been directed to do by the robber. We made our way to the vault and, thanks to Mike's skillful negotiating techniques, were able to extract the hostage and remove the bank robber from the scene in handcuffs.

Celebrating our victory over lunch in the academy's dining room, we anxiously anticipated viewing the tape and finding out what critical mistakes we had made during our apprehension of the bank robber. We all felt pretty confident that we had done a good job and that if this had been an actual case, our performance would have been applauded by FBI management.

As we walked back to our classroom, there was much chatter about the actors' performances in the mock scenario and how the one playing the role of the bank robber had gotten a little roughed up by one of the agent trainees. It seems that as the drama developed, the level of realism had escalated to a point at which the agent placing the handcuffs on the felon forgot that the whole thing was a training exercise. With adrenaline rushing through his veins like fast-moving lava, he had cuffed the guy with such force that the cuffs had dug into the actor's wrists, pinching the skin and causing swelling and an abrasion which had to be treated by FBI medical personnel. Although injured, the actor congratulated the agent on having done a good job, adding that since he was able to immerse himself so deeply in his role, perhaps he should give up on his FBI career and become an actor instead.

Back in the classroom, we settled quickly into our seats, anxious to see the tape. As we witnessed our screen debuts, it became painfully obvious that we were not quite the experts that we had envisioned ourselves to be. One agent could be seen to the right of the screen "covering" another agent with his gun. In other words, pointing the weapon at his fellow agent as he turned around. As you might imagine, this is a definite no-no in law enforcement. As the camera panned right, a rumble of giggles rolled through the classroom. Within seconds this escalated into a full-blown roar of raucous laughter. There on the screen was Special Agent Trainee Rick Berger, gun in hand, moving from the right to the left, all the while executing a perfect Broadway dance step. The step was, in fact, the same move that can be seen in act two of the world-famous New York production of the Broadway revival *42nd Street* when the tap dancers arrive on stage to begin their show stopping tap number. As I slunk down slowly into my seat, I could feel the blood rushing into my face. The flushed feeling immediately began to permeate my neck and shoulders. A nervous laugh erupted from my throat as I did the only thing I could think of to do at the moment. I rose to my feet and took a bow. I bowed deeply, first to the right, then left, and finally, turning around, to the "audience" behind me. As I took my seat, I could hear the comments, "Hey, Berger, nice dance step," "Whoa, look at Mr. Broadway," and "Where's your tutu?" I knew in an instant what had prompted my on-screen antics. When the announcement was made that our training exercise was being taped, my mind had immediately gone into the showbiz mode. Out came the tap shoes, top hat, and tails. It was time to give 'em the old razzle-dazzle.

The mood eventually got serious again as the review of the tape continued. We were told that we had done a pretty good job and that we should be proud of our lack of major screwups. Before releasing us and sending us off to an afternoon of firearms training, the instructor made one final announcement. He called me up to the front of the room to formally thank me for adding a little comic relief to an otherwise serious classroom session, adding that if I ever get involved in a real-life situation such as the arrest of an armed criminal, I should concentrate a little more on the arrest scenario and less on my histrionics. The room broke out in thunderous applause.

STUNT MAN

Did you ever hear an interview with an actor who says, "I do all my own stunts"? In life, we're all, in a sense, actors, and we all do our own stunts. There are no stunt doubles and no understudies. When we're thrust out onto life's stage, we are faced with the challenge of giving the best performance we possibly can, and that includes during our working years.

I must admit that I performed well during my FBI career, but I was certainly no superstar, and there were several times during which I wished I had a stunt double. One of these occasions occurred during firearms training and, in particular, during shotgun training.

When I started out in the Bureau, I didn't know the front end of a gun from the back end. I soon learned that shooting a shotgun is a unique experience. The power packed into that rod of steel is more impressive than you'd imagine. So the first time we were taught how to fire this weapon, I made sure to pay attention to everything the instructor had to say. After all, the last thing I wanted to do was to blow myself up and miss my next paycheck. I clearly remember how the shotgun looked in the instructor's hand. This guy was about six feet three inches—wide, not tall! The man was Frankenstein without the bolts in his neck. If I were a bad guy, opened my door and saw him standing there, I would have surrendered and admitted to every crime committed in the neighborhood in the past year. In his hand the shotgun looked like a Daisy air rifle, a mere toothpick with a hole in one end. I listened attentively as he spoke of the power wielded by the weapon. He said that proper positioning of the gun against your body would prevent injuries from kick-back, something the weapon had plenty of. He lifted the gun and demonstrated the correct way to place the wooden stock into the area where the shoulder meets the torso. If you do this right, the amount of kickback will be minimized so it would only feel like three bricks hitting your shoulder instead of six. Comforting words. He showed us how to lower our cheek down onto the gun's wooden stock so our eye would be lined up with the sighting device.

My first time up at bat with the shotgun was a little scary, to say the least. Standing on the firing line, I glanced left and then right, checking to see that I was lined up with the other agents who were also about to experience the shoulder pain felt 'round the world. I felt a hand on my shoulder. "Berger, why are you holding the gun on your left shoulder. Aren't you right handed?" "Yes, I am, but I'm left-eyed." "You're what?" "I'm left-eyed, sir. My left eye is the better one, so, in order to be able to site the gun well on the target, I'm going to shoot lefty." "You're ambidextrous?" "When I have to be." "Okay," he mumbled, as he walked away. God knows what he was thinking.

"Ready on the firing line?" echoed from the high tower where the range officer who gave the commands sat. Nobody said a thing. No hands were raised, indicating that all of the eighteen agents were ready to commence fire. I was ready. My ear protectors were in place, ready to muffle the explosive sound. My safety glasses were there to protect me from flying bits of brass and debris. I carefully raised my weapon, tucking it securely into the space between my shoulder and chest where the impact would best be cushioned. I lowered my cheek down onto the smooth wooden stock. The silence created by the "ears," as they called the protectors, was broken by the sound of, "Ready on the right? Ready on the left? Commence fire."

I sighted in on the bull's-eye target, some fifty yards away. I took a long breath and then slowly pulled the trigger. I heard blasts all around me, but paid attention only to what I was doing. Each agent shot just one round as instructed. Hey, man, I did it. In the distance, I could see that my target had a hole in it. It was off to the right of the bull's-eye, but there definitely was a hit on my target. As a matter of fact, there were two holes. Wait a minute. I had only taken one shot. I looked to my right and saw that the agent next to me was shaking his head. His target had no hits on it. "Thanks, Greg. I guess you gave me an extra hit." The poor guy. He had successfully hit my target, but missed his own. "Hey, Berger, what happened to your cheek?" I reached up to my cheek and felt a burning sensation just below the frames of my safety glasses. Within a second, I realized what had happened. I had pressed my cheek so firmly against the stock that I had wedged the glasses into my face just enough so that when the gun fired, the glasses ripped into my cheek. I thanked Greg for letting me know that I had become the first casualty on the firing line.

I wiped the blood away with my sleeve, returned the gun to its ready position, and got into position for the next round of shooting. "Look at me," I thought to myself, "well, if it isn't Barney Fife of the Mayberry Police Department!" At least I hadn't shot myself in the foot.

Well, one way or another I graduated from the FBI Academy. I passed all of the academic courses. I learned the law and how to apply it to real-life cases. I was taught how to present facts in a clear and concise manner in writing as well as in oral presentations should I be called upon to testify in court. I got through the physical training as well, although I was not particularly enamored with certain activities such as boxing, during which I found out what it's like to be hit square in the jaw by a guy with a forearm the thickness of a branch from a sturdy oak tree. I climbed, jumped, and ran around buildings with a gun drawn.

Graduation day at the FBI Academy was an especially proud event not only for the new agents, but for their families as well. The auditorium was packed with parents, grandparents, spouses, brothers, sisters, and kids—all beaming with pride as the newly appointed agents filed by the faculty and approached center stage where each one stepped up to the FBI Director, shook hands, and received his credentials. The speeches were not lengthy, yet each one stressed the fact that the new agents would be following in the proud footsteps of their predecessors and that the primary job of the FBI was to safeguard American citizens, their ideals and their freedom. In some ways, the ceremony paralleled that of a college graduation, yet there was something special in the air. All of the new agents were, of course, college graduates. Some possessed law or accounting degrees while others, like myself, had degrees in a wide variety of other areas—communications, science, psychology, etc. We all knew that unlike our college graduations, which were the launching pads from which we would set out to explore employment options, here, we had a career firmly established and were about to embark on the first step on our new career paths.

When my name was called, I rose from my seat, and, in an attempt to expand my chest so it would fill out my suit jacket, I took the deepest breath I could possibly muster. As a result, the room started to spin, and I almost passed out—not a good way to kick-start an FBI career. By some stroke of luck, I was able to regain my normal breathing pattern as I left my seat and strode up to the stage. I shook the Director's hand, making sure to use as firm a grip as possible. He returned a grip which damn near crushed my thumb. As I exited the stage, the thumb started throbbing, but, by the end of the ceremonies, I was able to focus on other things as the pain subsided. By the time I had met my family at the back of the room, smiled through a thousand photos, and shook hands with everyone in sight, I was ready to take my badge, credentials, and gun, and head home.

When I think back, I realize that all of the realistic hands-on training we received was really valuable—except for one thing. Upon graduation, I was sent to the New York office. What I had practiced on that quaint and quiet little Main Street in Hogan's Alley would have little application on the bustling streets of midtown Manhattan. There was virtually no chance of ever bringing an FBI car to a screeching halt in front of a bank in New York City, where you're lucky if you can reach a top speed of about four miles an hour during noontime traffic. Well, if we learned nothing else, we at least found out that in order to survive as an agent, you had to be flexible. I must give credit to most of the agents for having the good sense to realize this and to adapt to whatever circumstances they encounter during their FBI careers.

Once I settled in back at home in New York and reported to work at the field office, I was assigned to a squad which handled organized crime investigations. Prior to working on that squad, I never realized just how well organized some groups of criminals actually were or, for that matter, how accomplished and polished they were at plying their trade. I also learned how, in spite of efforts on the part of law enforcement to stop them in their tracks, quite often their crafty attorneys were able to get them off the hook. The mission of my squad was to investigate the activities of a particular organized crime family with a long history of violating every U.S. law on the books while claiming to be legitimate business people in the used-car and trash-hauling businesses.

I had the privilege of meeting a few of our subjects during raids aimed at uncovering their sports betting activities. I remember one occasion during which, armed with a search warrant, we were to enter the premises of a gambling den operating out of a downtown apartment. Since it was much more effective to hit a place during the early-morning hours, we packed up our equipment at about 2:00 a.m. and headed for the downtown location. Some of the guys carried shotguns. Others brought long, heavy battering rams to knock down the door if necessary. At the insistence of my supervisor, I brought—you guessed it—my camera.

We reached our destination at about 2:20 a.m. and assembled outside the apartment building. I was assigned to the group with the battering ram, since that would be the first team to enter the apartment, and I needed to start shooting photos as soon as we went through the door.

As we tiptoed up the staircase to the second floor of the six-story building, I pushed my weapon solidly down into the holster to make sure it would not fall out. I also checked to make sure that my camera case was securely closed. After all, I'm sure that I would have been slightly embarrassed if, while silently climbing the stairs, my bulky Speed Graphic did a swan dive out of the case and plunked down loudly onto the stairs.

When we approached the apartment door, we were faced with a dilemma. At the part of the hallway near the stairs was a door marked 2B. At the opposite end of the hall was another, also marked 2B. Apparently, the apartment had an entrance at each end. Playing apartment-door roulette, our supervisor decided to first approach the door nearest to where we were standing. He sent three other agents down the hall to secure the other door. He walked up to the door and motioned for me to position myself directly behind him. As I got behind him, two other agents placed themselves to his right and left. As he pounded on the door with a clenched fist, he shouted out loudly, "FBI, open up." Not a sound was heard from within the apartment. He banged once more, this time shouting his "FBI, open up" command even louder. No response was heard from inside. He motioned for the guys with the battering ram to take the door down. As they swung the heavy pipe into the door, the wooden doorframe began to buckle. On the second shove, the door swung open. Just as it did, out of the corner of my eye I noticed some activity at the other door. The agents readied their guns as the door opened. Standing there, in his pajamas, was a guy resembling Fred Flintstone. Through sleepy eyes, he stared at all of us, then calmly said, "Why did you guys have to break down my door? You could have just knocked on this one." "Sorry, sir," said my supervisor, striding down the hallway toward him, "but how were we to know which door to knock on?" "Anyway, what do you guys want? I didn't do anything wrong." "Well, sir, we have a search warrant for this apartment." "Come on in. I got nothin' to hide," said the mournful-looking soul.

We entered the apartment and began our search. It wasn't too difficult to spot the gambling slips with the names of baseball teams on them on the kitchen table. In the toilet were a few more slips. Apparently, we got in just prior to Mr. Flintstone flushing them down. As I photographed every nook and cranny in the room, a woman identifying herself as the girlfriend asked if she could sit down on the couch. I told her that this would be quite all right, but that first I just wanted to have a look under the cushions. As I lifted the cushion off the couch, I spotted some money—a lot of money. After taking shots of the bills from several angles, two other agents counted the money. The wads of hundred-dollar bills added up to a total of $5,000. The woman, upon seeing the cash, remarked, "Where did that come from?" adding that it must have been in the couch when they bought it.

We finally left the premises at seven that morning with four large cartons loaded with enough evidence, including many phone numbers of associates of theirs, to present an excellent case against them. Right to the very last day in court, the couple insisted that the couch must have contained the money under the cushions when they bought it. The jury didn't buy that story, and the couple was convicted. Subsequent to that case, I've purchased several couches over the years and have yet to find any money under the cushions. Some people have all the luck!

I SPY WITH MY LITTLE EYE

My entire career in the field of organized crime lasted eleven weeks. By the end of my third month in the New York office, the FBI decided that my keen investigative insights should be used toward headier purposes, so they reassigned me to a Foreign Counterintelligence squad. People frequently ask me what this means. I explain that "foreign counterintelligence" is fancy terminology for spy chasing. The spies are from far-off lands and have entered the United States for the express purpose of stealing our secrets. "What kind of secrets?" you ask. "Every kind you can imagine," I reply. "You know, like military and technical stuff." Next, they want details, so I explain that the FBI is mandated to neutralize attempts to pilfer U.S. critical high technology. That simply means that the FBI has to stop people from stealing our country's secrets, and that's where my job came in.

So how do you catch a spy? First, you have to identify the culprit, and then you have to find him. Once you've done this, you face the most difficult and challenging part of the process—you have to catch him in the act, then prove that he was actually engaged in espionage. It's hard enough to catch a cab in New York, no less capture a spy. Talk about a needle in a haystack. This needle is buried in a haystack of eight million people! So how do you do it? There are several ways to go about it. I'll outline a couple for you.

One method is to locate some particularly astute business people who employ foreigners in their company or deal with them through their business, or socially. You then seek their cooperation by explaining to them that by helping the FBI, they play a key role in protecting national security. I found that most business folks were willing to help out by providing information as long as it didn't adversely affect their business or their relationships with the individuals we were interested in. Here's how it worked:

I would find out that Mr. Alfred Krotz, the president of Krotz Manufacturing, was meeting twice a month with Vladimir Dumbashitsky, a Russian who owned the Moscow-based company Brokenski Widgetov. I would arrange for an appointment to meet with Mr. Krotz. At our first meeting, I'd explain to him that the FBI is not really interested in Mr. Dumbashitsky, but rather, a certain Russian diplomat who may be involved in some questionable activities in his off-duty hours. I'd tell him that we have developed information that Mr. Dumbashitsky is a friend of the diplomat and may be able to clarify certain bits of information regarding the diplomat's activities. The first question Mr. Krotz would usually ask was, "How did you find out that I deal with Dumbashitsky?" I would tell him that the FBI has a variety of sources which keep an eye on foreigners (non-U.S. citizens) who travel to America and that we heard that Mr. Dumbashitsky visits the United States about twice a month to conduct business dealings with Americans. In addition, we were told that he is a friend of the diplomat. I'd tell Krotz that our source also identified him as one of Mr. Dumbashitsky's business contacts. Once convinced that he was not in any sort of trouble, and that the Bureau will not divulge to anyone the fact that he is providing information, in most cases, a business person such as Krotz was usually willing to continue providing information as long as it did not affect his business.

I found that most of the people from whom I sought information kind of got a kick out of working with the FBI. It may be due, in some part, to a sense of patriotism, but it probably had more to do with the cool aspect of considering themselves sort of part-time spies for the FBI. Maybe it's that many people harbor a hidden desire to be James Bond, at least on a temporary basis. Taking a few seconds to imagine oneself as a secret agent gingerly stepping out of the electronic door of an Aston Martin while sporting a finely tailored suit would certainly help to break up an otherwise dull business meeting.

Another way to catch a spy might be to develop a widely varied group of informants who are either super patriotic or just want to get their hands on some quick government cash. Unlike a company president such as Mr. Krotz, these could be waiters or bartenders at eating establishments the suspected spy frequents. Even gas station attendants who regularly filled up his tank were good sources of information. On many occasions, I got more useful information from some lower-level employees than those in upper management. If you really want the dirt on some character that may be spying in his spare time, just ask the guy who fills the creep's tank each day or the mechanic that fixes his car. He can tell you whether the guy is preparing to take a long trip or has just returned from one, or what maps he inadvertently left on the front seat of his car, maps with little check marks on them which could identify sites where he may have received, or passed on, some classified information to a fellow spy. Sometimes the information would simply serve to identify other persons with whom he travels to work each day, but even that can prove to be valuable data. Knowledge about who associates with whom is very important in the spy-catching business. Sometimes the most innocuous details can provide the missing puzzle piece that points out whether a spy has been traveling extensively or, perhaps, meeting with someone in order to complete some espionage assignment that he has received from his superiors back in his country.

I took great pride in my ability to extract information from people who might otherwise be reluctant to cooperate. My method was simple. I reverted to the old showbiz method sung about in the show *Chicago*: "Give 'em the old razzle dazzle; razzle dazzle 'em." I razzle dazzled them with jokes, anecdotes, and whatever else it took to make them feel comfortable. I avoided presenting the image of the serious FBI agent who wanted nothing more than the facts. By the time I had finished a conversation with the person I was interviewing, we had developed the type of relationship that friends in the business arena possess. I didn't care if the guy was a bank president or parked cars for a living. I treated them all with dignity and respect, and they responded in a positive way by giving me the information I sought. They'd sometimes say, "Are you really an FBI agent? You're such a nice guy." Some would say, "You seem like an actor or comedian. You should be in show business." I knew in my mind and heart that they were right.

Since spies are often judged by the company they keep, information regarding associations between individuals suspected of spying sometimes served to identify additional cohorts. This information could have come from an "asset" (foreign counterintelligence jargon for informant), or it could have been gleaned from conducting a series of surveillances on the suspected spy. For instance, let's say that the FBI has potentially identified a particular foreign national as being engaged in intelligence-gathering activities. Let's further identify him as a diplomat assigned to one of the many foreign diplomatic establishments in New York. Since this person is a foreign national, in other words, not a U.S. citizen, the FBI is authorized to surveil, or follow, him to see what he's up to. When FBI agents conduct a series of surveillances on this person, they notice that he is frequently seen in the company of another individual from the same country, perhaps a fellow diplomat who is of a similar rank or seniority at the diplomatic establishment. This could indicate that these two are working as a team with one acting in a support capacity for the other. In such a case, there's the likely possibility that if one is actually caught in the act of spying, the other may be seen in the vicinity acting as a lookout, conducting countersurveillance, in an effort to find out if the FBI is on to them and in the area. Such was the case during a 1978 spy caper known by the FBI codename "Lemonade," which I detail in the section of this book entitled "FBI Cases—The Real Scoop." Throughout my years in this field of foreign counterintelligence, I found it intriguing that so many diplomats (and some business types), particularly from the Soviet Union, led lives with dual roles—that of a legitimate representative of their country by day and the role of secret spy by night (or sometimes on weekends).

I spent a good deal of time developing and analyzing patterns of daily behavior. Once an individual's routine (how he normally spent his days at work and leisure) was established, it was my job to identify and cite changes in these patterns. I don't want to dissuade you from watching FBI movies which make the spy game seem really dramatic, but to be honest, some of this analytical stuff could get pretty laborious. Even more tedious was the conducting of surveillances.

Picture yourself sitting in a car for an entire day watching a doorway in the hope that the potential spy might show his face, and if you were lucky, might actually go somewhere to engage in some suspicious activity. I spent many hours fighting cramps in my legs and numbness in my ass, hoping for some action as I sat in subzero weather trying to read a magazine while, at the same time, not removing my eyes from the view of that doorway—and all of this with a bladder that was about to explode.

I must admit that the FBI is damn good at this counterintelligence stuff, or was, until Bob Hanssen came along. You may remember him. He was the FBI agent who was caught spying for the Russians in exchange for cash and diamonds. In 2001, he pled guilty to fifteen counts of espionage and conspiracy charges in exchange for federal prosecutors agreeing not to seek the death penalty. In 2002, at age fifty-eight, he was sentenced to life in prison without parole. The FBI Director at the time, Louis Freeh, described Hanssen's activities as "the most traitorous actions imaginable against a country governed by the rule of law."[1]

To this day, I find it hard to believe that the Bureau was infiltrated by a mole. I remember one day, sitting at my desk and trying to decide how to properly phrase some descriptive data in a report. I looked up, and standing there was Hanssen. I was familiar with Bob's expertise in this area since his reporting skills were legendary in the office. "Hey, Bob, I'm describing someone here, in my report, as having possible links to the KGB. What's the proper Bureau language to use?" As he usually did, he looked down at me as if I were in his third-grade class and methodically spewed out a boilerplate sentence used by the Bureau to describe just about any Russian who could possibly be a spy. I asked him if I could get a little creative and change the words around a bit. He glared at me and said, in no uncertain terms, that the phrase had to be used exactly as he had stated it or my supervisor would not accept my report. As a supervisor himself, he was a stickler who regarded himself as the absolute expert in matters regarding the foreign counterintelligence field. I guess he was, since he knew the business from both sides of the fence.

At one point, without any explanation, the FBI conducted polygraph exams on all of the agents working on foreign counterintelligence matters. When I sat down for my exam, I jokingly remarked to the examiner that these tests were ludicrous. After all, I said who would risk his career, and, in fact, his life (espionage is punishable by death) by acting as a double agent—spying on his own organization while secretly working for the enemy? Pretty naïve of me, I guess. Bob Hanssen proved that.

Well, we all learn and grow as a result of experience, and so did the FBI. Because of the Hanssen affair, the FBI is more aware and certainly more cautious than it had been before. For the sake of the Bureau and the nation's security, I hope we never experience another episode like this again.

I thought you might enjoy hearing about a unique experience I had while in the FBI. Each lunchtime, if I were not out of the office on an assignment, I would leave the FBI building for a short walk on New York's ritzy Upper East Side. Unlike the downtown area with its bustling crowds and giant department stores, this part of town had small shops and many apartment buildings with families living in them. The streets were lined with classy children's clothing stores, small bookstores, and tiny restaurants whose windows beckoned with decadent desserts. These stores helped to bring a small-town feel to this portion of the city.

My usual route took me west on East Seventy-second Street toward my destination, Central Park. Upon arriving at the park, I would step up my pace and walk briskly down the pathway for about a half mile, then head back to the office. On most days, at about the same time and at about the same place, my path would cross that of a young man walking in the opposite direction. My intuition, coupled with my keen investigative skills, led me to believe that he was a fellow agent, also assigned to the New York office. I figured that his lunchtime routine was the same as mine and that he was returning to the office. Day after day, I'd see the same guy, same place, same time. After some time, I think he began to recognize me during our daily lunchtime rounds, so I decided to acknowledge his presence. My plan was to introduce myself and find out what squad he was assigned to in the office.

I distinctly remember that it was a slightly brisk day in early spring as I traversed East Seventy-second Street, heading toward the park. Coming toward me was the agent I had seen almost every day for months. As we approached each other, I stopped, turned to him, and said, "Excuse me, are you going back to the office?"

Looking at me as if I were one of the New York psychopaths that approach people daily in this city, he said, simply, "What office?" Well, I was no dummy. I knew that we agents were savvy enough to hide the fact that we were members of the elite and most powerful law enforcement agency in the world. "You know, our office, the one at the corner two blocks down." "What are you talking about?" he said. At this point, I felt that the charade had gone on too long. I said, "The FBI office." Without flinching, he looked directly at me and said, "I don't work in the FBI building." "You don't?" "No." "You're not an agent?" "No." "Then where do I know you from?" "Probably TV." "TV?" "Yeah, I'm an actor. My name is Tony Roberts. I play a lawyer on TV." "Oh, uh, hi, Tony. I'm Rick Berger, and I play an FBI agent. I mean I am an FBI agent, for real . . . and I work in the FBI building down by—" "Oh, I know where it is" he said. "Everybody in this neighborhood knows the FBI building." "Well, it's been nice meeting you, Tony. Uh, see ya around, and, uh, as they say in show business, break a leg!" As I walked away, feeling like the biggest jerk in New York, I kept thinking, "I hope someday someone will say to me, 'Good luck in show business. Break a leg!'"

Sometime ago, my wife and I went to see a wonderful show on Broadway called *The Tale of the Allergist's Wife*. Afterward, we met the stars of the show: Michele Lee, Valerie Harper, and another fine actor, Tony Roberts. Tony was good enough to spend a few minutes with us as I recanted the tale from the 1970's when a young FBI agent approached him on East Seventy-second Street and made an absolute fool of himself. Believe it or not, he remembered the incident! I told Tony about my new career in the entertainment field. As we departed the theater stage door area, guess what he said? "Good luck in show business and break a leg!"

IT'S COMING AND YOU CAN'T STOP IT

RICHARD CORY

by Edwin Arlington Robinson[1]

Whenever Richard Cory went down town,
We people on the pavement looked at him:
He was a gentleman from sole to crown,
Clean favored, and imperially slim.

And he was always quietly arrayed,
And he was always human when he talked;
But still he fluttered pulses when he said,
"Good-morning," and he glittered when he walked.

And he was rich—yes, richer than a king—
And admirably schooled in every grace;
In fine we thought that he was everything
To make us wish that we were in his place.

So on we worked, and waited for the light,
And went without the meat, and cursed the bread;
And Richard Cory, one calm summer night,
Went home and put a bullet through his head.

This poem, which was written in 1897, is a chilling glimpse into a man's life. In many ways, it parallels the story of an FBI agent with whom I worked for many years.

It was a bitterly cold December day. I was returning to the office after a six-block walk from the gym, where I had just completed a less-than-enthusiastic workout. I just couldn't seem to concentrate on lifting weights that day because I knew that I would be facing a mound of paperwork on my desk. Despite the paper mountain that I'd soon be wallowing in, I was glad to get back indoors. As I entered the squad area, I immediately sensed that something was going on. A pervasive air of silence hung above the squad area. Agents were leaning over cubicle walls, talking quietly to each other. Sporadically, whispered conversations were broken by the sound of ringing phones.

I passed Dave's desk, which was the nearest one to the doorway. I approached one of the guys standing nearby. "What's going on?" I asked. "Did you hear what happened down by the World Trade Center?" he replied. "No. I just got back from the gym," I said. "An agent was shot—with his own gun. They think it's a suicide." Holding my breath, I asked him who it was. He said just one word, "Dave." "Which Dave?" I asked. "Our Dave. Dave P."

Dave P. was a quiet guy—a real quiet guy. He was the type of person whom you just couldn't get next to. He had no close friends, male or female. He kept to himself most of the time and rarely let anyone into his world.

To all of us on the squad, he appeared to be an excellent agent. From the reports he wrote, it appeared that he had some good, strong informants in his pocket, ones who provided just the sort of information the Bureau wanted. It was the type of information that could prove to be of immeasurable value in catching a spy.

On the rare occasions that we worked as partners conducting interviews, I noticed that Dave knew just the right questions to ask. But most of the time, he worked alone. He wanted it that way. The words "team player" were not in his vocabulary.

I remember one instance that occurred when we were surveilling a foreign national whom we suspected of spying. On that rainy Sunday, we had a number of teams spread out in the vicinity of the suspect's home, which was located in a New York suburb. The teams consisted of two or three agents per car—except for Dave. He chose to work alone. With the exception of perhaps one quick trip to McDonald's for a bathroom break, he sat in his car staring at that doorway without hardly ever batting an eyelash during the entire eight-hour shift.

Now, a period of eight hours sitting in a car watching a doorway in the hopes that the person of interest comes out is not exactly what you'd call exciting. It's definitely not the stuff spy movies are made of. After reading the newspaper and a couple of magazines, I'd start to get antsy and begin to think of comparisons based on the time I was spending pursuing this mighty cause. For instance, I'd think about how, in this amount of time, I could fly to sunny Spain and be in my hotel room unpacking. I don't think Dave ever thought about comparisons like that. His focus seemed to be fixed on one purpose alone—to see the subject of the investigation exit that doorway and then to follow him, in the car or on foot, to wherever on earth he was headed. While doing so, he'd take careful notes in his head and on paper of the exact route the subject had followed and his final destination, noting every stop or move he had made during his travels. Dave took his assignment seriously, making the Bureau's mission his own.

As the shift drew to a close, the dreariness of the day began to wear on all of us. The gray skies were dotted with rain clouds, and the light drizzle had now become a steady pelting of heavy raindrops. We were within fifteen minutes of the shift ending, and we couldn't wait to get going so we could head home and enjoy what little was left of the weekend. The team leaders got on their car radios and agreed that we should call it a day and get going since most of us had to drive back to our homes in New Jersey, and with the worsening weather conditions, it would be prudent to get on our way. All agreed that if the guy hadn't left his house by now, chances were that, in this weather, he wasn't going to. Also, we all shared the opinion that since the investigation was not really the hottest thing the FBI had on its plate that week, leaving a few extra minutes early would not make or break the case.

The signal was given for us all to head out. As I drove past Dave's car, I noticed that he was not pulling out. In fact, he had not even started the engine. I backed up next to him and opened the passenger-side window. "Hey, Dave!" I shouted, attempting to get him to look at me. He just kept staring at that damned doorway. As he lowered his car window, I yelled, "Didn't you hear the message? We're all through for today. Go home." Without turning his head toward me, he said, "I'm on an eight-hour shift, and I'm not leaving until the end." I shook my head as I drove away, thinking, "Who was I to argue with a perfect FBI agent, one who obeyed the rules to a tee?" You can't fault a guy for being perfect.

Few of us knew anything about Dave's personal life. It was said that he had a law degree but had never practiced. Perhaps, like many other agents, he had gone into the Bureau right after law school. The only thing we did know is that he liked fly-fishing. During one of his rare conversations with anyone on the squad, he had revealed that, besides the FBI, he had one other interest, and that was fishing. Once or twice a year, he would take a week off and go to Montana or somewhere far from bustle of New York where he could enjoy some solitude while fishing—alone. When he returned from these adventures, someone on the squad, in an attempt at being friendly, would ask him about his trip. He'd say something to the effect that the fishing was good that year. That's about all that he'd say. Joe, our squad supervisor, being a personable guy who had a genuine interest in people, went so far as to read up on fly-fishing so he could have some sort of informed conversation with Dave on the subject. That, too, was to no avail. Even Joe was unable to get much out of Dave.

Once a week Joe would hold a squad conference to go over administrative and investigative matters and to discuss the cases we were working on. The get-together was always punctuated with some kind of levity. Once in a while, even Dave would let out a brief laugh or interject a little bit of dry wit or humor into the proceedings. That is, when he wasn't looking out the window. I always marveled at how Joe never lost his patience, as he'd calmly ask Dave, whose back was facing us, if he'd care to turn around and join in on the discussion. At times like these, Dave's actions indicated that he was interested in things other than a routine squad meeting.

I recall one occasion during which I had some dealings with Dave in regard to a case I was working on. One of his informants had provided some very interesting information regarding the person that I was investigating. I approached Dave, and he invited me to pull up a chair to his desk so that he could show me some documents. I couldn't help but notice how barren his cubicle was. Most of us had more junk on our desks than we needed. There were souvenirs and photos related to cases we had worked, trophies for sporting events, tons of colorful photos of family and friends, etc.—the same kind of stuff that folks surround themselves with in every office in America. But Dave's work area was different. He had one photo, an eight-by-ten of President George Bush and his wife Barbara, their dog, Millie, sitting obediently in front of them. Pinned to the muslin cloth on the front panel of his cubicle, facing his desk, was a page cut from a newspaper. Its bold white block letters, resting on a solid black background, decried the message "It's Coming and You Can't Stop It." Perhaps it had been cut out from an ad in the paper. Every time that I saw that thing, I wondered what it meant. Yet, for some reason, I never asked Dave about it. I guess I felt that asking about it would be some sort of invasion of his personal life. I did, however, ask a couple of other people on the squad if they knew what it meant. They all sloughed it off, saying things like, "Who the hell knows and who the hell cares? It belongs to Dave, so what do you expect?"

At one point, I remember telling Dave that although it was years away, I was already contemplating what I would do in retirement. With a sly little grin on his face, he said, "In eleven years I'll have enough money to last the rest of my life." I assumed that he was referring to his FBI pension. Perhaps this was a wrong assumption.

Dave knew that I was the coordinator of the FBI's DECA Program, DECA being the acronym for Development of Counterintelligence Awareness. He also knew that I had an interest in puppets. On one occasion, I had just returned to the office after having briefed a group of defense contractors on how they could protect their companies by working with the Bureau in identifying spies who wanted to steal U.S. technology. As I passed his desk, Dave said, "How'd the briefing go? Did you bring the DECA dummy?" Then, positioning his hand so that it resembled a little mouth, he began, in a falsetto voice, saying, "Hello, ladies and gentlemen, I am the DECA dummy. Today we are going to talk about spies." It was one of those rare occasions where he slipped out of character, showing that there was a side of him that few knew.

Over the years, most of us on the squad had tried to draw Dave out of his shell, befriend him, or at least attempt to make him feel comfortable with us. On several occasions I had attempted to engage him in conversations on topics such as current movies, politics, anything, just so he'd get his head out of his work. I knew that he worked out too, so upon his return to the office from the gym, I'd ask him how his workout went. His answers were always terse. "Pretty good," he'd say, then sit down at his desk, and begin to work on some report.

According to the rumors, Dave had left a note which said something to the effect that when his family found out what was going on, they'd be very upset and disappointed in him. What, in fact, was going on? Agents began to speculate. Questions arose: Was Dave a spy? Was he a double agent? Where did he really go on those fly-fishing trips? Was he gay and trying to conceal it? Was he just a quiet introverted person, or was he hiding something—a secret, which had become a burden he could no longer bear to carry around? It appeared that Dave was either a troubled guy or a guy in trouble.

Dave was fastidious. He dressed well each day. His outfits were not the type one would find in the pages of *Gentlemen's Quarterly*, but they were appropriate for an FBI field agent. Like his person, and his reports, his desk had a certain semblance of order which most of the other desks lacked. Even his suicide was planned and executed in a meticulous manner, with great attention being paid to detail.

One of the news headlines on that day, December 13, 1994, simply read, "FBI Agent Kills Himself."[2] It went on to state that on that afternoon, a veteran FBI agent had been found with a self-inflicted gunshot wound to the head. The weapon, a 9-mm semiautomatic handgun, was found next to the agent's body which was clothed in a suit, tie, and trench coat. The location given was the promenade behind Two World Financial Center. According to news reports, no note was found. However, according to office rumors, there most certainly was a note. In that precisely written document, Dave, in his typically careful and concise manner, had provided detailed information regarding the location of his FBI car, the whereabouts of the keys to his New Jersey apartment, and other information which would help speed the investigation along.

Prior to the funeral, our supervisor told us that Dave's parents would like any of us who had any personal stories, anecdotes, or other remembrances of their son to please approach them at the funeral and relate these stories to them. They expressed a great deal of interest in hearing anything and everything about Dave since they really didn't know their own son very intimately. To me this was a shocking and sad revelation. I knew that speaking to them about their son might help them in some way, so I didn't hesitate to approach them at the funeral.

The funeral can best be described as strange, the reason being the odd circumstances surrounding the death. The small New Jersey church, which was just across the river from New York, was packed with mourners. By the time I arrived, the thickening crowd was already spilling out onto the street. It was surprising to see that a guy with so few real friends in life had drawn, in death, an audience of this magnitude. To an outsider in the neighborhood, the event probably resembled a funeral for a rock star rather than an FBI agent. But that's the way it was during my years in the Bureau. If someone was sick, needed financial help, or died, FBI people were always there to lend support—either to the person themselves or the family. The turnout for Dave's final farewell was a clear demonstration of what it meant to be a member of the FBI family.

I had a mission that day. As my supervisor had requested, I would seek out Dave's parents and tell them whatever I could about their son in the hopes that they could get to know him a little better. Perhaps, it was an after-the-fact gesture, but I felt it might give them some solace, maybe a partial sense of closure, to learn things about Dave that they had never known. Not having ever met Dave's folks, I scanned the crowd looking for unfamiliar faces, folks who were not FBI people. I surmised that these might be relatives or friends of the family and that they would be able to direct me to Dave's mother and father.

"Good morning, sir. I'm Rick Berger. I worked with Dave. I was wondering if you could point out his parents to me. I'd like to speak with them for a moment." The tall gentlemen in the dark blue suit looked more like an FBI agent than I did. He introduced himself as a member of Dave's family, then, gesturing me to follow him, led me toward the front of the church. After briefly introducing me to Dave's folks, he whispered in my ear, thanking me for my interest in speaking personally with the parents. "This will mean a lot to them, hearing from guys like you." He shook my hand and walked slowly toward the back of the church.

I knew the service would be beginning shortly, so I made sure to keep my conversation brief. Dave's father shook my hand warmly as I introduced myself. His mom told me that it was wonderful to see so many of his coworkers here, knowing that they had taken a portion of their busy day to attend the funeral. I began by telling them that I was on the same squad as Dave and that, on several occasions, we had worked together conducting interviews. I told them of my position as coordinator of the FBI's DECA program and how Dave had made fun of me for giving my presentations using the DECA dummy, a character he had conjured up. They laughed at my impersonation of Dave raising his hand as if holding a dummy and making the little falsetto voice as the puppet spoke of the FBI's efforts to catch spies. They said that hearing something humorous at this time was just what they needed to give them a little break from the anguish and torment they were experiencing. Dave's mother, her voice cracking with emotion, thanked me for letting them know something about Dave's sense of humor. Then, Dave's dad expressed his appreciation for my telling the story, saying that it was important for them to hear things like this since they really didn't know much about their son. He thanked me for giving them a glimpse into their son's life. I could see people beginning to take their seats, as the service was about to get under way. As I walked away from Dave's folks, I felt a sense of inner peace, secure in the knowledge that in some small way, I had provided some solace for them. Perhaps others had also come forth and related little anecdotes about Dave—his success as an agent, his investigative skills, or, as in my story, his sense of humor.

Like Richard Cory in that ancient poem, Dave was "a gentleman from sole to crown." And, like Mr. Cory, he too possessed a troubled soul and found the ultimate solution resting in his hand one quiet day.

The sign on Dave's desk said, "It's Coming and You Can't Stop It." Whatever that meant to Dave, one thing is certain—all of us were not to blame. We tried our best to befriend him, draw him out of his shell. I guess some human lives are more frail than others. We tried our best, but in Dave's world, whatever it was, it was coming and none of us could stop it.

OFFICIAL QUIRKS

Little-known FBI Fact Number 1:

Until the death of FBI Director J. Edgar Hoover, in May of 1972, FBI cars had no air-conditioning and no regular radios, just police radios. As a young agent, I was told that the reason for this was that Hoover believed these two modern conveniences would interfere with an agent's concentration and ability to perform his duties. Is Hoover spinning in his grave at the thought of cell phones and CD players in current Bureau cars?

Little-known FBI Fact Number 2:

Every five years, the FBI conducts a reinvestigation of each agent. This is done to ensure that each agent is not engaged in any activities which could jeopardize FBI operations or cases, is not in any financial difficulties, is living within his means, etc. It keeps the agents on their toes and prevents any embarrassment to the Bureau.

Around the time of one of my reinvestigations, I had just returned home from working a 7:00 a.m. to 3:00 p.m. shift. The springtime sun was shining brilliantly as I began mowing my front lawn. Living on a cul-de-sac, few if any cars would pass my house during the day, so when, over the sound of my sturdy Toro lawnmower, I heard a car approaching, I naturally looked up. As the big white Chevy Caprice swung into the curve of the cul-de-sac, I surmised that the driver would soon realize that he had entered a dead end and would continue around the curve and head back out to the main road. To my surprise, he slowly stopped, just short of the driveway belonging to the house next to mine. I noticed that, in addition to the driver, there were three other male occupants in the vehicle. No sooner had the car come to a halt than the driver whipped out what appeared to be a powerful three-hundred-millimeter telephoto lens and began shooting pictures of my house. Letting the safety handle on the mower drop, the engine stopped, and I continued to scrutinize the activity while deciding whether to call the police or approach the vehicle. Since, like most agents, I rarely made it a practice to wear my gun while mowing the lawn, I decided that if there was going to be any kind of challenge or trouble, I was already marked to be the loser. As I squinted against the glare of the harsh sunlight, I saw the driver lower the oversized camera lens, and I recognized him from the FBI office. These were fellow agents! What the hell were they doing at my house? Without hesitation, I approached the car. Inside I could see one of the guys scribbling feverishly onto a pad.

"Hi, guys!" I said. Recognizing that these were agents assigned to the Applicant Recruiting Squad, I now knew what was going on. These guys, when not conducting background checks on potential new FBI agents, were assigned to conduct the five-year reinvestigations. Since I was about due for mine, it all made sense. They were taking pictures of my home to verify that I was not living in some mansion, because this might indicate that I was in debt up to my eyeballs, a condition which is not illegal, but one which is certainly not in keeping with the image and standards of an FBI agent. However, the guy with the pad really puzzled me. I could see through the car window that he was pointing up at the house and then marking down numbers. I asked him what that was all about. He said that he was counting the windows on each floor of my house. "Why," I asked, "would you be counting the number of windows?" He explained that his supervisor had told him to do this so they could determine if it was a really expensive house. After all, if an agent had a house that looked like it was far in excess of what an agent's salary could buy, perhaps the agent was selling secrets to the Russians for extra cash. Apparently, to the Bureau's way of thinking, there was a direct correlation between the number of windows in the front of a house and its value.

Now that's good solid FBI reasoning. I knew several agents whose spouses were doctors, lawyers, pilots, and God knows what else. Many of them had homes that would knock your socks off, and they weren't selling secrets to anyone! Sometimes the FBI's thinking puzzled me.

Here's another story involving a lawnmower. On occasion, an agent would choose to dictate a report instead of typing it himself. The tape of the dictation would then go the steno pool, where a typist would dutifully transfer the agent's spoken words to the printed page. Once in a while, a stenographer would take it upon herself to alter the dictation in some way. Sometimes it was a grammatical change, the addition of a comma, etc. However, sometimes what the agent had dictated seemed to take on a life of its own when placed in the hands of one of these "stenos."

My fellow agent, Jack, had submitted a fairly lengthy report on the goings-on of a subject whom he was investigating. One sentence stated that the individual had been seen in public, locked in a romantic embrace with his paramour. When he received the completed report from the young lady who had typed it, the sentence describing the activity stated that the individual had been observed "locked in a romantic embrace with his power mower."

One last little adventure I think you'll enjoy hearing about involved a little airplane ride from hell. Several FBI agents are licensed pilots. Some received their training in the military and continued to fly as a hobby. Others were licensed to fly commercial aircraft. Some of these folks had flown for major airlines prior to their FBI employment. One day I received a call asking me to accompany an FBI pilot on an aerial-surveillance mission in order to get some photos of a particular vehicle as its owner drove from his home to meet a person we suspected of being a spy. On the morning of the flight, I drove out to the small airport, which was located in one of the New York suburbs. For years I had known the agent who would be piloting the small Cessna, and I trusted his judgment implicitly. The flight lasted for a boring four hours during which we flew in circles waiting for the guy to leave his home, get in the car, and start driving. Throughout this entire period, the sound of classical music played in my headset. The pilot loved classical music. I hated it. Give me some good old rock and roll to break the monotony. About two hours into the Peer Gynt Suite, I politely asked if we could listen to something else. He switched to Verdi's "Aida." Some days you just can't win.

As luck would have it, the guy we were supposed to surveil never went anywhere during our time in the air, so we began to head back to the airport. My only thought at that time was how glad I'd be to see the men's room once we landed. On final approach, I noticed a sudden silence. Turning to the pilot and speaking slowly, in a vain attempt to hide my panic, I said, "Did the engine just cut out, or what?" "Oh yeah. That happens sometimes. If it doesn't cut back on, we'll just glide in." Hearing this almost caused a reaction which would have negated my need for the men's room. The good news was that as we approached the runway, the engine kicked back in. We had a bumpy yet safe landing. Needless to say, as I climbed out of the plane, I headed straight for the hangar and the room that meant the most to me at that moment. Our surveillance was a failure, but I was glad that at least I was around to write the report stating that.

I was a competent FBI agent. My reports were always in on time, and usually ahead of schedule. My investigations were complete and thorough. My ability to handle guns was proven by my scores in firearms practice sessions. What was lacking was a passion. Some of you may know the experience of owning a passion. It's a feeling, a sensation that totally engulfs you when you're engaged in an activity that is so much a part of you that you, in sense, become a part of it. As I said, I did a good job, but I'm sure that I could have done a better job playing the role of an agent on TV.

ALL IN THE FAMILY

"We're an FBI family!" You never heard that one in our house. Rarely was there even a mention of my work. The reason for this was simply that just about everything I handled was classified "Secret" or, at the very least, "Confidential." Once in a while, the Bureau actually trusted me to work on matters that had some super classification such as "Top Secret." However, that occurred on only a few rare occasions. After all, that info was as heavily guarded as the secret recipe for my wife's meat loaf.

My area of expertise, foreign counterintelligence, was vastly different from other types of investigative law enforcement work. The job of an FBI agent who spends his day profiling and chasing spies is quite unlike that of an agent on, say, a bank robbery squad. Those agents' kids can't wait till dad comes home so he can regale them with exciting tales of rooftop chases ending in the sound of handcuffs clanking onto gnarly wrists. What could I say, "Hey, kids, wanna hear about the Russian spy I caught stealing classified information from the Dataflop Corporation on Long Island?" What if they had answered, "Yeah, Dad, tell us." In order to avoid lengthy explanations as to why I couldn't talk about my work, I chose not to discuss it at all. Was that a copout? I guess in a way it was. I probably could have explained to them that my role in the FBI was to locate people who were trying to steal very important information and, if I caught them, to make sure that they were punished for what they did. In retrospect, I probably should have told them more about what I did in the FBI. There were always plenty of FBI dramas on TV, but they were rarely about espionage investigations. I guess there just isn't enough action and gore in catching a spy as opposed to tracking down, and arresting, a gang who pulls off a million-dollar jewel heist. Once in while, at home, I would mention something related to my work. I remember an incident during which my daughter, Sherry, who was about eight years old at the time, heard me discussing a case in which we had caught some guys attempting to get information from a company's computer system. Sherry chimed in with, "Dad, did you FBI 'em?" That was the first and last time I heard the name FBI used as a verb. All three of my kids—Sherry, Ilyse, and Todd—thought that I had a cool job but, due to my rarely speaking about it, never really found out much about the FBI other than what they saw on TV. Perhaps that's why they never showed an interest in pursuing careers in law enforcement. Sherry, although a busy mom, holds down a full-time job as a social worker. Ilyse followed her dream of becoming a registered dietician. Todd is a sought-after videotape editor and independent filmmaker, whose most recent film has won critical acclaim.

Unless they are working in an undercover capacity, most agents do not keep it a secret that they are with the FBI. They are, however, selective in choosing those with whom they share this information. The majority of agents I worked with, after having known their neighbors for a while, were not at all hesitant to let them know about their Bureau employment. The FBI is in the business of gathering information, and the more people that know what you do, the more information you'll receive. Of course, once folks know you as the local FBI agent on their block, they'll feed you more innocuous information than your little brain can process. At least once a week, some neighbor or friend would approach me with an FBI-related story. Maybe it was the one about how his friend's uncle had helped the FBI catch a spy during World War II. Sometimes it was a question about whether the FBI really knew the identity of the person that had killed President John F. Kennedy, or whether it was true that J. Edgar Hoover had been seen at a party in a red dress. (I always told them that this was a ridiculous story since everyone knew that Hoover's favorite color was blue.) However, once in a while, a neighbor or friend would actually come up with some valuable information that the FBI was able to use in a particular investigation. Besides providing information, people who knew what I did were able to help in other ways. I recall incidents in which realtors, who were friends of agents, provided assistance in locating suitable housing for spies who had defected. Thanks to these folks, on several occasions, we were able to obtain vacant homes to use as safe houses in which defectors could be hidden and protected during ongoing investigations.

It's interesting to note that when agents move into an area, in most cases they blend quickly into the neighborhood, particularly if they have their family with them. However, throughout the country, there are several "agent ghettos" which consist of clusters of FBI agents and their families who find a safe haven in living within close proximity of each other. There are several reasons for this. One is that when an agent receives an assignment which takes him to an area of the country with which he or she is not familiar, most agents find it reassuring to locate in a neighborhood where other agents already live. For one thing, he will immediately be welcomed into the brotherhood. Also, in this way, he feels confident in knowing that the school system in the area has already been checked out and determined to be good. Agents are also pretty savvy when it comes to real-estate values, so there's a pretty good guarantee that the locations and homes chosen by the agents living in that area provide a sound investment. Then, there's the matter of instant car pools. When an agent moves into a place with other agents already living there, he will have no problem finding a ride to work, and most agents travel to their office in cars. Few agents that I have worked with take public transportation to work unless they live within a short distance of the field office they work in. In New York City, for instance, the few agents that traveled to work on the city subway or bus system were, for the most part, single and lived in an apartment in the city or a short train ride away. This was usually across the Hudson River, in a predominantly "singles" neighborhood in New Jersey.

The success of most FBI agents lies not only in their investigative skills, but in the patience and understanding of a loyal and devoted spouse. Husbands of female agents and wives of male agents are very unique individuals. They must possess the sensitivity and good judgment to know that, at times, they must stifle the urge to let a friend in on some secret about where their spouse is working or to blurt out something at a party which could possibly change the course of an investigation or affect someone's life. Due to the nature of spousal relationships, FBI agents will at times share with their spouse information, which, although perhaps not actually classified, is nevertheless sensitive and may not be suitable for dissemination to the general public. Husbands and wives of agents are damn good at keeping secrets and deserve to be applauded for their efforts at doing so.

So you see, FBI families are really no different than any other families except that one or both of the parents spend a portion of their time keeping secrets, chasing spies, or hunting down murderers or international terrorists!

FBI CASES—
THE REAL SCOOP

I am often asked about interesting cases that I was involved in during my FBI career. A few of these instantly come to mind:

"Crayola"

One oddball crime fest that stands out in my mind occurred back in the early 1970's, during the period in which I served as a photographer. It involved a cat-and-mouse game initiated by a true New York whacko that the Bureau referred to as "Crayola." This guy was involved in some illegal activities, which caused several agents to scurry around the city looking for clues. He would plant these clues in the most inconspicuous place. He would write them on the walls of the tunnels of the New York City subway system. Whenever he successfully eluded capture by the Bureau, which proved to be several times over a period of a few months, he would leave a scorecard of sorts in the classified ads section of a popular New York City newspaper. He would do this in the form of a coded message. It would read like a sports score, "Crayola One, FBI Zero." The next one might read, "Crayola Two, FBI One." These little messages were intended to taunt the agents who were diligently scouring the city in an effort to find him.

Due to my photographic skills, I had the luck to become a part of this game of hide-and-seek. It happened in this way: I was finishing up my morning's work, busily printing an eight-by-ten-inch glossy of some "grip and grin" scene. This is one of those corporate-type photos in which some high-level muckety-muck is seen handing an employee a certificate for a job well done. Both are wearing those plastered-on smiles that disappear the moment the flash goes off. I had just placed the print onto the large heated drum, which dries the photos, when I was summoned to the boss's office. He told me to grab my jacket and report to Tom, the case agent handling the Crayola investigation. I had heard about the case, found it interesting, but knew that it was not the hottest thing on the FBI blotter. "Oh, what the hell," I figured. "At least it'll get me out of this lab and into the streets of New York, where the action is." I grabbed my coat and camera and raced off to meet Tom.

Within minutes, we were out of the building and heading to Tom's car, which was parked about a block from the office. As Tom skillfully navigated the FBI car through the clogged New York streets, he explained to me that we were heading uptown where Crayola had left one of his latest messages for us in the subway. They were always written in crayon, hence the name, Crayola.

After much jockeying around in a search of a parking space, we located a spot about two blocks from the subway entrance. As we jumped out of the car, I noticed that Tom simply ignored the expired parking meter. I guess feeding the meter was futile since it would run out of time anyway while we were on our assignment, and we'd be facing a windshield full of tickets when we got back to the car. So Tom just flung his official FBI parking placard onto the dashboard. Imagining myself in the role of an FBI agent in a Hollywood flick, I grabbed the door handle and gave the door a sharp shove with my shoulder, attempting to exit the car FBI movie style. Unfortunately, the door was still locked. I heard a sharp crack as my shoulder met the locked door. I unlocked the door and, like a brooding puppy, got out of the car and followed Tom down the block on our quest to locate Crayola. Okay, so it isn't like in the movies.

After a two-block walk, we approached the entrance to the subway station. A large mass of slow-moving commuters blocked the entrance. I artfully dodged my way through the crowd. I knew that yelling out "FBI, get out of the way!" or something to that effect would have created pandemonium, so instead I calmly forged on through the crowd as Tom blocked for me. We made our way to the entrance and began to wend our way down the staircase and onto the train platform down below.

As the cop on the platform slowly turned in our direction, Tom whipped out his FBI credentials and announced that we had an ongoing investigation in the area and needed access to the electrical tunnel below the main tube that the train goes through. The cop seemed unimpressed. He asked Tom if this was an emergency. In response, Tom simply told him that it was a routine investigation related to an ongoing case. In typical NYPD fashion, the cop now seemed even less impressed. How come in the movies everyone jumps when they hear the words "FBI"? Do you want to know a secret? In New York, no one jumps about anything except when someone yells "fire!" in a crowded movie theater. The cop went on to ask Tom if there were any suspects down there or if there would be any chance of weapons being drawn. Tom informed him that there was little chance of this and that what we were after were some pictures of writing on a wall. "Sounds pretty exciting," said the cop dryly.

Officer Exuberance then said that we would have to wait until he could secure authorization for us to enter the area we needed to access. After making a call on his radio, he told us that we had received clearance to enter the area. "Well, have fun, guys. If you need anything, just come back up. I'll be here. I'm on until three." He then pointed to a door at the end of the station on which through thick black smudges of grease, the words "Authorized Personnel Only" were barely visible. Since we were now "authorized personnel," we made our way toward the door. As the roar of an approaching train grew louder, we heard the cop yell out, "You guys have flashlights, don't ya?" "Yeah, we got 'em," Tom responded. Switching the clumsy camera case to my left hand, I reached for the doorknob. I found it almost impossible to turn since it was heavily coated with thick black grease. I finally had some success, opened the door, and wiped my blackened hand on a nearby pillar. As we made our way past what looked like miles of bundled wire hanging on the wall to our right, I reached around to my back pocket, checking to make sure that the flashlight I had brought was still there. It was. Actually, the bare bulbs located every few yards were sufficient to light the small tunnel, which reminded me of a similar space that I had been in when I took a tour of Howe Caverns in upstate New York.

Tom suddenly stopped a few yards ahead of me. He pointed to the wall just in front of us. Clearly written on the wall, in what appeared to be red crayon, were some directions, locations, and times. Tom explained that Crayola, in his last message to the FBI, had identified this as the place where he would be providing his next clue. I knew that I had to get some really clear photos of the area and the writing itself. I reached into the camera case and pulled out the cumbersome Speed Graphic press camera. Since it was the same type that I had used for four years in the air force, I was familiar with its every detail, so much so that I could make all the necessary adjustments, like setting the lens aperture and securing the flash attachment, in the dark. I carefully connected the flash unit, its gleaming chrome bowl reflecting what little light there was around us. Then I began my calculations. You see, these cameras had no meter, no automatic settings, or any of the other features that we're all so used to on today's cameras. In order to get a good exposure, I had to do all the calculating in my head. It was all a matter of math—and I was lousy at math. I asked Tom to aim his flashlight at the writing so that I could focus. With each shot, the flash lit up the tunnel, just long enough for us to catch brief glimpses of shadows darting up and down along the opposite wall. We knew that we were not alone down there since these tunnels are home to the famous New York rats. Our main concern was the danger of being bitten and having to endure a painful series of rabies shots. As I shot my photos, Tom, who had by now put himself in charge of the rat patrol, kept a watchful eye on the swiftly moving shadows. As I shot various angles and close-ups, I wondered how this Crayola nut had gotten down here. Had he convinced the cop upstairs that he, like us, was a member of the secret society known as "authorized personnel"? With the sound of the rats conducting their frenetic Olympic races just feet away from us, I shot a few last photos of Crayola's hieroglyphics. The smallness of the space around me had made it difficult to compose the shots as I had really wanted to, but I reasoned that since these were not art photos, they'd serve the purpose. I knew that as long as they clearly documented the writing and the surrounding area, my assignment was complete.

As a train rumbled overhead, we began to make our way out of the cavelike tunnel. I imagined how my daughter's pet hamster must feel as he enters and exits those plastic tunnels. We left the maze and reentered the subway platform area. Tom laughed, remarking that I looked like a chimney sweep. I told him that he resembled a Santa that had gotten caught halfway down the chimney. As we approached the cop, we saw him shaking his head as he asked, "You guys going back to the FBI office looking like that?" I gave him a quick lesson in how to use the camera and had him take a picture of us, two grease-covered ragamuffins who represented the nation's premier law enforcement agency.

When we got back to the office, we took plenty of ribbing about how Bureau employees should take pride in their appearance. Tom thanked me, and I told him that I'd have the photos processed and ready to be picked up later that day. For all the tribulations we had experienced, I must admit, the pictures came out pretty damn good.

Crayola's game of hide-and-seek continued for several weeks. Then, one day, I got a call from Tom. "Guess what?" he said. "We got that Crayola jerk. It turned out that he's a writer and was trying to drum up a little controversy so he could get some publicity." "We're going to use your shots as photographic evidence in court and nail the bastard. Good work, Rick, and thanks."

A couple of weeks later, there I was, in the office of the special agent in charge, shaking his hand and being photographed for one of the "grip and grin" eight-by-tens as I received my certificate of appreciation.

A Cold Lemonade

Most of my years in the FBI were spent in the field of counterintelligence. A great deal of it was interesting work, this spy-chasing stuff. Let me give you a little background.

Although J. Edgar Hoover had died in 1972, the Bureau continued throughout the entire decade to follow his mandate, which ordered us to keep a close watch on any and all government officials representing the Soviet Union. Echoing Hoover's sentiments, the agents sometimes joked, "You just can't trust those Commie bastards." The Bureau's approach to dealing with these Commies was to assign several hundred agents to investigate their activities, particularly in large cities such as New York and Washington DC—cities which hosted diplomatic establishments. Keeping track of this large group of Russians proved to be a massive undertaking. The FBI had reason to believe that several of these individuals were actually intelligence officers who operated under the guise of representing their government, the Soviet Union. The Bureau realized that it was dealing with a group of highly trained professional spies who were quite experienced in gathering information and recruiting others to aid them in accomplishing their goals. The FBI also knew that the Soviets were aware of the Bureau's interest in them, their contacts, and their activities. The whole affair was, in essence, a cat-and-mouse game, at the end of which was a trap loaded with bait in the form of sought after U.S. information, some of which was classified. It was a case of spies spying on spies.

The assignment was challenging. After all, how does one go about identifying and catching a spy? This lofty endeavor reminded me of the *Mad* magazine spoof "Spy vs. Spy." There was the bad spy, all in black. Then there was the good spy, all in white. Each spent his day trying to outwit the other. Sure, it was just a magazine comic strip, but basically, that's the way it actually worked in the real world of espionage.

The Russians who were living in New York were there on what was purported to be legitimate business. As I mentioned before, several of them were stationed in the Big Apple as representatives of their government, the

Soviet Union. Some worked as employees of the United Nations while others spent their time at the Soviet Mission to the UN, which was located in New York's Upper East Side. The FBI regarded both the UN and the Russian Mission as nests of spies. Years of surveillance, coupled with information obtained from a variety of sources, demonstrated to the Bureau that these Soviet citizens had dual jobs. Apparently, in their eyes, the more rewarding one was their intelligence-gathering activities.

Picture a spy. What image immediately comes to mind? Surely, a dapper James Bond-like fellow sporting a sleekly tailored outfit reeking of style and pizzazz. In the case of the Russians, that mental image was skewed. The Russian spy of the 1970's looked more like someone who had raided a collection bin for the homeless. If these intelligence officers, as they are known to the Bureau, were attempting to blend in with the crowds on the streets of New York, they were miserable failures. Like my fellow agents, I could spot a Russian on a New York street in a New York minute. Their baggy black suits would have made excellent grain sacks. Their clownlike appearance suggested that perhaps they were on leave from the Moscow Circus. Each of them had the amazing ability to walk down a crowded New York street without tripping on the cuffs of their oversized trousers. No slave to fashion, these spies. The balloonlike legs of their pants rested sloppily on the insteps of their ungainly black shoes. The clopping sound of their thick heels meeting the pavement easily gave them away, making short work of tailing them down the block and into a building. As professional spies, they were a dismal failure when it came to hiding from us as we surveilled them on the street. My thanks go out to those spies of yesteryear who helped make my job so much easier.

Okay, so we knew that the spies were here. And we knew why they were here. Their mission was to pilfer any kind of secrets they could get their hands on: technology, military information, scientific data—that kind of stuff. As for the FBI's role, it was to determine which ones were the spies and then to "neutralize" their attempts to get their dirty little hands on our material and information. Sounds like a fun way to spend your day, right? Well, that's how I earned my living in the FBI. Did I catch any spies? Certainly, but not by myself. Catching spies is a team effort and the FBI is a team.

If I had to comb through decades of memories stored in the hard drive in my hard head and pick out one espionage case that leaps out as my favorite, it would be one from the late 1970's known as "Lemonade." Don't ask me where that name came from. I haven't the slightest idea. There's a highly classified method by which the Bureau assigns code names to cases. Agents joked that the method involved a monkey at FBI Headquarters who threw darts at a board with potential code names on it. Anyway, the Lemonade case was a classic example of a spy drama. It featured espionage tradecraft including encrypted messages, clandestine locations and meetings, and all the other accoutrements of a film noir spy movie.

The principal player in the drama was Navy Lt. Commander Arthur Lindberg. Art, as everyone called him, stepped right off a navy recruiting poster. His tall well-proportioned frame proudly displayed his carefully pressed navy uniform. His face was highlighted by gleaming blue eyes which perfectly complimented his sandy blond hair. His was the image of a mature California surfer in a Navy uniform. In addition to his good looks, Art was an upstanding family man and a credit to his community, with involvement in the Lions Club and the parent-teacher organization. His naval career took him on several adventures, including a mission which placed him aboard a ship that was stationed in the Bay of Pigs right in the heart of the Cuban missile crisis.

By 1977, Lindberg's successful naval career was drawing to a close. He was looking forward to the day, in about two years, when he would embark upon a well-earned retirement. He contemplated spending his remaining time in the navy at the Lakehurst, New Jersey naval base, where he was in charge of purchasing equipment and supplies. This seemed like a secure and logical plan. It was just that, until the April day when he received a phone call from his friend, Terry.

Terry Tate was an agent of the Naval Investigative Service and a good friend of Art's, so there was certainly nothing out of the ordinary about Art receiving a call from his buddy. During the couple of weeks that followed that call, Terry asked Art some routine questions including ones regarding how certain types of information could be obtained from the base. Then, the questions began to become more serious. Finally, Terry jolted Lindberg when he asked him if he would like to take part in a secret assignment. His involvement, explained Terry, would be so secret that he would not be permitted to discuss it with anyone, not even his wife or his boss at the base. Lindberg, sensing that this was the chance for the adventure of a lifetime, accepted the assignment.

Within a week, in a secret lunchtime meeting that took place at a Howard Johnson motel in the area, Lindberg was introduced to two FBI agents. Several more meetings took place over the next two months during which the agents found Lindberg to be not only a willing participant, but also a genuinely friendly person whom they felt they could trust.

The first portion of the assignment immediately presented challenges. Lindberg was told by the FBI that he was to take a pleasure cruise to the

Bahamas on a Russian-owned vessel, the MS *Kazakhstan*. I can't imagine how he explained that to his wife. But one way or another, he was able to convince her that he was off to Detroit on business for the navy.

Art's mission was to determine whether the ship was being used by the Soviets for spying and to identify the individuals on board who were involved in this activity. This was quite a formidable task for someone untrained in these matters. But Art was up to the challenge.

During the first week of July, Art traveled to New York where he met with an FBI agent who provided the money for him to purchase a ticket for the trip. His instructions were simply to write a note, which he would leave on board as he departed the ship. The note was to state that he was interested in making some extra money prior to his retirement. He was to say that he was in a position to provide information which might be of interest to the Russians. At the end of the note, he was to direct them to call a certain phone number at a particular time of day on August 30, 1977 and ask for Ed. (The Bureau told Lindberg that for the duration of the operation, he would refer to himself as Ed.)

As the trip drew to a close, Art mentally prepared himself for the action he was about to take. After the ship docked, several crew members stood near the gangway smiling at the well-tanned passengers as they departed. Lindberg slowed his gait, allowing other passengers to exit ahead of him. Watching from the terminal, FBI agents carefully observed Art's every move as he approached one of the ship's officers, and handed him the folded paper. The officer, perhaps anticipating a tip, smiled. Art quickly walked down the gangway, looking straight ahead, never turning to look back.

Less than two weeks later, with the FBI in the vicinity, Art rolled his car window down as he pulled up to a phone booth located in front of a New Jersey diner. Within five minutes, the phone rang. Art knew the phone call meant that the Russians were receptive to his offer. As he answered it, a caller with a heavy foreign accent asked for Ed. When Art told him that he was speaking to Ed, the caller, who identified himself as Jim, suggested that they meet that very evening in New York. Art declined this initial invitation. The caller attempted to set up a meeting on the following Saturday instead. Once again, Art refused. He knew that attending these meetings would result in his being away from home too much and that he would not be able to account for these times away from the family. However, he did agree to another phone contact for the following Saturday.

Saturday arrived, and Art reported back to the diner, this time minus his FBI handlers who had decided that it was too risky to show up at each contact. After all, the Russians were in this business too, and there was always the danger that they could be conducting countersurveillance, looking for the FBI in the area.

As Art anticipated, the phone at the diner rang precisely on time. The deep voice on the other end asked if he was speaking to Ed. Art, once again identifying himself as Ed, listened carefully, as Jim informed him that, for security reasons, he should go to another phone. This next phone would be located outside of a Sears store. Art began to realize that this spy game could be time consuming.

Not wanting to jeopardize the operation, Lindberg raced off to the Sears store, carefully following the directions that Jim had given him. Within a short time he found himself lost. Now, these Russians may have been trained intelligence officers, spies from the KGB, Russia's elite security service, but they couldn't give directions worth a damn, not in this country anyway. In the name of national security, Art violated the cardinal rule regarding men who find themselves lost while driving: he asked for directions. In a mild state of panic over the minutes that had been lost, he arrived at Sears a bit stressed, but nevertheless in time to receive the call. Over the phone, Jim instructed him to reach under the shelf in the phone booth where he would find a metal container, the kind used for hiding spare keys. The container would be held to the shelf by a magnet. Inside the container would be a note with further instructions.

Reaching under the shelf, Art located the container, removed it, and slid the thin metal top back, revealing the folded-up note inside. He returned to his car where he sat and read the message. As he digested the words on the paper before him, he realized that this special assignment that he had agreed to take on was blossoming into a full-blown spy drama. The typed note proposed that he, accompanied by his family, if he so desired, use his vacation time to take an all-expense paid trip to Finland, Guyana, Columbia, or Jamaica, where matters could be discussed with greater security.

The next phone call was set to take place in September in a booth along New Jersey's Garden State Parkway. On that date, as Art approached the designated area, he noticed two cars sitting in an empty parking lot near the phone booth. As time went on, Art had become more confident and adept at this spy stuff. By this point, he probably would have made a damn good FBI agent working in the foreign counterintelligence field. He memorized the license plates so he could later give them to the agents working on the case. As he drove by one of the cars, he could see an individual behind the steering wheel raise a bottle in an attempt to cover his face. These cars, plus a third one, were traced to three Russians who had been assigned by their government to work in New York. Two of them were employees of the United Nations and the other, an employee of the Soviet Mission to the UN.

Over the next nine months, a series of meets, as they're called in spy lingo, took place. These were accompanied by drops, where the American would drop off some information, then, usually within a short time, the Russian would "clear the drop," picking up the desired material and leaving a cash payment secreted in the immediate vicinity. This seemingly crude method of exchange, though certainly not high-tech by today's standards, had been a tried and true method of espionage tradecraft for eons.

On one occasion, Art had to drive to a railroad station where he "dropped" an orange juice carton containing information onto a loading dock. While doing so, he spotted one of the Russians' cars. Following instructions he had previously received, he then drove to a wooded area near a gas station where he entered a phone booth and received a call from Jim. He was told to look on the ground in front of his car. There, he would find a dirty crushed milk carton inside of which would be his payment. Following the instructions, Art bent down, picked up the carton, and carefully opened it. Inside was $2,000.

If, by now, you're wondering why our government would supply classified information to be given to the enemy in the name of catching a spy or two, don't fret. The information that Art passed to the Russians was not exactly hot stuff. In fact, it was information which had been cleared by the government and okay'd for passage due to the fact that it was often old stuff that was no longer pertinent or valuable.

At this point, Art was growing more concerned that his wife would become suspicious of his time away from home. This was especially true since he was involved in community activities and was missing the meetings. In addition, the things he had to do in order to comply with the Russians' instructions were becoming complicated and almost comical in nature. After all, how do you get your hands on empty orange juice containers? Art had to keep buying OJ and dumping the stuff out or rifling through the family garbage in search of empties. ("Hurry up, kids, drink up! Daddy needs another container!")

The powers that be finally decided that if the operation were to continue, they had to let Art's wife in on the deal, so they arranged for a discussion to take place where they could tell her about her husband's secret mission. In a clandestine meeting at a motel, an agent from the Naval Investigative Service spilled the beans to Art's wife. She expressed her total support, adding how proud she was of his involvement. She understood that in some instances, this meant that she would have to make excuses for Art missing family events. She turned out to be so cooperative that she even ended up emptying and cleaning orange juice containers for him to use in the operation!

Although real life FBI cases don't always reflect the excitement and drama of a Hollywood production, in this case, there actually were a few touches of the James Bond brand of intrigue. In the Lemonade case, a concern arose that at some juncture it might become necessary for Art to stall for time during his travels. Enter the creative crew to save the day! With their talents and expertise, they devised and installed in Art's car, a button which he could press to make one of the tires go flat. The time needed to change the flat would give him a ready excuse for a delay should the FBI need some additional time to conduct a surveillance or perhaps take some photos at the next site.

As the meets with the Russians continued, Art became aware that they were trying to conceal their identities by making sure that he never saw them. However, on one occasion, Art showed up early in order to receive a phone call. His instructions brought him to a group of booths which were located in a highway service area. He had been given the phone number of the particular phone that he was to answer. In order to determine which booth contained the right phone, he poked his head into each booth, glancing at the number on each phone. As he approached the second booth, he saw that it was occupied by a man. He immediately recognized him as the fellow that he had seen in September when he had received a call on one of the phones along the Garden State Parkway. He recalled that he was the guy who had covered his face with a bottle in order to avoid Art's gaze. Art immediately backed away and left the area, returning a short while later to continue checking for the number. Just as he located the correct booth, the phone rang. He heard Jim's familiar voice directing him to go to an adjacent booth where he would find something of interest. The booth turned out to be the one previously occupied by the Russian he had recognized. In it he found a package containing further instructions. He probably laughed to himself, thinking, "Gotcha!"

Money and documents were exchanged in a variety of curious places and in equally curious containers. On one occasion, Lindberg found himself attempting to locate a fence that was supposed to be next to a railroad track. He traversed the area several times, at one point sliding down a mud-covered hill. He finally located the fence on the opposite side of the tracks, next to a dirt-covered parking area. Recognizing that this scene fit the description of the place where he was to pick up his cash payment, he began a search for the money. According to his instructions, the dough was to have been hidden in an old radiator hose which was covered with grass and dirt. It took him quite a few minutes to locate this proverbial needle in the haystack, but persistence won out, and he finally found it. Inside the cleverly disguised black hose was $5,000. Little did the Soviets know that before long that money would be in the hands of the U.S. government, only to be used later as evidence against them.

Several types of disguised containers were used in the case. There were squashed coffee cans and even crushed cigarette boxes. Giving credit where it's due, I must admit that throughout this case, the Russians maintained a pretty good record of not losing any money. They must have surmised that very few people would pick up something like an old radiator hose.

As the months went by, the Russians' trust in Art grew stronger, and so did their demands. They began to request more detailed, precise, and of course, more valuable information. Throughout this time, the FBI had carefully monitored and documented the meets, drops, contacts, and telephone conversations between Art and the Russians, all with an eye toward building an ironclad case against these spies.

By the spring of 1978, the Bureau decided that it was time to put an end to the Russians' blatant espionage activities. An arrest was going to be made. On May 20, 1978, Art's car approached an A&P food store in Woodbridge, New Jersey. He was there to retrieve a whipped cream container inside of which was to be a note. (It was later revealed that the note requested that Lindberg travel to Austria for a personal meeting with the Russians.) The backseat of Lindberg's car had been removed and filled with bags of peat moss. Under these bags were FBI agents ready to spring into action.

The Russians never got to complete their mission. Jim, as he had come to be known, and his accomplices, were surveilled on land and from the air that day, as they left their homes and drove to the site of the drop. All three were arrested in the vicinity of the drop site. A Russian-speaking agent read Jim his rights in both English and Russian. The other two were also afforded the same opportunity. The arrest was accomplished successfully and without incident.

Following the trial, which took place in federal court in Newark, New Jersey, the two KGB officers assigned to the UN each received a fifty-year prison sentence. Neither of them ever served a day. An unusual agreement was made between the two governments, by which the spies were exchanged for five Soviet dissidents. The third Soviet was picked up but not charged since his assignment at the Russian Mission afforded him diplomatic immunity. He left the United States, as did the others, with the proviso that none of them was to ever set foot on U.S. soil again.

Upon the return of the spies to the Soviet Union, interesting news filtered back to the FBI office, saying that articles had appeared in the Moscow newspapers stating that "FBI monsters carrying Colt pistols" had manhandled and arrested three innocent Soviet citizens working in New York. It was also reported that these Russians were declared national heroes and given promotions.

Art Lindberg is regarded as a true patriot. He received no monetary reward for his efforts and accomplishments other than a small sum as compensation for his time and the inconvenience this endeavor created in his life.

Where did I fit into this drama? Well, once again the Bureau decided that I could best be used for my photographic knowledge and skills.

It was determined that in order to prove its case against the spies, the FBI needed some really good photos to introduce as evidence. As I mentioned, on many occasions, the Russians chose to communicate with Art via instructions and maps left in telephone booths located along New Jersey's Garden State Parkway.

The FBI decided that on one particular occasion, it would make an all-out attempt to document the spies engaged in their dirty work. As always, as soon as Art found out the location of his next contact with them, he would notify us. The location on the targeted date was a group of four public phone booths, which were connected with one another. I knew that my photos would be scrutinized in court and that I would probably have to testify regarding my photographic knowledge. This did not faze me in the least. I had confidence in my ability to take photographs, my background in the field was extensive, and I had a big mouth, which I would gladly use to toot my own horn in the courtroom. Maybe I'd even be discovered and asked to act in a TV drama about an FBI photographer!

When the day of the meet arrived, the weather was not on our side. It was an extremely cold and blustery February day with gusts of wind-driven snow blanketing the area. The previous week's snowfall had left miniature mountains and drifts in the immediate vicinity of the phone booths. With the snow continuing to accumulate, the snowbanks grew higher and higher until some of them were as tall as a person.

A short distance from the phone booths was a trailer that had been used to house a construction crew, but which was now vacant. I was to be situated in this trailer along with another agent, whose assignment was to videotape the Russians' activities.

Two days before the event was to take place, I began to assemble everything that I could possibly need for the assignment. Among the many necessities, my photographic survival kit included an extra tripod, masking tape, flashlight, batteries, and the savior of twentieth-century life in America, duct tape.

Early in the morning on the day the operation was to take place, I checked my camera gear, making sure that the telephoto lens was working properly. I also packed enough rolls of film to have documented the entire Russian Revolution.

When I entered the trailer, I could see that this was not going to be a Hollywood production. As an experienced photographer, I knew that my first consideration had to be, to quote an old real-estate adage, "location, location, location." Since I had to shoot through one of the two windows, and Rich, the agent who would be shooting the video, already occupied the one on the right, I positioned myself at the other window.

Between my Boy Scout training and my mother always saying, "Better to have it than wish you had it," I was sure I had brought everything I needed. That was until I noticed the condition of the window through which I would be shooting. The glass looked as if a four-year-old had smeared chocolate ice cream cone drippings on it. The one item I had failed to bring with me was a bottle of window cleaner. However, I must say, when the Bureau plans and prepares for an operation, the agents always expect the unexpected, so when I looked around the room, I was gratified, but not surprised, to see a bottle of Windex sitting on a small table in the corner. Within minutes I had that window glistening like a newly polished diamond. Now it was just a matter of setting up my camera gear and getting all of the accompanying equipment in place. I was ready for action!

"Our main interest is crossing the bridge now. He's in his usual," came across the radio located at the far end of the trailer. That meant that the surveillance team had the Russian in sight. He was driving his usual car, a Dodge Dart, the one he drove every day. He had not switched cars for the occasion to throw us off should we be following him that day. Coincidentally, that Dodge was the same model car that I drove at the time. I guess professional spies and spy catchers have the same taste in automobiles. From the radio transmissions echoing through the trailer, we knew, at this point, that he was crossing the Hudson River and heading from New York into New Jersey. Ground surveillance teams reported that the other two Russians were also on their way. Their job was to conduct countersurveillance—in other words, to keep an eye out for the FBI in the vicinity of the meet so they could let Jim know that he should change his plans if they spotted us.

The snow let up for a brief period. Through the trailer window, I had a fairly good view of the phone booths where the meet was to take place. I felt confident that my photos would be good, providing that a blizzard didn't suddenly whip up and obscure the view.

"Well, between your video and my stills, we should be able to nail the bastards," I said. "Which booth is he supposed to go into?" Rich told me that it was the one down on the end next to the garbage can. "Okay, I'll focus on that one," I replied.

"He's heading onto the parkway now," said the voice on the radio. The snow was beginning to fall faster, and the gusts of wind were beginning to increase in intensity. Within a short while, we were told that the subject of our investigation should be arriving within a few minutes. His Russian partners were now scouring the area for any signs of us. Because we had carefully ditched our cars and all of our agents in the area were hidden, the Soviets never detected our presence.

With all precautions having been taken, we felt confident that our efforts would lead to success. The one thing that none of us had considered was an intervention by Murphy, the guy who wrote the law that says, "If anything can go wrong, it will." Well, it did.

Staring through the lens, I saw movement. Someone was approaching from the left. "Wait a minute," I thought, "based on where he would have to park, Jim, our Russian friend, is supposed to be coming from the right. This guy is entering my frame from the left!" As I peered through my 200 millimeter eye on the world, I saw the individual approach the group of phone booths followed by three other men! "That's no Russian. That's not Jim!" I had seen countless photos of Jim, and I knew that the person I was looking at was someone else. "Who were these guys, and what were they doing out in the middle of a snowstorm?" I wondered. "Holy shit!" I blurted out. "Shut up, Berger, this tape has sound on it. When they use it in court, the world is gonna hear you cursing," yelled Rich. "Sorry," I mumbled, as I began clicking away, not knowing what the hell I was documenting. I figured that I had better keep shooting, just in case the goings-on had anything to do with the case. The plot thickened as I noticed that the four men were carrying buckets and squeegees. They walked up to the phone booths and put down their buckets. Each then dipped his squeegee into one of the pails of soapy water and began to clean the windows on the booths!

Just then, a radio transmission was received announcing that the Soviet should be arriving at the site within approximately six minutes. We had to act fast. Two of the agents ran from the trailer, snow and wind assaulting their faces as they ran toward the phone booths. The cleaning guys dropped their squeegees and stood still, not quite sure what to expect. The agents whipped out their badges, announcing that they were FBI. The group's leader explained that they were cleaning personnel hired by the phone company and that their supervisor had ordered them to clean the windows on the booths regardless of the weather. The agents told them to leave immediately since some police activity was about to take place. Figuring that within seconds they would be caught in the middle of a gun battle, they quickly picked up their equipment and ran off, hot soapy water sloshing out of the buckets, causing volcanic eruptions of steam as it hit the frozen New Jersey tundra. The scene was reminiscent of a surrealistic clip from a Fellini movie or, better yet, a *Three Stooges* skit.

"Here he comes," the agent on the radio announced. From our vantage point, we could see the Russian get out of his car and begin to walk toward the phone booths, stopping every few feet to glance over his shoulder. It was Jim, Art's contact.

"Oh shit, I'm outta film!" "Shut up, man, I told you, there's sound on this video!" "Oops, sorry, Rich. I forgot." I realized that I had wasted a whole roll of film on those guys cleaning the windows. My brain screamed, "Grab the other camera quick! No time to load up another roll!"

By now our Soviet spy buddy was approaching the first of the four phone booths when he suddenly disappeared from my camera's view. Thank you, Mr. Murphy. The star of the show had just walked behind a five-foot-high mound of snow. My view of him was now completely obscured. As he continued walking, he appeared from behind the show bank, and once again, I could see him heading toward the booth.

I kept clicking away as Vladimir (his real name) entered the booth which he and Art had agreed upon would be the one in which Art would leave the classified documents in exchange for a map and further instructions. Although the wind-driven snow ruined several of my shots, the fact that the window in the booth was clean helped quite a bit. I guess Murphy's Law was kind of on our side that day, since the cleaners had washed that particular window just prior to the agents scaring them away.

I enjoyed watching the professional spy at work as he constantly turned to look in every direction in an attempt to locate his enemy, the FBI. I photographed Vladimir retrieving the Hide-A-Key container which contained film with photos of the classified documents on it. I wondered if the inventor of these containers that were designed to hold an extra car key would ever have dreamt that his invention would someday play a role in an historic FBI espionage case.

The spy deftly removed the container that Art had left and placed it into the deep pocket of his woolen coat, then quickly walked over to the predetermined area where he would drop the payment. Looking around to make sure that he was not being observed, he placed a crushed coffee can, which held the cash payment, into the pile of loose dirt next to the base of a tree located several yards from the phone booth. Since this particular area was sheltered, it had not yet become covered with snow, so the can was visible enough for Art to see and retrieve quickly. Kicking a few twigs onto the can completed the process of making it look like just another piece of rusty, discarded litter. With one last glance in all directions, Jim assured himself that no one had seen his spy charade. Lifting his collar even higher to shield him from the bitter wind gusts, he quickly began to walk back toward his car.

"Great, we got the bastard on film!" I shouted. "Berger, shut the hell up! How many times do I have to tell you, this video has sound!" I thought to myself, "I had better stifle my enthusiasm and show some professionalism here. Act like an FBI agent." In the meantime, racing through my mind were thoughts of, "Hey, man, this is cool. Just like the movies, but better 'cause this is real!"

As it turned out, I did have to testify at the trial. When questioned about my experience as a photographer, I regaled the court with tales of my photographic background. In order to make sure that no one could trip me up on some technical details regarding camera settings, lighting, etc., when asked to describe my level of expertise, I said that I was a "qualified" photographer as opposed to labeling myself an "expert." My still photos, combined with Rich's videotapes, virtually nailed the Russians. Of course, their attorney claimed that we had doctored up the photos and that the FBI had created nothing more that a Disneyesque charade. The judge said that there was no need to play the sound portion of the videotape since it added nothing to the case. Perhaps this was because it consisted mostly of some wiseass FBI agent using foul language.

I found it interesting that when the Russians were questioned in court, they consistently feigned lack of comprehension due to their inability to speak English. At times they were even heard to say, "I don't speak English." This was quite comical as the FBI tapes of the phone conversations between Art and the Russian revealed that, in fact, they (at least Jim) spoke English very well. The Russians also said that they didn't like my photos very much and that the persons in the pictures were not them anyway. To this day, I remain highly insulted by their remarks.

TWA Flight 800

The seats sit in silence, awaiting the next bustling group of airline passengers to jostle through the cabin, feigning politeness as they jam their hand-carried luggage into overhead compartments. But the passengers are not to arrive. These seats will never again transport excited travelers eagerly anticipating their arrival in Paris. No, these seats will instead rest on a wooden structure, built to resemble an airline cabin. They are now pieces of evidence from what may have been a crime or, at the very least, one of the most horrific airline tragedies in our nation's history. These are the seats from TWA Flight 800, a Boeing 747, which took off from New York's Kennedy Airport on July 17, 1996, carrying 230 people. The destination was Paris. The flight got only as far as a few miles out over the Atlantic Ocean when it fell from the evening sky and plunged into the waters just off the Suffolk County shore of Long Island.

Initial reports contained eyewitness accounts of a "giant orange ball of fire," which lit up the darkened sky as it plunged into the ocean. Within hours, rumors arose espousing the now famous "missile theory," which declared that the event was the result of shoulder-fired missiles which were targeted at the aircraft. Further speculation pointed toward our own U.S. military, which had allegedly fired the missiles in error. Surfacing at the same time were reports that the projectiles had been fired by terrorists, who had timed the disaster to occur just two days before the opening of the Olympic Games in Atlanta. While speculation ran amuck, official statements released to the public described the cause as a mechanical failure attributed to a spark in the center fuel tank.

Officials of several agencies, including the FBI, U.S. Coast Guard, National Transportation Safety Board (NTSB), New York City Police Department, Suffolk County Police Department, and others launched a massive investigation, which included the careful scrutiny of the passenger manifest to determine whether anybody suspicious, or the target of a terrorist plot, might have been on board. Pilots who had been flying in the vicinity at the time of the incident were interviewed regarding what they may have seen. While this went on, the 255-foot navy salvage ship, the *Grapple*, was brought to the waters of East Moriches, Long Island to retrieve whatever pieces of the wreckage that it could obtain. The salvage operation was reported to have been the largest one the navy had undertaken since the effort after the 1941 bombing of Pearl Harbor. In addition, several commercial trawlers joined in and were successful in recovering debris. While this activity took place at sea, the Coast Guard base in East Moriches became the temporary workplace for rescue workers who would place the deceased into body bags. While all of this was going on, the families of those on the flight were arriving in the area to try to find out details and attempt to cope with their losses.

The destination of the recovered debris became a story unto itself. If you had had the opportunity, as I did, to view the tableau that had been created in a former Grumman aircraft plant in Calverton, Long Island, I'm sure a look of amazement would have crossed your face, as it did mine. The scene took place in an enormous hangar where F-14 fighter jets had once been built. It is difficult to accurately describe the immense size of the building's interior. Some of the areas had ceiling heights of eighty feet. Certain sections on the sprawling floor contained the aircraft's engines. They reminded me of the engines that I had become so familiar with during my air force days. I remember having to take pictures of them to document damage, some of which had been caused by starlings and other birds getting caught in the rotary blades during flight. These eight-foot-tall TWA engines towered above the investigators as they scrambled through and around them, looking for anything that might provide some insight into what could have caused the crash.

Placed carefully in specifically designated areas on the hangar's floor were the thousands of pieces of recovered wreckage. Some were actually quite small, the size of a person's hand, while others took up the space a car would occupy. Built on a specially constructed platform about eighty feet in length was a mock-up of the plane, which created a ghostly frame that resembled the carcass of a picked-over holiday turkey. Attached to this were pieces of the actual airliner. As additional pieces of the airplane's skin were found, they were attached to the structure. It reminded me of the plastic model airplanes that I put together as a kid. Perhaps the most striking sight was that of the partially reconstructed fuselage of the aircraft. Bizarre and somewhat ominous was the scene as investigators, including engineers, pilots, and other experts climbed in and out of the wreckage. Adding to the sense of surrealism were the many people scurrying from one location to another on, of all things, bicycles. The NTSB had determined that the most efficient way to get around in the three-hundred-thousand-square-foot building was on a bike, so the purchase order was signed, and the bikes were bought.

On several occasions, I rode a bike over to the area housing the mock-up of the central fuel tank. I'd stare at it, gazing intently at the portion which most clearly showed the result of an explosion, wondering if this piece of evidence really held the answer regarding the mystery of the plane's demise.

In an adjoining building was the reconstructed interior of the cabin. This, I found to be the most disturbing area to look at. The seats were positioned just as they had been on the airplane. Autopsy information was studied in an effort to determine just what had happened to each particular passenger in whatever seat that person had occupied. Walking down the center aisle and between the seats created vivid recollections of the time I had flown home from Japan on the military flight during which I slept between the coffins being flown back from Vietnam. As I walked among the seats, I could hear the cries of the passengers as they realized that the front of the airplane had fallen off and that they were speeding toward certain death. I tried to imagine what decompression felt like. Did it hurt, or were they completely unaware by that point because they were already unconscious? At times like these, I told myself that as a professional investigator, I should not become emotionally involved. That line of reasoning failed—particularly when I would come face-to-face with some family members who had been brought to the sight to demonstrate the immense effort that had been launched to determine just what had happened to their loved ones.

My job was far from the most glamorous one in the investigation. I was assigned to the security detail whose sole purpose was to make sure that no unauthorized individuals were allowed to enter the area. This included uninvited spectators, press people, and vendors. Vendors, did he say vendors? Yeah, I did. If you're an American, I'm sure you're familiar with the tee shirt and baseball cap phenomenon that has swept the country over the last several years. If there's an event, a rock concert, a rally, a sports event, or even a death penalty execution, you can be sure that some creative entrepreneur will be there selling tee shirts and caps commemorating the event. The TWA investigation was no different. Every day, some vendor would show up, just beyond the end of the security lines, with an abundant supply of souvenirs. How, you ask, could someone take advantage of a tragedy such as this to make a few bucks? Well, you know, as well as I do, that some folks think nothing of exceeding the bounds of decency in the name of going home with a fat wallet. It happened in the same fashion with the 9/11 tragedy, and it continues to this day. I still see vendors on the streets of New York hawking their 9/11 artifacts—cheap wall decorations, neon paint-on-velvet scenes of the Twin Towers, automobile decals, and bumper stickers covered with American flags with the smoking towers in the background. I am embarrassed to admit that at the TWA site, I too, fell prey to the underhanded tactics of these below-the-belt business people. I bought a tee shirt—from a guy who sold them from the back of his van, just beyond the gate that I was guarding. As I write this, I'm looking at the shirt. On the front is an American flag which is partially covered with a ribbon. Above the flag it says, "TWA Flight 800." Below the flag are the words "Investigative Task Force." Emblazoned on the back, in full color, are the insignia of the many organizations that took part in the investigation. Above these logos is a full-color drawing of the scaffolding on which is hung the reconstructed airplane. Running across the top are the words, "Search for Answers." I never wore it.

Like the numbers "911," the name "TWA Flight 800" will remain in the minds and hearts of Americans. If we are to remain healthy in our outlook on life and search for the glass that is half full, not half empty, we must try to find something positive in these tragic events. Because of what was learned from this horrific airline tragedy perhaps better-engineered and safer aircraft will be designed and built. Nothing can replace the innocent people that were lost on Flight 800. I doubt if there is any real closure for the families. It is not my place to speculate on the cause of the event. The final Aircraft Accident Report of the NTSB states that "the probable cause of the accident was an explosion of the center wing fuel tank resulting from ignition of the flammable fuel/air mixture in the tank."[3] Based on my peripheral role in the investigation, I cannot, nor will I, confirm or dispute this conclusion. I will, however, attest to the fact that a great many dedicated people spent countless hours attempting to find out just what did happen on that fateful July evening in 1996. I saw the massive effort firsthand and am proud that, if even in a small way, I was a part of that dedicated workforce.

Now that I look back, it seems that a majority of the cases that I found most interesting involved the use of my photographic skills. It's kind of ironic that after having made my meteoric rise from photographer to special agent, in so many of my assignments I found myself serving less as an FBI agent and more in the role of an investigative photographer. Come to think of it, the Bureau could have saved itself a lot of money by simply keeping me on as a photographer since that salary falls far below that of an agent's. However, had they not permitted me to become an agent, I probably would have pursued other employment options—like becoming an entertainer.

MISPLACED AGENTS

You may be wondering why, during my Bureau years, I didn't work at performing part-time. After all, there are plenty of entertainers who have never given up their day job as waiters or cab drivers. The reason is that an FBI agent is not permitted to have a second salary-paying job. That's not to say that an agent can't volunteer to work on his or her neighborhood's rescue squad or help run a church service. In fact, over the years, I have appeared in several community theater productions—but never for money. The Bureau makes a concerted effort to ensure that no agent will ever be involved in a conflict of interest situation. However, support employees of the FBI, such as translators, photographers, secretaries, etc., are permitted to hold jobs outside of the Bureau. Did this frustrate me? Sure. It's difficult to reign in one's desire to burst forth when being held on a short leash.

Were there other agents in the FBI who were misplaced like I was? Were there others who wondered what they were doing in the Bureau and whether they should remain in the FBI? Sure, there were. I distinctly remember three. One was a guy who loved the outdoors. He was a native of Florida who longed to be home, outdoors in the Florida sunshine. For a year or so, I was in a carpool with him and several other agents who also lived in New Jersey. Each morning we would gather for our trip into New York in our official FBI car. As we'd hop in, one of us would offer up the morning prayer, which went something like this: "Dear Lord, please let this government hunk of junk get us to the city without breaking down in the Lincoln Tunnel. Amen." Each day, as we watched the magnificent New York skyline grow larger in the windshield, this guy would say (in his slightly Southern accent), "There she is. Ain't she beautiful?" No snide comedian or talented actor could have possibly spoken this sentence with any more sarcasm. This agent despised New York, and day by day grew less tolerant of the FBI and its bureaucratic ways. One Monday morning, the car pulled up to the corner as it always had, ready to whisk my fellow agents and me off to another fun-filled day of investigation. I noticed that, as always, the engine sounded as if it were about to breathe its last gasp of gas. I also observed that on this particular day, there was one less occupant. "Morning, guys. Hey, where's John?" "You mean you don't know?" said Greg. "Know what?" I asked, feeling like I had missed the headline of the week. "He quit. Friday was his last day." "Quit? Where'd he go?" "He went home to mow lawns in Florida. He said a bad day mowing lawns in Florida was more fun than a good day investigating crime in New York."

Then there was the writer. In order to be a successful FBI agent, you must have good investigative skills and insight, but far more important is the ability to get it all down on paper. Reporting and documenting are the food on which the Bureau subsists. During the early 1980's, I worked with an agent who was known more for his way with words than for his investigative acumen. I'd see this fellow sitting at his desk for hours on end composing great works of government documentation. I would sometimes leave the office for the better part of a day only to return to find him still typing away on his trusty IBM Selectric typewriter (you do remember those, don't you?). While the rest of us struggled to get our paperwork in on time, this fellow was always ahead of the eight ball. His work was not only in on time, but usually way ahead of the deadline. And it was voluminous. The guy could turn out volumes on the simplest subject. For instance, in reporting that during the course of a surveillance, he had seen some suspected spy leave a building, he'd turn out pages of description rivaling the juiciest portion of a Hemingway novel. I'd have a hard time getting out even one paragraph on the same subject. One day, after returning from lunch, the office was abuzz with some rumor. This was nothing extraordinary, since this happened at least twice a day. Like the rest of the gossipy agents, I had to know what was going on. When I asked the guy at the next desk, he simply said, "Steve's leaving." "Leaving the Bureau?" I asked. "I thought he liked being in the FBI, and he's such a good writer." "That's why he's leaving, Rick. He's going home to California to write novels. He figures at least that way his literary skills will be appreciated, and there's the chance that his work will be seen by thousands instead of ending up in a dusty file jacket in the Closed Files section." Another career change. Another one bites the dust.

Next up at bat is Ed. He was a nice kid from Jersey. He had graduated with a law degree simply because his mother thought that she'd like to have a son who was a lawyer. After graduation from law school, Ed did not relish the thought of becoming an attorney, so he applied to become a Special Agent of the FBI. His father, a fireman in his local town, was as proud as could be of his son's decision to pursue a career in the nation's premier investigative agency. However, after a few short years chasing Russian spies, Ed decided that he had loftier goals. He confided in me, telling me that his true desire was to become a recreation director at Club Med. I knew that he was an East Coast surfer dude, but thought that his interest in this was only a summer pursuit which he used as a method for meeting girls. To this day, I don't know what happened to Ed, but I sincerely hope that he was able to pursue his dream. Perhaps, today, instead of writing his Bureau memoirs like someone I know, he is basking in the warm glow of a sunlit afternoon on an island in the Pacific. Good luck, Ed, wherever you are!

Finally, there's the saga of the FBI actors. I remember the first fellow, Henry, from back in the 1970's. I was new in the FBI and was still trying to figure out how to work my way through the paramilitary structure of the Bureau without becoming lost in its midst. Henry had been in the foreign counterintelligence field for decades and was an expert in the area. He helped me by lending his expertise to a few of the cases I was working on. He was well liked and looked upon by his coworkers as a great guy and a fine agent. Toward the end of his career, he sported a head of silken white hair which looked too perfect to be real, but it was. Rumor had it that when he retired, he pursued his dream of becoming an actor on the New York stage.

One evening, about a year after Henry retired, I traveled into New York to see the off-Broadway hit, *The Fantastiks*, a show that had been running for years and had several casts over that time period. There were only five cast members, since the story revolves around two fathers, their two children, and an on-stage narrator. Before the show started, I glanced at the *Playbill* to see what actors would be performing in that evening's show. There in bold type was Henry's name. The copy stated that Henry was a former FBI agent who had become an actor and was playing the role of one of the fathers. I couldn't believe my eyes! Then and there, I vowed that some day, I, too, would be on the stage.

After the show, I went backstage and spoke with Henry. He told me, in no uncertain terms, that I should stick with the Bureau, retire, and then pursue a show business career. "After all," he said, "I'm the only one on this stage with a steady income. The rest of them are waiting tables." As Henry donned a black leather jacket, we walked out of the stage door. He hopped onto his motorcycle and sped off into the cold New York evening.

Then there was Ernie, another FBI actor. Ernie seemed to be an agent on another planet. He, too, was involved in the spy-chasing game, but always seemed to be studying a notebook or something that looked like one. One day, I finally asked him what he was reading. "It's a script," he said. He had let me in, if ever so slightly, on his secret. He, too, was preparing to become an actor upon retirement. I found out that in his off hours, like me, he was involved in community theater and other semiprofessional productions. Apparently, Ernie chose to keep his little secret to himself, but I would often see him in a quiet corner of the cafeteria, eating his lunch while intently memorizing lines. Ernie retired at about the same time that I did. He is now an actor and director of a major theatrical production company.

Was there some strange connection between the fields of foreign counterintelligence and going into show business? Why did agents such as myself, who chased spies for a living, turn to acting as their next profession? I don't know, but the scenario certainly has the makings for an interesting screenplay.

"So why didn't you just quit?" I'm often asked. The answer is simple. Like many of you, I was stuck. Most of us know the feeling. It's the desperation we experience when we have a job that's not bad, but we'd really rather be doing something else. However, little things—like a family, a mortgage, a car payment—get in the way. In my case, all of this was accompanied by fear and insecurity. I was used to being coddled by the system—one which provided the security of a steady paycheck and raises granted by the Congress of the United States. Of course, there were no Christmas bonuses and few financial incentives other than an incentive award every so often for a job well done. I mean, really well done. To get one of those babies, you had to go way beyond the parameters of being a good FBI agent. To pry one of those out of some of the squad supervisors, you had to go into a nearby phone booth and, like Superman, change into a cape and emerge as SuperAgent, one who is able to leap tall buildings at a single bound or, at the very least, bring to justice a really bad guy or, even better, a whole posse of bad guys. So, like so many others, I remained in place, proud of what I was doing, but suppressing a secret desire to pursue my life's dream.

Over the years, I've met many folks who were stuck in place, running on a career treadmill with no end in sight. In the military there were the lifers. These guys and gals had gone past the first four years of enlisted time and were now into their second period of enlistment. By the time they had been in eight years, they figured that it was too late to leave the military, since they had only twelve years to go until retirement. Twelve years! That's a long time. Think of what you can do with your life in twelve years, yet they perceived themselves as stuck.

OK, You Dummies, Up Against The Wall!

At the conclusion of my shows, I often play a little audience participation game with them, asking them to guess what I had done for thirty years prior to my meteoric rise to ventriloquial stardom. They offer answers running the gamut from insurance salesman to accountant. When I tell them that I had been an FBI agent, half of them laugh in disbelief. The other half sound just like the school kids I perform for by crooning, "Ooh." After one show, a gentleman came up to me and said in a rather solemn tone, "You're so lucky to be doing what you love. For forty-two years, my wife and I owned an upholstery shop. We made a good living, but I hated every day of it." There are countless stories out there just like that one. So many lives are lived out in quiet desperation, waiting for the weekend to arrive. My life's weekend has arrived, and I am savoring each and every moment of it.

9/11

I thought that my FBI career ended with my retirement on January 1, 2001. Officially, it did. Then 9/11 happened. In our lives, there occur certain events which are permanently etched into our memories. Along with these memory etchings goes a distinct remembrance of where we were at the time the event took place. Those of you who experienced the assassination of President Kennedy most likely remember exactly where you were and what you were doing when you got the news. The tragedy of the World Trade Center had the same effect on me. When the horror of September 11, 2001 took place, I was working out in my local gym. At the exact moment that the first plane hit one of the towers, I was running on the treadmill. I will never forget looking up at the TV above the treadmill and watching the coverage of the first plane hitting the building, only to be followed by the live scene in which the second plane ran into the other tower. As the events of the week unfolded, many people commented on just how lucky I was to have retired from the Bureau. They saw the immense task the FBI was facing in investigating the catastrophe. The more I heard about how lucky I was not to be involved, the angrier I got. The tragedy took place on Tuesday. By Saturday, I had reached my limit. I knew that, in some way, I had to help and could no longer view the goings-on via television. Living within a short distance of what had been termed Ground Zero, I had little excuse not to go there and offer my help. The quandary, however, lie in the fact that I was no longer an active FBI agent. My badge and credentials (the wallet-size document agents show to identify themselves) were now neatly mounted on a plaque hanging on our family room wall. Spanning the document was a collection of small punch-outs which clearly spelled out the word "RETIRED." Obviously, it would have looked less than professional to show up at the site with an eleven-by-fourteen-inch framed plaque as identification.

Desperate times require desperate measures. I carefully ripped the mounted credentials from their resting place, removed the glue from the back of the thin black wallet which holds them, and tucked them back into the breast pocket of my shirt. The feel of the little wallet against my chest felt familiar. After all, that's exactly where it rested for thirty years of my life. I had no intention of attempting to pass myself off as a working FBI agent upon arriving at Ground Zero. I would, however, proudly display my credentials and announce that I was retired, as the document showed, and was volunteering my time to work, in any capacity needed.

My wife, Audrey, a caring person who had been a teacher for over thirty years, felt a need to do something to assist the victims, firemen, or whoever needed help. New Yorkers constantly get a bad rap for being rude and uncaring. The nature of this tragedy brought out the best of us New Yorkers as well as others throughout the country that helped out in countless ways. After hearing announcements on television advising the public as to what supplies were needed at the site, we made a list of items to bring there. These included food, flashlights, clothing, and even dog food for the canines that were sniffing for bombs and bodies. We had recently received our tax refund and could think of no better way to use this money than to purchase the items on our list. It took visits to several stores to get all the items on the list, but we eventually had everything we needed.

With the supplies jammed into our van, we set out for Ground Zero. The acrid air engulfed us as we approached the police roadblocks. Before I could even bring the van to a complete stop, a cop yelled out, "Hey, Rick, I thought you retired." My wife and I found it incredible that in a city with a police force the size of New York's, I had immediately connected with one of the cops that I had worked with! No need to show those credentials now, I thought, as he ushered us into the area. Other police officers guided us to the spot where we could drop off the supplies. Our donation, as well as those of all the others who had contributed, was well received. It was heartening to see the huge amount of goods that had already been donated and to view the steady stream of vehicles dropping off even more supplies.

Within a short time I was working at the site, helping firemen pull hoses into position while my wife dispensed needed drinks and other supplies from a Red Cross truck. Throughout our time working at Ground Zero, I met many folks whom I recognized and who remembered me from my FBI days. It's difficult to describe the feeling I experienced when some of them thanked me for "unretiring." What we did was certainly not heroic. We met hundreds of others who had done the same thing. We did what we could to help in our own way. Once you're in the FBI, even in retirement, you're always a part of the organization. During the brief period of time that we helped out at the site, I felt a sense of pride in once again being part of the team. However, I doubt whether I will ever "unretire" again and certainly hope that no circumstances arise which move me to do so. I have gone on to the next chapter in my life's journey.

"KEEPIN' BUSY"

A short time after retiring from the FBI, my wife and I were having dinner at a local diner when we noticed a familiar-looking couple a few tables away. I turned to Audrey, who, anticipating my next comment, exclaimed, "Oh, there are our old neighbors, Sue and Bob Denner! Let's go say hi to them." We hadn't seen them for at least five years, so we got right up and went over to say hello.

After all the usual pleasantries, we got down to brass tacks, the interrogation. I asked, "So where do you guys live now?" "Oh, we're 'snow birds,'" said the wife. "We spend the winters in Florida and the spring and summer here in sun-filled, fun-filled New Jersey." (She always did fancy herself the queen of sarcasm.) Bob now asked the question I hear every time I meet someone whom I haven't seen for a while, "Still with the FBI?" (Nobody ever seems to forget what my former career was.) "No, Bob," I answered, "my FBI days are over. I retired from the Bureau about a year ago. You know, I investigated the hell out of just about everything, so I decided to check out." "So what are you doing now?" he asked. "I'm an entertainer," I replied. Staring at me as if he had just heard Noah say that he can't stand animals, he burst out into a sarcastic chuckle, through which he spat out the question "What?" "I'm an entertainer," I repeated. "I'm a singer and comedy ventriloquist." His face riddled with a look of utter disbelief, he listened, as I briefly described my act. As I turned toward his wife, I noticed that she, too, looked surprised.

By now, Bob's brain had had an ample amount of time to digest my story. He shrugged and said, "Okay, so you're keepin' busy." Now, you may be thinking, "What makes this statement important enough to use it as the title of this chapter?" Well, here's my reasoning: When Bob referred to my current career as "keeping busy," my immediate reaction was one of anger. I became enraged. I was about to explode, and my wife knew it. I had made a serious career change and someone was ridiculing it, tossing it off as inconsequential and nothing more than a way to fill the gap created by retirement. I realized that at this point I could exercise any one of several options. I could turn and walk away. I could tell him to go to hell, or I could simply inquire as to what he was now doing, feign interest, then say good-bye, and return to our table.

Opting to be a gentleman, I decided to conceal my rage and politely said to Bob, "And what are you doing?" His answer was simple and to the point. "Golf." My first thought was to say something like, "Oh, now that's something that will help save the world." But deciding to take the high road, I simply replied, "Oh, that sounds like fun!" I lied. It didn't sound like fun to me—not in the least. That's because I'm not a golfer. See, to Bob, golf is a way to pass time. But that's my whole point. He's passing time. There's nothing wrong with that if you're enjoying yourself. But that's not me. Like other creative types, I have a drive to produce—to do, make, build, shape, create—and finally, to end each day asking, "What have I accomplished today?" If my answer is "nothing," I go to bed feeling like I've wasted a precious day of my life. I guess it's kind of a curse that creative people learn to live with. I've also noticed that this driving force and abundance of anxious energy that drives people to pursue creative activities in one area often leads to them to tackling creative endeavors in other areas. Very often, these folks excel in more than one area. For instance, Tony Bennett is a talented artist as well as a dynamic singer.

Well, Bob just didn't get it, and neither did many others when I first made my career change. They couldn't understand that I wasn't just "keepin' busy." I've entered another phase in my life. With each day, my new career unfolds and blossoms. Not every day is a resounding success. Sometimes it's a process of taking two steps ahead and one step back. The work is self-motivated, challenging, and never ending. My son-in-law, Jeremy, noticing the constant whirlwind in which I operate, recently posed this question, "Do you ever stop working?" I stuttered and stammered, answering, "Uh, yeah, I mean . . . no." The truth is that in this business, unless you have someone else providing you with material, writing your scripts and songs, handling publicity, etc., you're a one-man band with the entire weight on your shoulders. There's no supervisor, manager, or anyone else to formulate ideas for you to execute, no one e-mailing you the latest instructions or guidance on how to handle a project. However, the work is truly rewarding and gratifying, and I love it.

Well, that's the end of my angry chapter. I'm no longer pissed off. Now that I've been an entertainer for a few years, I realize that some people will just never get it. That's okay. I know who I am and what I'm doing. My audiences reward me with applause. I'm glad that I'm not just "keepin' busy."

FBI ENTERTAINER

At least twice a week, someone says to me, "How in the world did you go from being an FBI agent to an entertainer?" When I explain, they say, "You ought to write a book about it." I tell them that I'm doing just that. They laugh. Hey, out there, stop laughing and read on!

The truth is, my abrupt career change didn't just happen. In fact, it took a good deal of planning, spiced with a pinch of luck.

During my last two years in the Bureau, I decided that it was time to begin launching my showbiz career. I had been a successful public speaker while serving as the Bureau's coordinator and representative of a program known as DECA (Development of Counterintelligence Awareness). This was a vehicle designed to heighten private industry's awareness of the danger posed by foreign spies who desired to steal technology from U.S. companies. It was my job to visit firms that had government contracts, many of which contained classified information and details regarding the manufacture and/or distribution of similarly classified materials. I would speak to the employees about the spies who were out to gain access to the products or data their companies handled. Sometimes I would speak on a personal basis to the firm's security officer, who, on several occasions, turned out to be a retired FBI agent. At other times, I would find myself addressing groups as large as five hundred in an auditorium brimming with people who were eagerly waiting to hear what the guy from the FBI had to say. After a couple of years of putting on the Bureau's best face in front of the private sector, I found myself pretty comfortable with public speaking and could face a crowd of any size with little or no stage fright.

Retirement from the FBI is mandatory at age fifty-seven. At fifty-three, the itch to move on was growing stronger by the day. Since I had served in the military and had been with the Bureau since my days as a photographer, I had accumulated enough time to retire earlier than age fifty-seven. However, in order to secure a larger pension, I decided that I had better stay on the job a little longer. Realizing that my Oscar nomination would just have to be put on hold, I entered the final phase of preparation for stardom. Here's how I did it.

Based on my experience as spokesman for the FBI's "How to Identify a Spy in Your Company" program, I was able to secure an assignment as the Community Outreach Coordinator for the FBI's New York office. A major portion of this job entailed visiting New York City schools and talking to the kids about the evils of drugs, the role of the FBI in our society, and various other topics designed to mold the little Americans into better and more productive citizens. Some of these events were billed as career days. On these occasions, representatives from a wide variety of local and government agencies, and from the private sector, would present their programs to the kids. For example, firefighters would demonstrate their latest gear, talk about fire prevention, and answer questions about careers in their field. The children always enjoyed the law enforcement folks who would bring a dog to show how the canines worked with the cops in finding drugs, missing persons, etc. Professionals from such diverse fields as medicine, science, theater, art, etc., would all explain and sometimes demonstrate what they did in their careers. It was a great way of exposing the kids to career choices.

Although I was a part of the law enforcement contingent, I always seemed to find my way over to the entertainers, where, like one of the little kids, I stood in awe of some man or woman who was an actor on the Broadway stage, in movies or on TV. It was ironic to me that they had a similar reaction to me, always asking what it was like to be a real FBI agent! On more than one occasion, I met an actor who played an FBI agent on the stage, screen, or TV. He, or she, would ask me if they were playing the role correctly. I would tell them that I too was an actor and that I was also playing the role of an agent, only for real! I confessed to them that I sometimes questioned myself as to whether I was playing the role correctly.

My presentations consisted of a forty-five-minute nonstop effort to hold the kids' attention while getting my point across. From this experience, I gained an understanding of what a teacher goes through every school day. As my wife, Audrey, a retired teacher, will tell you, sometimes it's a roller-coaster ride of dips and climbs. As the kids departed the classroom, visions of becoming an FBI agent, veterinarian, or whatever would stream through their minds as they sped off to the next presentation on their schedule.

On one occasion, after a grueling four-session morning, I began my journey down the stairs to the library where a luncheon was to be held for the presenters. Negotiating one's way down the crowded staircase was not an easy task, since, at the same time, throngs of kids were barreling down the same steps, heading to their next class or the cafeteria. How I remember that scene from my school days. The roar of the thundering herds was deafening. I couldn't wait to get to the library where I was guaranteed some peace and adult conversation.

I always enjoyed the lunch portion of the day since I knew that I would meet a diverse group of professionals, all of whom had stories to compare about the kids in their classroom. I especially relished hearing about some of the absolutely off the wall questions the kids had asked the other presenters. It was pretty predictable that at least once during each session, some kid would ask me if I slept with my gun on, not to mention the all time classic, "You ever shoot anybody?"

As I made my way through the crowded halls, I heard the sound of laughter escaping from one of the classrooms. Apparently, one of the presenters was running a little late and was just finishing his program. My curiosity got the best of me, so I stopped and glimpsed into the noise-filled room. Inside was a magical scene. In front of the class was a New York City police officer. Dressed in a light blue sport shirt with a New York Police Department insignia emblazoned on the pocket, he had the kids mesmerized as he placed red, yellow, and green balls into a clear plastic cylinder. He then covered the tube. When he removed the cover, the balls had mysteriously changed places and were now in the order that they appear on a traffic signal. As he performed his magic, he talked to the kids about traffic safety and the importance of obeying the traffic lights. The expressions on the kids' faces, as they watched the magic, clearly demonstrated their amazement and delight. It instantly hit me that this guy was an expert at attracting their attention, then holding it, while getting his message across to them through the use of magic. The combination of visual and verbal statements really did the trick! At that moment, I had a revelation; I had to change my FBI act.

Wandering into the library where lunch was being served, I spotted a table at which three cops were attempting to eat between jokes that had turned their meal into a laugh fest. I quickly grabbed a turkey sandwich and approached the cops' table where I waited to speak, hoping to catch a break in the laughter so that I could introduce myself. Just after the laughter died down from a punch line, one of the cops looked up and said, "Hey, aren't you the FBI guy?" Enjoying my star status, I nodded, and then told them that I was indeed from the FBI and that I was, in fact, the FBI director. From this reply, they gathered that I was at least as crazy as they were. Having passed the test which proved to them that I, too, was a fellow law enforcement whacko, they invited me to join them.

Allow me here to briefly tell you a little about cops. People perceive cops as serious gun-totin' law enforcers. To a certain extent, this is true. However, some of the funniest people I have ever met are cops. For them, perhaps, humor is a release from the daily stress they face in a job in which one's life is constantly on the line. If you're privileged enough to listen in on some of their conversations, which, by the way, can get pretty raucous and raunchy, you'll hear stories of arrests gone wrong, inept criminals, and detectives that can't detect where they left their own car keys.

Taking the first bite of my sandwich, I looked up to see the "magic cop" approaching our table. I knew instantly that I liked this guy because of the wide grin that seemed permanently affixed to his face. I sensed from his demeanor that he didn't take himself too seriously and was certainly not trying to impress any of the other visitors with the fact that he was a cop. Even his choice of clothes for today's event demonstrated this. I'm sure that he could have worn the official uniform of the New York City Police Department, with its impressively tailored dark blue jacket and highly polished brass buttons. Yet he had chosen to go the casual cop route, sending a message to the kids that he was their good friend, the neighborhood cop who was here today to have some fun with them while teaching them something of value.

As the cops looked up, the one with the deep operatic voice sang out, "Here comes the Dog!" In response, the Dog rolled his eyes, loudly announcing, "I'm not the Dog today!" I motioned for him to sit directly across from me and he extended his hand saying, "Hi, I'm Bob Statler. I'm a cop." "Hi, Bob. Rick Berger, FBI. Nice to meet you." I couldn't wait any longer, so, without any restraint, I asked, "Why'd these guys call you the Dog?" Statler grinned widely, explaining, "Oh, that's because part of the time, I'm a dog. See, I'm the NYPD's official crime dog, McGruff. Ya know, the one in the trench coat and dog mask that tells the kids to 'take a bite out of crime.'" Bob went on to explain that he was assigned to the unit that handles community affairs and that his job was the equivalent of mine since he attends these sorts of events in an effort to explain to the kids how law enforcement works in the community, how drugs can hurt them, and that kind of thing. "It's fun sometimes, but mostly, it's hard work," he said. He also spoke of how, every so often, some wise guy kid would take a poke at the dog's long snout, sending his head spinning around with a sharp jolt. Sometimes there were jabs to the stomach while the kid shouts, "You're not a real dog!" "How do you handle that?" I asked. "At that point, I extend my big furry paw and gently drag the kid off to the side. Then, even though the dog is not supposed to speak, in my deepest cop voice, sounding like Darth Vader, I let him know that he's correct, I am not a dog. I tell him that I am a cop and that if he doesn't cool it, I'll make sure that he is sent home from the event and that he'll have to explain his behavior to his parents. (A few months later, I witnessed this very scene at a neighborhood picnic sponsored by the police department, and by the time Bob was done reading the kid the riot act, the young man was shaking in his sneakers.) I guess I had never pictured a cop in this role, but as I later learned, from watching Bob sweat through numerous performances as McGruff, he was a real expert, worthy of donning a Disney costume with the best of the Mickeys.

I knew I liked this cop and thought it would be great to work with him. During the next couple of years, I saw Bob frequently at various schools around the city. At one of these events, I suggested the possibility of us doing a joint presentation some time in the future. He seemed receptive to this. He said that he would continue to do his magic and suggested that I come up with some shtick that would compliment his portion of the presentation. Bob told me I should call him when I had the idea formulated. We would then check with our superiors to see if they were amenable to the joint FBI-NYPD concept.

Driving home that day, excited by the prospect of working with Bob at some upcoming events, I began to wonder how I could fit in and lend entertainment value to the program. Perhaps, I thought, I could be the foil in Bob's magic act. Imagine how the kids would react when, instead of the pretty assistant, he sawed the FBI agent in half. I quickly nixed that idea. The drill sergeant in my head barked, "Okay, Berger, let's get with the program." "Come on, man, I thought, you claim to be so attuned to what kids like. Think of something they'll find funny, amusing, anything that'll get their attention."

As I pulled away from the school, the city streets became a blur of color. Yellow taxis fused into streaks of mustard. As I passed through the tollbooths I said out loud, "What can I be? What can I be?" For some unknown reason, I stretched the word "be" out, each time, making it longer and longer. "What can I be?" became "What can I bee?" which evolved into "What can I beee?" Looking up at the rearview mirror, I noticed that as I held the sound "beeee . . ." I was not moving my lips. Without making a conscious effort, I was doing what I had seen so many times on TV as a kid. I was performing ventriloquism!

Like a lightening bolt, it hit! I would be a ventriloquist! That would be my contribution to the act. My brain started racing, "I gotta call Statler as soon as I get home. Great idea. What a concept!" Reality then began to set in. As I pulled into my driveway, I had one thought, "I don't know how to do ventriloquism."

By the time I closed the car door and started walking toward the house, I had decided on my plan of action. One way, or another, I was going to learn ventriloquism. Little did I know that this plan would alter the direction of my life.

As I walked into the house, it began to dawn on me that what I was about to tackle could be more than I had anticipated or imagined. Opening the door, I could barely contain my excitement. I blurted out "Hi" to my wife and immediately launched into a diatribe describing my encounter with McGruff, the crime dog, and how I was about to enter a new phase of my life. As I spoke of how I was going to reinvent myself and become a ventriloquist, Audrey began to beam with delight. "If anyone can teach himself to be a ventriloquist, it's you!" she said. "But," she continued, "it's going to take some time to develop the skill." She pointed out that since I was fifty-three years old, I would have only a few years to do my little act before facing mandatory retirement. I told her of my plan to leave the Bureau early and get started on the road to stardom. Always supportive of my harebrained schemes, she said simply, "If performing for the kids while you're still in the FBI is your goal, go for it," adding, "and whatever you want to do after that, that's okay too. After all, it's your retirement."

Well, now I had the okay from the real boss, not just some FBI supervisor. I felt confident that my plan would work. "You know," I thought, "if I do this the right way, I can use this as a training ground for the pursuit of my life's dream—to become an entertainer." "Damn good idea," I said out loud as I dialed Statler's number, "damn good idea."

Since there are no schools of ventriloquism, I figured I'd have to teach myself. I began by reading books on ventriloquism, its origins, history, and how it was used in different societies. I learned a lot. For instance, did you know that this art (and it is considered an art) derived its name from a French word with an origin in the Latin word "venter," which means stomach or belly? That was combined with the word "loqui," which means "I speak." Eons ago, folks believed that ventriloquists were born with a double throat or that they spoke from their stomachs. Not true. Sorry to disappoint you, but I have only one throat and only talk through my stomach when I have indigestion. Also, you don't "throw your voice" as some people believe. I cannot make my voice come from somewhere at the end of the block or from the men's department in a store at the mall. I can, however, create the illusion that my voice is coming from a source other than my throat.

So how did I learn all of this stuff? Mostly from books and TV. Thinking back to when I was a kid, I recall the fun of Sunday nights. I remember how my family would gather round the TV, anxiously awaiting the start, in glorious black-and-white, of course, of *The Ed Sullivan Show*. Ed loved ventriloquists. In fact, most of us thought that he, himself, looked like a puppet, being controlled by some guy with his hand up his back. Every man, woman, or child that could skillfully talk, or even sing, without moving his lips, was invited to appear on the show—and most of them were pretty damn good. Some were already famous, like Edgar Bergen and his monacled partner, Charlie McCarthy, who had gotten their start on the radio. Others went on to fame after their TV appearances. There were names like Paul Winchell and his wooden friend, Jerry Mahoney, Senor Wences, with his buddy, Pedro, a talking head encased in a box. There was Jimmy Nelson with his little friends, Danny O'Day and Farfel. Arising from the female ventriloquial arena was the perky Shari Lewis and her pet, Lambchop. Thanks to Ed Sullivan, they all became household names. Ed, the newspaper reporter turned TV celebrity, is no longer with us, but there exists an extensive library of his shows on tape and DVD. In my quest to learn the art of making inanimate objects come to life, I began to study those tapes. I watched and scrutinized the nuances in every move made by the ventriloquists on those shows. I studied the way in which they told their jokes and how they manipulated their little partners in just such a way as to make them appear real.

Using the bathroom mirror, I began to learn and practice the language of ventriloquism, and, believe me, it isn't all that easy. Try it! Stop reading right now and say the alphabet without moving your lips. You'll probably find, as I did, that certain letters, like *a* and *c*, are easy to say. However, letters like *p*, *m*, and *b* are a bit of a challenge. It took a while, actually many months of practice, to master this skill, and it's a never-ending learning process. To this day, I am learning new and better ways to make certain sounds.

I decided that it was now time for me to go out and get a dummy. That, in itself, was a challenge. Where, even in New York City, one of the great shopping centers of the world, does one go to buy a ventriloquial figure? I scoured the telephone book from cover to cover until I discovered that the primary source for ventriloquist figures was magic shops. I picked one of the largest suppliers of magic in New York, and not having the slightest idea of the cost of one of these puppets, I visited the store.

For any of you who have never visited a magic store, let me tell you, it's a real experience. In addition to magic supplies, this particular store is one of New York's principal suppliers of costumes. They have outfits not only for actors, but also for anyone else who wants to pretend that he is someone else, be it for Halloween, Mardi Gras, or whatever the reason. After walking through what seemed like miles of ghosts, headless horsemen, and at least one ghoul that resembled a girl I knew in high school, I made my way to the back of the store, where, the salesman had told me, I could find a dummy. I'd like this little story to read like one in which the kid enters the pet shop and points out, to his mom, the perfect puppy that he wants to bring home for Christmas. Unfortunately, it didn't happen just that way. Very quickly, I learned from the salesman that "real" dummies, the professional models like I had seen on *The Ed Sullivan Show*, were not only hard to come by but were individually handmade and generally very expensive. "However," he said, "we do have this little Danny O'Day whose mouth is controlled by a string in the back of his neck." He picked the little guy up and demonstrated how this worked, remarking that the price was $65. I stared at little Danny with his black-and-white checkered sports jacket and the mischievous grin painted onto his plastic face and thought, "This is it?" Oh, he was cute enough all right, but he certainly was not the kind of dummy that I had imagined would launch my showbiz career.

"Is there any way to make him do a little more, like turn his head?" I asked the salesman. "Sure," he answered. "For an additional $40, we can send him out to the factory. They'll cut out a portion of his back (this sounded painful) and install a headstick like the pro models have. Then, instead of pulling the string, you'll be able to turn his head and control his mouth from inside the figure."

"What the hell," I figured. I told him to go ahead and do it. About a week later, my wife told me there was a message on our answering machine saying that the dummy was ready. I was really glad that I had opted not to give the guy my work number. I could just see Grace, our squad secretary, saying, "Rick, I got a message for you from some guy saying, 'Your dummy's ready'—must be some kind of secret code, right?"

The next day, I went to the magic shop and picked up my new son. He looked no worse for the surgery. I turned him around, and sure enough, he now had a hole about the size of my hand cut right into his little suit jacket. I reached in and grabbed the wooden control rod. The salesman asked me if it looked like it was going to work for me. I said, "Yeah, this feels okay." I turned Danny's head to the left, then to the right. I gently pulled down on the little plastic lever attached to the stick. I felt the string pull down Danny's jaw as I quietly said hello in my newly acquired language. The salesman laughed as he said, "That's pretty good. You didn't even move your lips." With my new kid tucked safely into a plastic shopping bag, I left the store feeling like a nine-year-old about to embark on a new adventure.

As I traveled back uptown to the FBI office, I decided to make my little star a miniature FBI agent. That way, he could help McGruff, the crime-fighting dog, take a bite out of crime, and he'd fit in perfectly with Bob Statler's magic. I began my search for a name, a name that would be, in some way, related to the Bureau. Names went flying through my head like fireworks exploding in a July 4th sky. All of a sudden I had it. I would name him after the most famous of all FBI directors. He would be J. Edgar Hoover. "No. That won't work. Scrap that idea. It's ridiculous. Wait a minute. I'll shorten it to Jedgar Hoover. No, too disrespectful. My supervisor will not find it funny. Wait a minute, shorten it to just 'Jed!' That's it! I certainly won't get into trouble for having a puppet named Jed!" Jed was born, and so was my new career.

Statler and I eventually got the whole thing together, and the team approach worked well. The kids were, as always, mesmerized by Bob's magic and kind of stupefied by my little plastic guy telling them not to use drugs because "users are losers."

As the time rolled on, both Bob and I began to turn our thoughts toward retirement. Both of us had enjoyed our careers in law enforcement, but felt that the time was approaching where we should make changes in the directions of our lives. Bob still had a couple of years left to complete in the police department and wasn't quite sure of what his future held in store for him. He was semifamous for some magic handcuff tricks he had invented and was known for them in the magic field. I, on the other hand, knew where I was headed—I was going to pursue my dream. Jed and I were going to be lit by footlights and spots. It was time to set the wheels in motion.

I began to study my art relentlessly. I dug up the names of ventriloquists and performers from whatever sources I could locate. I picked their brains for information. I asked them a lot of questions and found them to be very accommodating, fascinated, and in some cases, honored by the prospect of an FBI agent entering their field. Armed with more information than I could absorb, I began my quest to find a replacement for my partner. I had outgrown my little plastic friend and was turning pro, so it was time for some professional equipment. I eventually located and bought my new Jed, a real professional ventriloquist dummy—one made of wood, just like the ones I had seen on TV when I was growing up. I got him from a guy who, himself, had been a

TV performer years ago. He still performs and, like many of the professionals in the field, had a side business of selling puppets. He mentioned that he had for sale a brand-new wooden figure that just might fit my requirements for the new Jed. We arranged to meet that following Sunday.

When Sunday morning arrived, I jumped out of bed extra early, excited by the prospect that that this could be the day that I get my first piece of professional ventriloquist equipment. I remember thinking that I wasn't half that excited getting my first gun in the FBI!

The trip to his home in Pennsylvania was filled with chatter about my new career. Audrey especially liked the part about how, for the first time in decades, I would actually be able to talk with my family about what I did for a living. As we approached the house, my sense of anticipation began to get escalate. I felt like a little kid traveling to a pet store with his parents to go pick out the puppy they were buying him for Christmas.

Mike greeted us at the door. As we walked in, we immediately noticed that, like us, he and his wife were into nostalgia. The house was filled with memorabilia from the fifties, sixties, and seventies. Reminders of the bygone days of *Howdy Doody* and *Leave It to Beaver* were everywhere. My wife and I quickly realized that we were not the only incurable collectors around. My curiosity and excitement was now reaching a fever pitch. I wanted to see my potential new partner. I spotted a carved wooden figure nestled in one corner of the couch, resting comfortably against a plump pillow. Since Mike had been a ventriloquist for years, I surmised that he had many dummies and that this was one of them. He saw me looking at the figure and said, "Well, there he is. What do you think of him?" My immediate reaction was, "Is he dead?" For those of you who have never seen a ventriloquist dummy in repose, let me tell you, it is one of the most frightening and bizarre-looking things you'll ever see. No wonder there were episodes of *The Twilight Zone* and movies featuring little Chuckie and other dummies who could scare the daylights out of the audience by merely sitting in a chair motionless.

Mike suggested that I pick him up and try him out. I turned to the lifeless figure with his big boyish eyes and sandy orange hair and gently lifted him from the couch. I placed my hand though the hole which had been torn in the back of his shirt and grabbed the wooden headstick. It felt much larger than the one that controlled the head movements of my little plastic Jed. This was my first encounter with a professional vent figure. (Ventriloquists use the abbreviation "vent" when talking with their peers.) I felt two levers. Pulling down on one, he slowly opened his mouth. I gently released it, and his mouth closed. "Not really rocket science," said the little voice in my head.

I tried the other lever. Pushing it to the right made his eyes look toward the right. Guess what happened when I pushed it to the left? You got it. See, now you too can be a ventriloquist! When I let this lever go, his eyes miraculously returned to the center. An engineering marvel! Now just add talent and the mix is complete!

In ventriloquism, size matters. Now, hold on there, what I'm referring to is the size of the puppet. Of course, some are little hand puppets, but the professional figures used in shows vary from about thirty inches to about forty-four inches in height. This new guy was of the larger variety, so he felt a lot bigger and heavier than my original little plastic partner. However within a few minutes, I had him talking up a storm. I said, "Okay, Mike, you've got a deal. I'll take him." My wife and I drove off that afternoon with our new little kid sitting quietly in the backseat. I knew he'd be perfect. Not once during the long ride back to New Jersey did he ask, "Are we there yet?"

I find it hard to believe, but that was several years ago. Since then I've acquired several dozen figures which I use in my shows today. But Jed is always waiting, ready to leap from his case and get back into the act.

People sometimes ask if the dummy actually becomes a person who seems to talk on his own. Yes, this does happen. I sometimes laugh at what my little friends blurt out, especially when their statements are spontaneous and not things which I had consciously planned on them saying. Maybe only Rod Serling, or a good therapist, would understand this. I have even dragged my wife into this mania. On occasion, she engages in a conversation with my grandma puppet, Ceil. All three of us become completely engrossed, forgetting that Ceil's responses are actually coming from me!

DOES ANYBODY KNOW I'M HERE?

"Oh, man, this is great! I don't have to be at the office today or, for that matter, ever again!" With those words, my retirement began. It was a bitterly cold January morning in 2001. The air was still—both outside and in the house. Audrey had left for work. Ilyse was away at college. I began to think things like, "I wonder if they miss me yet at the office. The phone on my desk is probably already ringing." I could hear Grace, our squad secretary, saying, "No, Rick's not here. He retired last week." I got to thinking, "Maybe I should just call the office. Not to gloat or anything like that—just to say hi and see if the place was falling apart without me."

"Okay, Berger, let it go. This is the first day of the rest of your life. You're going to be an entertainer. Drop the FBI stuff. It's over, man. Get it? It's *over*." My brain was spinning as reality set in. Sure, I had a plan. But where do I start? As I looked around the family room, I felt anxious. No phones ringing. No e-mails to read. Nobody trying to reach me. I decided that the best way to rid myself of this desperate feeling of emptiness was to do something physical. I quickly jammed my exercise clothes into my bag and headed for the gym. I had been working out since I was seventeen, and now was when I needed the workout most.

Driving to the gym, I was overcome by feelings of guilt. I felt like I was being watched, surveilled. I thought, "I don't belong here—not on a workday. I belong back in the office in New York. What the hell am I doing in New Jersey on a Monday morning?"

With my heart racing, I rushed into the locker room and changed. The gym felt strange. I was used to the New York branch of this health club. The equipment on the gym floor was familiar, but not the faces. I didn't know anyone. I grabbed the pull-up bar and began a slow ascent until my chin reached the bar. This was the same exercise that I had been tested on at the FBI Academy. I remembered how I had struggled to squeeze in that last pull-up in an effort to pass the physical exam. Not passing could have cost me the agent position. "Damn, Berger," I thought, "stop thinking about the FBI. You're not there anymore. You're retired!"

"Hi, Rick!" I recognized the voice. I lowered myself from the chinning bar and turned around. It was Dan, a fellow FBI agent. "Hey, Dan, what the hell are you doing here? I can't get away from the Bureau, can I?" Dan explained that he was working on a case in Jersey and decided to get in a workout at this branch of the club. He asked me how my retirement was going. "Well, Dan, it's been a whole forty-eight hours since I retired, so I really can't tell you yet. I'll give you a call back at the office when I have the answer," I replied. Dan wished me luck and expressed how much he was looking forward to his retirement in three years. "Don't worry. It'll be here before you know it," I said. As Dan headed for the locker room, I thought about the strangeness of the event. I had been out of the Bureau for a total of two days, and already I had encountered a reminder of my FBI days. There just seemed to be no escape—physically or mentally.

When I arrived back at home, I once again faced the stillness. In a desperate effort to break the silence, I turned on the TV. The noise helped, but I couldn't watch. I knew I had to start working. But where was I to start? I opened my briefcase, the one that I had carried throughout most of my FBI career. In it was a list of schools that I had visited as the FBI's Community Outreach Coordinator. I began calling the schools. I spoke to guidance counselors, secretaries, anybody who would listen. "Oh yes, Mr. Berger," they'd say cheerfully, "I remember when you came and did the FBI show about drugs. The children loved the puppet. Oh, you're retired. I wish I was. Well, send us the information about your show, and we'll make sure the principal gets it. Nice speaking to you."

I must have made over a hundred of those calls that week—all to no avail. Combining my design background with Audrey's skill, talents, and expertise in the field of education, we produced a flyer describing the show I had written for the schools. I dutifully sent one to every school I had contacted. I then expanded the list and sent those flyers to virtually every school in New York City. Then I waited, and waited. I got no response. Nothing, not one response. I became angry and depressed. The days turned into weeks. I refined the show. I wrote new scripts, catchy songs, created new skits, made the jokes funnier. And I practiced ventriloquism. I worked tirelessly at it, staring into the mirror for hours, making sure my lips didn't move. But the work didn't come. I began to wallow in despair. Even the visits to the gym didn't help.

"If I don't get work soon, I'm going to kill myself. I'm not kidding." "Okay, Rick, that's not funny," said Audrey, looking at me in amazement. "I've never heard of anyone committing suicide because they retired." What she said kind of set me back on my heels. I thought it over for a while, then admitted that my statement had been pretty extreme. "I guess you're right, but I am so damn anxious and depressed." With a look of understanding, she said, "Okay, let's just start from scratch and come up with a better plan." That's my wife, always there with a sensible way to handle life's situations. She's Dr. Phil, Dr. Joyce Brothers, and Ann Landers all rolled into one—simply amazing!

Well, we did come up with a plan and it worked. The key was in identifying a second target audience, diversifying my act, and networking. Audrey's grandmother had lived in a nursing home for several years. That gave us the idea to create a show specifically for senior citizens, one which I could perform in addition to my school shows. I began by developing a club act complete with costumes, props, humor, music and magic. We scoured lists of places where seniors lived, congregated, or visited. Then we devised a marketing strategy which included mailings and phone calls to these facilities.

During this time Audrey ran into a friend who was a school guidance counselor. The woman asked her what I was doing since retiring from the FBI. When Audrey told her about my school show with its messages about substance abuse, bullying, etc. she immediately booked it. That was the break I needed to begin presenting my school program.

Within a year, I was performing in both schools and senior-oriented venues. I no longer contemplated suicide. I was much too busy with commitments— bookings for shows, creating scripts and song parodies, rehearsals, recording studio appointments, and organizing my ideas for this book. Sure, when things got rough, I could have gone out and gotten a job. With my FBI background, I could have obtained employment in the security field. But that's not who I am and, in fact, never was. I'm most comfortable with a microphone in my hand and a script in my head.

Several years have passed since I retired from the FBI. Now, when I walk into the place in which I'm appearing and I hear, "Are you the entertainer?" I no longer stammer, "Uh, yeah, I guess I am." The catharsis is complete. I don't think twice about it: I am "the entertainer" and proud to be so.

THERE'S NO BUSINESS
LIKE SHOW BUSINESS!

"Excuse me, are you the school custodian? Well, I'm glad to meet you, Charles. Can you tell me where is the nearest electrical outlet to this stage? On that wall? That's the nearest one, huh?" I'm thinking, "How the hell could they build a stage and place the nearest outlet so far away you need a passport to reach it? Well, it's a good thing I brought my own extension cord. Gotta carry all my own stuff. Be prepared for the worst. That's my motto." I flip the mic switch to ON. "Hey, is this thing on?" I say out loud, giggling at how cliché that sounds. Oh hell, no joke here. It's not on. There's no damn power in this outlet. I turn the mic off again to prevent a power surge when I flip it on again once I finally get power. "Huh? Oh, hi!" I mumble as I see a figure standing in front of me, just below the stage. "Yes, honey, I'm going to do a show. No, it's not really a magic show. I mean, well, there's some magic in it. So you're in the third grade? What's your name? Tahisha, that's a beautiful name. No, the show's not going to be after lunch. It'll be at nine thirty this morning. Well, you better go up to your classroom, or you'll be late." The little girl with the big brown eyes and the red jumper quickly turns, her bright blue backpack swinging wildly behind her, as she runs up the aisle of the auditorium, glancing up at the big black-rimmed school clock on the back wall, realizing that she is already late. "Oh God, I hope no more kids come in now. It's almost 9:05. Assembly starts in twenty-five minutes. Gotta think. Try another outlet. Oh good, here's another one. Yes, this one works! Hit the Power button on the amplifier. Great! The power's on. Hit Play. Okay, we've got sound! Music, booms from the speaker—too loud, turn it down or the music will overpower Jed and me. Now, quick, key the CD so it starts on the first song. Turn on the mic. One, two, three. Is this thing on? Yes! Walk stage left. No feedback. Now stage right. Sounds okay. Look at this place. This auditorium must have been built during Shakespeare's time. Stained glass ceiling panels, carved plaster, and oh no—here they come. They're early!"

Suddenly a roaring tidal wave of sound erupts from the rear of the auditorium as the heavy brown doors swing open. As each door opens wide, a teacher enters the room. The one on the left with outstretched arms forms a human dam, determined to hold back the onrushing tide of third graders behind her. The teacher on the right appears to have already lost the battle as kids stream past her in an attempt to capture a better seat up front. A thundering voice suddenly pierces the air. "Excuse me!" There is silence. "Did we forget our manners?" Mr. Cox, the principal, sweeps the room with a glaring stare. The students quickly take their seats. Not a sound is heard except the clattering of ancient wooden auditorium seats. My one thought is, "Imagine, they're all here to see me!"

Okay, one last check—Jed's sitting quietly in his case, looking every bit like a real kid with the exception of the opening in the back of his shirt through which peeks the wooden stick that I use to control the movement of his head. Tommy Turtle, who talks a little too slow for today's fast-paced world, yet is an expert in how to handle bullies, is lying quietly behind the long table on stage. The large royal blue tablecloth safely shields him from the anxious eyes of the young audience. Snuggled next to Tommy is Wild Thing, a nervous fluorescent-haired creature whose protruding lips glisten with shocking red lipstick. Wild Thing is the inner soul of us all, the gutsy little voice that yearns to scream out how we really feel. Unlike us mortals, he is not afraid to tell it like it is. Yet his message for the kids is a serious one. He talks about stranger danger and how the kids can protect themselves from those who would cause them harm. Also quietly waiting for my hand to make its rude intrusion and bring him to life is Big Mouth, the school bully. He's the over-the-top edgy one, the loudmouth who proclaims that he's the "coolest guy in the sky" and that "he's no fool, he's cool in school." His looks do not quite fit the image of a traditional puppet, since he has no body. He's merely a large latex mouth with big white teeth and a tongue that could lap up a whole meal in one fell swoop. Sitting atop Big Mouth Loudmouth is a pair of the coolest sunglasses in the universe. Helping to support the cool shades is a pair of lips only Mick Jagger's mother could love. Then there's Ratso, the bug-eyed rodent whose task it is to let the kids know how to handle a bully like Big Mouth. Ratso's real interest, however, is in finding the nearest wedge of cheese. Character Ed, the rapper who raps out a tune explaining the principles of character education (caring, citizenship, fairness, respect, responsibility, and trustworthiness) is impatiently staring at the floor, anxious to make his entrance.

After Mr. Cox introduces me to the students I start with a little magic designed to get their attention. I turn a bright red silk scarf into a three-foot-long metal cane, then immediately proclaim that they'll have to pay attention, or they might miss something. Apparently, they're pretty impressed. Comments like "did you see that?" are spreading through the audience. The few who were not looking are saying to the others, "What did I miss?" Okay, now I've got them. That's half the battle won. Now all I've got to do is keep them with me for next forty-five minutes.

I'm about to say "good morning, boys and girls" when my brain clicks. I think about former FBI Assistant Director John Malone, years ago, addressing the agents as "boys and girls." I won't make the same mistake. But hell, I reason, these really are boys and girls; for goodness' sakes this is the third grade. I'll just play it safe. I begin, "Good morning, everybody!" Looks like I'm off to a good start.

In keeping with the theme of my show, "I Am Special," I now I launch into my interactive discussion with them about things which make them special—being a good citizen, recycling, not using drugs, etc. I hold up large colorful posters, which I have enhanced with my own artwork and photos. Each placard bears a word like "Caring" or one of the other principles of character education. I ask them how this particular trait makes them special. They respond with hands waving wildly in the air. Their answers are thrust back at me with the rat-a-tat of a machine gun. Now they're getting into it, and so am I! Even in the lower grades, kids today are a fountain of knowledge. Maybe it's the Internet or TV. Maybe some of them are actually reading, just like we did in the prehistoric days before Gameboy and video games. They seem to know much more than I knew in the third grade. God knows what they'll know by the fifth grade!

I scan the audience, looking for the most enthusiastic hand wavers since these are the ones that answer immediately. This keeps the show moving at a rapid pace. Once in a while, however, this theory falls flat on its face. You see, sometimes the wild and crazy hand wavers, when called on, deflate like a Macy's Thanksgiving Day Parade balloon with a puncture. I'll point and say, "You, the person in the blue shirt." After the standard "who me?" the kid freezes up. He looks at me, as his hand ceases its rapid fire waving, and then slowly grinds to a halt. As the hand begins its descent into his lap, he slowly lowers his head and begins to stare at the auditorium floor. I quickly move on to the next enthusiastic hand waver, hoping that this doesn't happen again. After all, the clock is ticking, and I have to perform my miracles before their attention span turns them all into a room of squiggly worms anxious to crawl out of a rotten apple. As I continue to call on kids, I constantly remind myself to refer to them as "neuters," calling them the "person" in the blue shirt rather than the boy or girl in that shirt. I learned to do this the hard way; on more than one occasion, as laughter broke out, I realized that the "girl" I had called on was a boy with long hair or that the "boy" that I had pointed to was a girl with extremely short hair.

Following Character Ed are Jed, who talks about substance abuse prevention and stranger danger, Tommy Turtle, the slow talker whom the bully picks on; Ratso Rizzo, the cheese devotee; Big Mouth; and the rest of the menagerie. Last of all, if time permits, I introduce the magic drawing board on which I draw a character named Michael, who mysteriously comes to life, announcing, "I'm Michael. I recycle." I must admit that I'm really adept at convincing the kids that these characters are living, breathing beings.

I sometimes find myself comparing the way in which the time passes nowadays to the way it moved in the Bureau. It always amazes me how forty-five minutes spent doing a school show goes by in a flash. Yet, at times, forty-five minutes sitting at my desk in the Bureau, writing a report, seemed an eternity. However, believe it or not, this showbiz stuff is exhausting. In fact, I find it far more tiring than investigating violations of federal law. In addition to the ventriloquism, there are magic tricks, music, and some other visual shenanigans during the show. Keeping constantly aware of the time remaining, audience reactions, waning attention span, and things like that also add to the tension. I'm glad I have an abundant supply of adrenaline. It sustains me throughout the performance.

Well, the show's over. I don't know how I got it all in. Mr. Cox comes bounding up onto the stage. "Wasn't that a terrific show? Let's all give Mr. Berger a big hand to show our appreciation for his coming to our school today!" Applause, applause. "Thank you, everybody. You've been a great audience!"

I assumed the children would then quietly exit the auditorium. But oh, no—here they come! They're charging the stage! In a split second, they've gone from grade-school kids to fanatic fans at a European soccer match! The verbal barrage begins. "Hey, how'd you make that cane show up?" "Where'd the red handkerchief go?" "Let me try the dummies." "How'd you make 'em talk?"

"Hey, guys, please don't touch my stuff. Put that down. Leave the turtle alone, or his head'll fall off!"

"Okay, everybody, let's go. Back to class," orders a teacher as she attempts to quell the insurgency and guide her class toward the door. "Oh, come on, Miss Fulton, can't we just ask some questions?" "Not now. Get moving!" she shouts.

"Thank God, they're leaving." By now my head is spinning, a result of the tension created by the postshow pandemonium. Ah, the auditorium is now filled with blessed silence. Oh no, the doors are beginning to open! A teacher spreads her arms, attempting to stem the tide. A roar erupts as the next group begins to flow into the room like molten lava on the run. I dash to reorganize my props. It's time for round two!

"Another triumph," I mumble to myself. Cox approaches with the guidance counselor. "Great show. The kids loved it. We'll have you back next year. We'll mail you the check as soon as the paperwork is processed." I smile broadly, shaking hands firmly with each of them. As they leave the auditorium, I feel the adrenalin begin its slow descent to normal levels. I begin the massive task of repacking all of my stuff into its proper place, being careful to take inventory of each and every item. The puppets and props are expensive, and I can't take the chance of leaving anything behind. If I'm lucky, I'll be able to find the custodian who, if he has time, may offer to help me haul the load back out to my car. This rarely happens, so I begin to drag the heavy bags of equipment up the auditorium aisles, wondering if they purposely built these at an angle to torture those carrying equipment from the stage. "Need some help?" I guess I lucked out. Here comes Charles. He helps me carry everything out to the van. After it's loaded, I offer Charles a handshake. As he shakes my hand, he says, "I heard the kids talking in the hallway. They really liked your show. I'm sure the principal will call you back." "I hope so. Thanks for your help, and have a great weekend." As Charles walks back into the school, I stand there for a minute before entering the car. I take a look at the school and think, "Nice kids, good school. I think I made a difference, maybe changed a few young lives. Good job, Berger."

I begin the drive home, realizing that I have a rehearsal this afternoon for Monday's show before an adult audience in a theater at a "Y." I've been told that they're expecting some kind of record crowd. In addition to my regular set, I'll be doing two new songs and introducing a puppet I've never used in front of an audience. I also have to pick out music for next week's recording session at the studio. I'd better get home. I've got plenty of work ahead of me.

Folks ask me, "This is easier than being in the FBI, isn't it?" My answer, "Hell no, but it's a lot more fun."

OVER THE HILL

"It's a puppet show." "It's puppets." "He's got puppets." "It's a puppet show."
I thought it would never end—the drone of these four women in wheelchairs, endlessly repeating themselves, two facing each other, two facing the front of the room, speaking out into the empty space ahead of them. A nurse's aide in a freshly starched white pantsuit approaches. Walking toward them at a snail's pace, she puts her hand on one of the wheelchairs and announces with the authority of a tank commander, "Cease and desist." Silence follows immediately. The soldiers have received their orders and are obedient—except for one. Not another word is heard from three of the troops, but from the fourth member of the brigade, a low mumbling sound emerges. I am just about able to discern the words. "It's a puppet show. It's a puppet show. It's a . . ." The mumbling churns into a low roar much like the sound of a car engine attempting to start on a February morning. "It's a pup . . ." "Okay, Susan, that's enough. We know—it's a puppet show. Thanks for telling us." Speaking as if addressing a third grader, she says, "Now please settle down, or there won't be any show for you. We have to have respect for the other people here." As I insert a karaoke version of a Frank Sinatra tune into my CD player, I realize that the nurse's lecture on respect is a familiar one. I've used it several times myself while performing in a school auditorium which had become so noisy as to make it impossible for me to continue with my show. I would stop the program, then, in a loud and commanding voice say, "Okay, everybody, let's quiet down and show some respect for our fellow classmates." The parallel between the seasoned seniors and the kids is obvious: Life is a vicious cycle. We're babies. We grow up. We become babies again. It's a puppet show.

So here I am, about to play before a full house at one of the many nursing home facilities throughout New Jersey. These shows are essentially a nightclub performance during daylight hours. I refer to these shows as "dayclub" performances. By the time I'm ready to begin, several audience members are snoozing away. I haven't even started my standup routine, and half of them are out cold. Well, it's not my fault. Perhaps they're a little overmedicated. Oh well, maybe they'll wake up when I start to sing the oldies rock number. If that doesn't wake them up, someone better dial 911.

When it comes to performing in nursing homes, one of the biggest challenges is the art of balancing the sound. Properly balanced sound in a nightclub, theater, or a school auditorium will reach all members of the audience at a level which is neither too low to be heard with clarity, nor so loud that it assaults the ear. People in all areas of the room should be able to hear both the music and my spoken words clearly. However, when it comes to doing shows in nursing homes, all of these considerations go out the window. Instead, the goal is simply to satisfy as many audience members as possible without creating the war of the wheelchairs. What happens is that if the sound is too loud, the woman in the first row covers her ears, and then begins screaming (and I mean screaming), "It's too loud!" The minute I lower the volume, some meek little blue-haired lady in the back lets out a raucous, "I can't hear a damn thing!" I do what I can to please them all, but I realize that I can make some of the seniors happy some of the time and some of them happy all of the time, but I can't make all of them happy all of the time.

By now you may have noticed that all of the audience members I refer to are woman. Startling, as it may seem, there are many more women in nursing homes than men. Why? It's simply because fewer men make it to old age. According to the nursing staffs, another reason I see few men at these shows is that the men are extremely reluctant to attend a puppet show. I guess they think it's just not a macho thing to do. (Like a guy who's eighty-nine has to worry about his image as a macho man.)

Now don't get me wrong, I have no objection to entertaining these almost all-female audiences. For one thing, it gives me the perfect opportunity to sing love ballads. If there happens to be a small contingent of men in attendance, I keep them happy with a couple of quick choruses of "Take Me Out to the Ballgame."

In light of the fact that I perform so frequently for senior citizens, I've been told that I've become the "darling of the senior set." As the resident darling, I've come to realize that performing in nursing homes and other senior facilities makes me more than a mere entertainer; I am a therapist. Now, never having been trained in geriatric care, I've had no guidance as to the correct method to employ in stimulating elderly people, so I've designed my own plan. My goal is to jolt their mental state so as to remove them from what I refer to as the "nursing home trance." This state is caused by the sameness of daily life in these residences. As full-functioning adults in a busy world, we encounter more stimuli in one day than these folks see in a week. Their lives are completely structured and regulated. Whereas we may choose to have a late dinner on Saturday evening, they have no such choice. Mealtime is the same every day. Simple choices, such as what type of food we'll eat, are not always an option for them. Our activities, particularly on weekends, are many and varied. They, on the other hand, become so enmeshed in a web of sameness that many of them don't know what day of the week it is or, for that matter, what month we're in.

As the entertainer/therapist, I make an all-out effort to connect with my senior audiences in order to get their juices flowing. I've found that one of the most successful ways to do this is by reminding them of things from the past. I dish up a potpourri of happy music and corny old jokes. To this, I add a blend of colorful props and costumes. Finally, I spice up the recipe with a dash of ventriloquism and magic. I must admit that many of the magic tricks I perform are ones they saw hundreds of times on the old *The Ed Sullivan Show*, but they seem to love them anyway. Professional therapists have told me that what I'm doing in my shows stimulates the oldsters, brings joy into their lives, and gives them something to look forward to (my next show, I hope!).

One of the things I enjoy most about performing for seniors is their appreciation for things from the past. They love to reminisce about the "good old days." During my performance, I'll sometimes spot someone whose lips are moving in sync with mine as I sing a Sinatra ballad. On another occasion, I'll notice that the frail lady with the bright blue eyes sitting right in front of the mic is singing in perfect harmony with my grandma puppet, Ceil. Her warm smile and body language indicate that she identifies with each move Ceil makes and every joke she tells. I have transported her back to the living room in the house that she lived in for forty years. It's a Sunday evening, and she is gleaming with glee as she watches Ed Sullivan introduce Senor Wences, or some other ventriloquist with his little wooden partner. Folks like these often come up to me after the show to say how much they enjoyed me and my little friends, adding that I really "took them back" to happier times. I leave their little theaters feeling fulfilled in the knowledge that I brought a bit of sunshine into their lives. That feeling of fulfillment makes all the hard work worthwhile.

Performing for the nursing home crowd provides an endless series of experiences, some of which are not at all that pleasant. For instance, in my summer show, I do a set of Caribbean island tunes. Some of these call for audience participation. During one number, Isabelle, a tall, thin woman who I'm told was in her eighties, walked up on stage and started to dance with me. The dangling gold bracelets on her thin wrists accented her elegance as she swayed gracefully to the island melody. The smoothness of her steps indicated that she must have been a wonderful dancer in her younger years. At the end of "Matilda," the Harry Belafonte ditty about the woman who took my money and ran away to Venezuela, Isabelle stopped abruptly, reached into her pocket, and withdrew some change. As I thanked her for joining in on the number, she began to force the thirty-four cents into my left hand. At this point, I was attempting to remove the CD from my karaoke machine and replace it with the one I was going to use for the next segment of the show. She grabbed my hand, insisting that I take the "tip" she was offering me. I made a polite gesture with my hand, indicating that she should exit the stage. Apparently, she didn't get the message. As she stood her ground, refusing to move, I saw a change come over her facial expression. She began to resemble TV's *The Hulk* as the metamorphosis continued. The look on her face changed from one of joyful pleasure to one of seething rage and anger. In vain, I searched the room for the recreation director or someone of authority who could remove her from the stage. Most of the aides in attendance seemed to be amused by the little drama and remained in their places watching the scene unfold. I decided that I had better begin the finale or the standoff would go on indefinitely. Perhaps, if I ignored her, she would finally go back to her seat. I pumped up the music to an acceptable level and began the number. The song was the wild and crazy Peter Allen number "Rio." Prior to the Caribbean portion of the show, I had handed out several pairs of brightly colored maracas so that the folks could join in and make a lot of noise. I find that they enjoy this, since it's something that they rarely get to do.

Picture this: I'm standing on stage in white Capezio dance shoes, sun-bleached white pants, and a wild turquoise Hawaiian-print shirt covered with pictures of surfers. The music is blaring, and I'm shaking a pair of orange fluorescent day-glo maracas while pounding a tambourine against my hip and singing, "When my baby smiles at me I go to Rio . . . de Janeiro." While all of this is going on, the audience members, some of whom can barely raise their arms, are making feeble attempts to shake their maracas. Poor Mrs. Goldfarb is screaming from her wheelchair because she dropped her maracas on the floor and can't pick them up. Meanwhile, on stage, standing in front of me, is Isabelle, growling because I am refusing to take the damn thirty-four cents from her. I finally relent. While continuing to sing, I put down the maracas and tambourine, grab the change, and put it in my pocket. While retrieving the noisemakers, I once again gesture for her to leave the stage. At this point, I spot the director of recreation enter the back of the room. She immediately notices my onstage dilemma and comes to the rescue. Racing onto the stage, she grasps Isabelle firmly by the wrist and escorts her back to her seat. After the show, as I gave her the "tip" Isabelle had force upon me, she apologized, saying that this occurs at almost every show at the facility. She promised that the next time I appear there, Isabelle would be held in check and not permitted to leave her seat.

A recent incident is a classic. A nurse's aide pushed her patient's wheelchair into place just in front of the area in which I'd be performing. I walked over to greet the lady. As I approached, the aide said, "She's going to love your show. She's deaf, but she reads lips." "We have a slight problem," I remarked. "What's that?" she asked. "I'm a ventriloquist." As I stated in my book *It Ain't Broadway,*[4] performing in nursing homes can be an adventure to remember.

In the wonderful Broadway show *BKLYN* [Brooklyn], *The Musical,*[5] these words are spoken: "Change somebody's life, you change your own." It's true. Although performing in senior facilities is often a daunting and challenging experience, it is one that has changed my life. My understanding of the aging process and the state of the elderly has become much more clear. Also, I've come to realize that what I do as an entertainer has a profound effect on the lives of the seniors for whom I perform. The laughter in their eyes indicates to me that I have brought joy to them during what might have otherwise been another dull day in a residence which will probably be their last stop on life's journey.

CONVENTION FEVER

It might surprise you to learn that there's a fairly sizeable group of men, women, and children around the globe that practices the art of ventriloquism. Some do it for fun, and some for profit. I'll bet you didn't know that ventriloquists hold a convention—actually a couple of them each year. One takes place in Las Vegas and one in Ft. Mitchell, Kentucky which is about five miles south of Cincinnati, Ohio. Almost every year, I attend the convention held in Ft. Mitchell. That convention is known as the Vent Haven ConVENTion. "Vent Haven" is the name of the museum of ventriloquism that is located a short distance from the hotel where the convention is held. This museum is a "haven" for all sorts of memorabilia related to the art. Its two buildings house hundreds of figures, some of which are extremely old and rare. Some are one-of-a-kind masterpieces which were created by skilled woodcarvers, costumers, and mechanical craftsman. You would probably recognize some of them from TV or movies. Among the more famous ones are Paul Winchell's Jerry Mahoney and Knucklehead Smiff, and Edgar Bergen's Charlie McCarthy. Also on view is Farfel, Jimmie Nelson's renowned dog. Although not the originals, these are museum replicas of the ones that appeared on TV. In the case of Farfel, the puppet is the original stunt double that was used in several commercials. Duplicates of the dummies are on display since many of the originals are housed elsewhere. Jerry Mahoney, for instance, has his own comfortable little nook in the permanent collection of the Smithsonian Institution.

A few years ago, when I approached my wife with the suggestion that we attend our first convention, she blanched at the idea, looking at me like I was nuts. "Why would I want to spend four days with a bunch of whackos who play with dummies?" I guess I can't blame her for reacting this way. I, too, questioned the value and validity of taking a trip all the way to Kentucky to spend time with a group of people I had never met—people drawn together to do what? What, I wondered, did they do at this gathering? Is there enough to discuss about ventriloquism to occupy several days in the middle of a beautiful summer?

"Oh, come on, Aud, it might be fun. And besides, if we don't like it, we just won't go again next year," I proclaimed. Reluctantly, she bought the idea, and we went. And we went again the following year, and the year after that, and continue to go to this day.

The convention is not what you might imagine. No, it's not a bunch of crazies running around a hotel comparing dummies and doing little skits to show how adept they are at not moving their lips. Rather, it's a well-organized four-day event that celebrates the evolution of an ancient art which has been successfully brought into our own time by some extremely talented individuals. In attendance are approximately five hundred people from around the world who attend workshops on subjects such as comedy writing and improvisation, the ventriloquist as an actor, using ventriloquism as a vehicle for teaching religion, performing for school children, seniors, etc. Several lectures are devoted to topics which, although not as glamorous as performing, are necessities for those of us who earn a living as performers. These include the areas of advertising and marketing your shows, dealing with agents, venues suitable for ventriloquists, and so on.

Many of the attendees bring their kids to the gathering. Man, do they have fun! Imagine what a cool time a kid can have going to a place with indoor and outdoor pools, people running around the hotel all day and night with puppets in tow, and several dealers' tables covered with magic tricks even a kid can master. And, to add to the excitement, each night, there's a show featuring performances by vents of every age group and level of expertise. For the adults, the convention is a sharing and learning experience. For the kids, it's a solid four days of summer fun.

When I began to perform, I didn't realize how many venues are available for ventriloquists to perform in. I figured that kids' birthday parties were basically it, unless you got some TV exposure and could get into a commercial or two. At the convention, you attend lectures from vents that work full-time in a wide variety of venues. I've become aware that the field is virtually limitless for a good performer and his little partner. Several ventriloquists make an excellent living performing in comedy clubs, on cruise ships, and in religious arenas. Others, such as myself, earn a living by performing in schools, in clubhouses at retirement communities, for senior citizens organizations, and at corporate events. Still others are in constant demand as opening acts for major celebrities in shows around the nation and, for that matter, all over the world. The most accomplished performers, such as the immensely talented Jay Johnson, are headliners in their own right. Jay, whom you may remember as the ventriloquist on the TV program *Soap*, received critical acclaim and won a Tony award for his performance on the New York stage, in his own one-man show, "The Two and Only." The show was a poignant look at Jay's own life and how, from the time he was a young boy and still today, he possessed the unique ability to bring joy to people through the use of puppets. Another highly acclaimed entertainer is Jeff Dunham. Comedy club and TV audiences roar with laughter at the snide comments dished out by Jeff's geriatric alter ego, Walter. Ventriloquists such as Jeff also do well performing on college campuses. As long as the material is fresh and hits upon topics with which college students identify, a good ventriloquist can fill every seat in the house in a college theater or auditorium. A big boost to ventriloquism was the recent success of Terry Fator when he took first place on the TV show *America's Got Talent*. He and his little friends are now booked into Las Vegas as well as several other venues throughout the country.

I'm often asked where I get my puppets. The convention is an invaluable source for me when it comes to puppetry equipment. There are twenty-six dealers' stations set up in two rooms. At their tables are an amazing array of one-of-a-kind soft puppets, hand-carved hard figures made of wood, plastic, and other materials. Also on hand are tapes, records, CDs, DVDs, photos, and volumes of books on every conceivable aspect of ventriloquism. At the 2004 convention, my own book *It Ain't Broadway* was a sellout success! I'm happy and proud to announce that a record number of copies were sold. You can find new and old scripts, books on how to perfect your skills, and others on the history of the art. There's even a booth dedicated to ventriloquial collectibles and memorabilia. This is the kind of stuff that my wife and I collect: photos from old TV shows, advertising posters, mugs featuring decals of Jimmy Nelson and his puppet dog Farfel, and even original copies of Paul Winchell's book on how to do ventriloquism. If you're willing to shell out the big bucks, you can sometimes find a vintage figure carved by master craftsman Frank Marshall, the guy who created such legendary figures as Paul Winchell's Jerry Mahoney and Jimmy Nelson's little buddy Danny O'Day. Some of the dealers sell sound equipment to enhance your performance. Magic tricks can be purchased from several vendors, who are magician-ventriloquists themselves. Like many other vents, I, too, use magic in my act. It adds variety to my show and gives me a chance to rest my voice while my hands are doing all the work.

The after-dinner shows give those in attendance a chance to see what others in the field do—and how well they do it. Young performers are given a chance to work in front of a large audience, something which they may not get to do at home on their own turf. During some of the shows, a panel of professionals jots down constructive criticism while a videographer tapes each performance. The comments and tape are presented to the performer at the end of the show. It's a great learning experience, although it can cause the *American Idol* jitters.

So there you have it—an insider's take on a yearly convention that few, if any of you, knew exists.

VOICES IN MY HEAD

Ever since I was little, I've had an ever-growing group of personalities in my mind. I enjoyed the fantasy of different characters coming to life in my imagination. Now, as an adult, as an entertainer, I get paid to bring these personalities into the lives of others.

The inspiration for several of my little friends came from characters that I was exposed to when I was growing up in New York. During the 1950's and '60's, I listened to radio station WNEW on which *The Klavan and Finch Show* aired each morning. The remarkable Gene Klavan and Dee Finch created some of the brightest comedy on the radio airwaves. When Finch retired in 1968, Klavan went solo but was always accompanied by some imaginary, irreverent souls who were so true-to-life that I was convinced that they existed. Gene stimulated my mind into creating some characters of my own. These imaginary folks have occupied a special little corner of my brain for decades, surfacing briefly every now and then when I'm in some crazy mood. Now, I draw on them to inspire me to create additional zany personalities to use in my act.

Steve Allen, Jackie Gleason, Ernie Kovacs, and a host of other comedians also provided a background upon which I continue, to this day, to build ideas which eventually make their way into my shows.

At almost every performance, people ask about the puppets. They want to know if I design and build them, who writes the scripts and song parodies for them, etc. Although I would love to make the figures myself, I have little time to do this, and at present, lack the expertise to even attempt it, so I purchase them from professional puppet makers such as the incredibly talented Mary Ann Taylor, the creator of Ceil and her husband, Murray, as well as several other puppets in my act. In designing them, I consulted with Mary Ann, describing each figure, in detail, as I envisioned them. This included body type, hair, facial expression, eye color, clothing, jewelry, etc. Mary Ann then took my vision and created the wonderfully whimsical yet realistic-looking figures that would become the grandma and grandpa in my show. I then began a series of rehearsals designed to make me feel comfortable with the figures. I would simply maneuver them around until the manipulation became natural and the image of them which I saw in my rehearsal mirror convinced me that they were living people who just happen to be smaller than most of us. Then I began the voice process, creating voices to match the personalities. Once that was complete, I wrote scripts and dialogues they could use to interact with each other as well as with me. Incidentally, the process of conducting a dialog with two puppets at the same time is known as "splitting." It's a real challenge, but the audience seems to enjoy it, and I get a kick out of hearing someone whisper, "Hey, this guy is good!"

The next step was in figuring out how to work some music in with the script. I decided that a duet would be the right approach. In my current act, Ceil usually does a solo and then is joined by Murray for a duet. I vary the songs from show to show, but usually use some old tune like "Love and Marriage," since tunes like this are familiar and recognizable to the senior audiences. Once in a while, I get goofy and allow Ceil and Murray to go completely out of character and sing the Sonny and Cher hit, "I've Got You Babe." After all, it's a variety show, so why not add some variety?

A constant dilemma I face in is that of conjuring up new personalities and envisioning how they will look as puppets. For instance, when I decided that I needed some senior citizens in my program, I took a look around at ladies in this age group. I studied people in restaurants, on TV, on the street, and in my own family. I eventually based Ceil's appearance on a combination of my mother-in-law, Thalia, and Doris Roberts, who played the mother on the hit TV sitcom *Everybody Loves Raymond*. Ceil's whiney New York voice and accent is derived from the voice of Fran Drescher's character in the popular television series *The Nanny*. Ceil's husband, Murray, is a combination of Peter Boyle's character, Frank, on *Everybody Loves Raymond*, and Carol O'Conner's timeless portrayal of Archie Bunker of *All in the Family* fame. (However, unlike Archie, Murray does not even know the meaning of the word "bigot.")

The collaboration with the puppet maker is, in many ways, as important as the show itself. It is a sharing of ideas and concepts with the common goal of creating a figure which an audience finds believable. It's important that the puppet presents itself to the viewers as a real, living person, animal, or whatever it's supposed to represent. The process is an evolutionary one. As the puppet is being made, changes continually take place. Sometimes the figure is near completion, or, in some cases, actually finished when I, or the puppet maker, realize that something has to be adjusted or changed completely. It could be the hairstyle or hair color that just doesn't fit the personality. Sometimes it's the clothing or even the shape of the body. For instance, once Murray was complete, I took a look at him and realized that there was something that was just not right. He was supposed to be the retired stay-at-home husband who indulges in too many snacks while watching the football game on TV. Murray's flat little belly just didn't reflect this lifestyle. When I told this to Mary Ann, she graciously went ahead and added a little paunch just above Murray's belt. "Perfect!" I proclaimed when I saw Murray after his "surgery." I'm sure that Ceil would have loved him even without his little doughnut belly, but as I keep reminding her, it's my show, and we'll do it my way!

Scriptwriting is fun, but tedious, to say the least. Just when it seems that I've captured the essence of a character, I'll realize that the joke I've written for him or her, is not that funny. Back to the drawing board. At the outset, some jokes seem like they'll be great, then when you put 'em out there, they bomb. Often, it depends on the audience and their sensitivity. Most are attuned to current events, but headlines and headliners change daily, so I try to avoid material that is too topical. A joke that's based on Monday's headline may be stale by Friday.

In addition to my life as a puppeteer, I make my living as a singer. My audiences tell me that I'm pretty good. Both my wife and my puppets agree. If any of you decide to become professional singers, my advice is this: Always have some puppets on the stage with you. That way, if you forget the lyrics, or anything else goes wrong, you can turn to them and blame their dumb little asses for the tragedy.

THE CAST OF CHARACTERS

My cast of whimsical whackos is divided into two touring companies. The first group is comprised of the crew I use for my school shows. You already met most of them in the chapter describing the school performances. Nowadays, since I perform mainly for seniors, I sometimes incorporate one of my school show characters into my adult act. For instance, I'll change Wild Thing from a kids' puppet with a message about stranger danger into an alien who drinks Metamucil. This character has now become one that appeals to the seniors.

Company number 2 is made up of adult puppets. The conversational antics of the husband and wife team, Ceil and Murray, are reminiscent of dialogs between George Burns and Gracie Allen. However, there is a distinct reverse twist. George played straight man to Gracie, who always seemed to be just a couple of degrees off in her reasoning. In contrast, Ceil, the wife in my happy little couple, plays it straight while Murray usually exhibits thinking akin to that of a third grader. To add a bit of variety, I sometimes reverse the formula. On these occasions, Ceil presents her thoughts in true Gracie Allen fashion while Murray shakes his head in bewilderment. The senior audiences, as well as their adult children, who sometimes attend the shows, readily relate to these two who are today's quintessential grandparents or great grandparents, the ones who still play bingo and mah-jongg while the rest of humanity is exploring the Internet.

In some shows, I introduce Murray's cousin, Bernie Lovestein. Bernie is the ultimate loser—a ne'er-do-well who changed his name to Bernie Love to pursue a career as an Elvis impersonator. When he sings, "I'm a hunk, a hunk, I'm Bernie Love," we're convinced that some folks really need therapy.

Nick, with his black turtleneck and gold chain, is the mob guy who fancies himself a "professional lounge lizard." His nightclub act leaves a lot to be desired. Listening to Nick sing rock and roll from the '60's is the equivalent of getting a root canal without Novocain.

Biblical Man, a.k.a. Howard Ino, is the personification of a guy from the year 0002. When asked about the derivation of his name, he explains that when he was born, his mother asked his father what they should name him. His father's response was, "How would I know?" From that point on, he was called Howard Ino. His big claim to fame is that, unlike his neighbors who are tent dwellers, he owns a condo. After his rendition of an oldies rock number, I have a difficult time convincing him that he really has no need to thank the academy, since his performance will never win an award. He insists, however, that I hand him "the envelope, please." He is truly a disaster of biblical proportion.

Mrs. Wes Chester, the wealthy blue-haired widow of the late Dr. Wesley Chester, hails from the affluent New York county, Westchester. She is the ultimate society matron. She truly believes that the world would be a better place if we all spent our time playing croquet or shopping. In her spare time, she serves as an environmental volunteer who diligently rids her neighborhood's streets of dog poop. She performs this admirable task with the ladies of her group, the Pooper Scoopers. Her dog, Lollipop, can't stand the old biddy and is constantly trying to pee on her leg.

Whoopie Goldstein is the R&B singer who just flew in from LA and is pissed off because the airline lost her luggage. Her new CD *Love On the Internet* has gone platinum. She threatens that in the coming year her hair will do this too.

Dino Suaveti is the suavest guy around. He sings about going back to Houston but is, in fact, from Secaucus, New Jersey. His rendition of the Italian tune "That's Amore" makes you want to upchuck a canolli.

Dino's twin brother, Mr. David, the decorator, is a flamboyant maven of current styles and trends. For some reason, he is bent on giving my home a makeover. He insists that we must "go bold" and "accessorize," by lining the room with Lucite vases of cascading roses. He sings about how he will redesign your toilet seat so that it's "comfy for your tushy."

Another buddy of mine is an aging hippie biker named Mercury Speedhead. In his black motorcycle outfit, he continues to live as if it were the 1960's. His weekend plans include a trip to Woodstock to attend a naked love-in. He refuses to listen when I tell him that Woodstock is now a piece of history and that his chances of hearing Janis Joplin sing or Hendrix play are null and void. When he sings about "feelin' groovy," I remind him that nowadays the only thing about him that's groovy is his wrinkled skin.

These are just a few of the miniature folks that I share the stage with. There are many others. In fact, there are closets full of additional crazies in our house, leaving no room for our clothing. Just ask my wife.

STAYING IN TOUCH

Since I'm in the business of entertaining children of all ages (prekindergarten to approximately ninety-six), it's imperative that I stay in touch with just about everything that's happening, particularly on the current entertainment scene. For the senior crowd, I have to stay abreast of current events, or my opening stand-up routine will fall flat on its face. When it comes to music, I must stay attuned to who's hot and who's not in the recording industry, or the kids will label me some old guy who's not with it. If I'm to relate to them and their world, I'd better be familiar with every current and upcoming new recording artist, rapper, hip-hop star, and American Idol. I'm familiar with almost every jokester, cartoon character, and superhero on both the big and little screen. I sometimes have to remind my wife that this process of staying in touch is the reason why I'm staring at Sponge Bob Square Pants on TV, or watching some computer-generated superhero clobber a robotic dinosaur with his intergalactic laser sword. For the seniors and Baby Boomers like myself, I have to know the lyrics to every Frank Sinatra and Tony Bennett song, all of Bobby Rydell's lyrics, and every song that ever stopped a show on Broadway. It's imperative that I remember the oldest Milton Berle joke from *The Ed Sullivan Show* and the newest political punch line from Leno or Letterman. I have to be able to rattle off the names of the characters on the latest reality shows. In addition, I must keep my magic skills honed so that I can perform a few eye-catching tricks to mystify the audience while, unbeknownst to them, what I'm really doing is resting my voice between verbal duels with my puppets.

Sure, it's a lot of hard work. But it's fun too. I find that when the brain is constantly challenged, it reacts in the same way that a muscle does when you work out; it remains healthy and grows stronger. Of course, there are times when I really don't feel like watching cartoons and couldn't care less about who's eating insects to survive on reality TV. At these times, I try to relax. To date, I haven't been too successful at this thing called "relaxation." In speaking with other creative types, I find that we share the same problem. Our brains never seem to take a rest. I often wake up at two in the morning with an idea for a script, song parody, or some crazy new character. I can see the puppet in my mind, even though it doesn't exist. The following day I start scouring catalogs of companies that sell puppets. If I'm not successful at finding one that fits the bill, I'll call one of the talented folks who make these figures.

Another aspect of this whole creative process is the writing. In order for me to write scripts that flow, jokes that are truly funny, and song parodies with catchy lyrics, I have had to undergo a complete transformation from FBI report writer to creative scriptwriter, author, and musical lyric composer/arranger. Anyone who has worked in government or a corporate environment knows exactly what I mean about writing those reports. There's the shop lingo, the acronyms which no member of the outside would understand, and the overall corporate way of putting things in writing. The FBI way of stating things on paper was, perhaps, even more challenging than what one might encounter in the private sector. How often did I find myself pounding out words that comprised an entire paragraph when what I wanted to say could have been said in one sentence? For instance, a typical FBI description of a man and his dog leaving his house at about two o'clock on an April afternoon, wearing a tan raincoat, would read, "At approximately 2:00 p.m. on April 24, 2004, the subject of the aforementioned investigation was observed departing his residence, described as a single-family dwelling located at 14 Filbert Street, Brooklyn, New York. At the time, said individual was observed wearing a tan garment, described as a raincoat, which appeared to be closely secured to his waist by a cloth belt. Accompanying the above-described person was a large-breed dog, white in color, around whose neck could be seen a chain bearing a metal object identified as a dog tag." See what I mean? My writing style needed a major overhaul if I were to come up with a humorous script for Tommy the Turtle.

Besides a complete makeover in writing style, in order to give my shows variety, I've learned how to do some basic magic, breathe properly when singing, and execute a few dance steps without falling on my rear end. In order to follow school mandates and make my school performances educational as well as entertaining, I've had to do research in several areas in order to write the scripts. These topics include character education, bullying, self-esteem, conflict resolution, etc. When a school requests a particular theme, such as space travel or American heroes, it's imperative that I not only write an appropriate script, but compose music for the shows as well. I find this especially important, since there's nothing like a catchy melody to keep the kids' attention.

In answer to the many folks who ask, "Wasn't it harder to be in the FBI than to do what you're doing now?" my answer is a resounding NO! You see, in the FBI, I was given an assignment. I did it to the best of my ability. Period. What I'm doing now is self-motivated. I've learned how to be my own boss. I must come up with the ideas and execute them. I must do the advertising. It's up to me to sell myself and my talents. The rewards are plentiful. For the first time in my life, the accolades and the financial rewards go directly to me, not to the organization that I work for. The feeling of success is mine. I am the one who receives the applause at the end of a performance. And, as any entertainer will tell you, that's a really good, no, make that a really *great,* feeling.

REWARDS

There are many rewards that I receive as a result of my current career but they're not the kind that I received in the Bureau. These rewards are not mounted on a plaque with an engraved brass plate decreeing that I had performed admirably on a particular date. These are internal rewards such as a sense of pride in knowing that I have done something to enrich and enhance somebody's life, if even for an hour or so. Here are some examples:

One of the most important portions of my school shows is the part designed to reinforce what the kids have been taught about character education. This consists of discussing, with the kids, values such as caring, citizenship, fairness, respect, responsibility, and trustworthiness. At one school show, while engaging the kids in an interactive discussion about caring, I asked them to give examples of people they care for. Most of them responded with, "My mother, my friends," etc. Then I asked for examples of other living things they could care for. Their answers were things such as "my cat, my hamster," etc. Next I asked for examples of things that they cared for that were not alive. Most said "my computer, my video games, etc." Typically, these answers refer to inanimate objects. However, one girl raised her hand and said, "My grandmother." I had never received a response such as this before. She was correct in her answer. She had named something that was not alive, yet a thing she cared for and, in fact, loved very much. However, in this instance, it was not an object but, rather, a person. I was quite taken aback, but, seeing that she was anxious to explain, I let her continue. She let all the kids in the auditorium in on her personal life and feelings, telling us that she still loved her grandmother even though she was no longer here. That young lady had offered an excellent example of how you can care for something, or someone, that is no longer with us. We can learn a great deal from kids.

At the conclusion of one show in an inner-city school, a teacher approached me with one of her students, a blind boy named Jorge. She asked if it would

227

be okay for him to touch one or two of the puppets. I was more than willing to allow him to do this. First, I brought out Tommy Turtle, a green and brown mass of soft plush material with an expressive mouth. In his Southern accent, Tommy softly said, "Hola. Como esta?" I guess the teacher was as surprised as little Jorge was to hear the turtle speaking Spanish. This, for me, was one of those definitive moments in life when some particular knowledge, or experience, paid off. Right then and there, I realized how glad I was that I had diligently studied Spanish in school and had, in fact, continued to use it throughout my life. I was barely able to hold back my tears as Jorge excitedly played with Tommy, Ratso, Big Mouth, and a few others. I had made his day—and he had certainly made mine.

Over the past few years, I have performed countless times for senior citizens, and I have a storehouse in my mind of stories related to members of these audiences. However, there is one experience I won't soon forget. Although many of my shows are for "with it" seniors, periodically I perform for patients in Alzheimer's units. These are lockdown facilities, which are equipped to handle the problem of patients who wander off their ward, sometimes attempting to leave the grounds entirely. After having completed a show at one of these facilities, I was packing up my props and sound system when a well-dressed gentleman, who appeared to be about sixty years old, came up to the stage. He congratulated me on doing a fine show and said that I belonged on television. After thanking him and asking him if he would act as my agent, I asked him whom he was visiting there. I was quite surprised when he told me that he was not a visitor, but was a resident. He went on to say, "I've been living in this prison for about two months," adding, "you understand." I guess I did. Apparently, since he was in the initial stages of the disease, he knew exactly where he was and why he was there. I wish I could have done something to help him. Maybe my show did help, in some small way.

In order to leave my audiences with a "feel-good" feeling, I end each performance with an upbeat song. Often, I sing something such as "Wonderful World," a tune made famous by Louis "Satchmo" Armstrong. "Wonderful World" is a particularly appropriate song for seniors since it reflects on the positive aspects of life. I find it important to remind these golden agers, particularly those in nursing homes, that there is a bright and positive side to living, regardless of your age. As I concluded the song for a group of seniors from a local organization, I noticed teardrops gently flowing down the cheeks of a lady sitting in the fourth row. As I backed away from the front of the stage, I saw her dab the tears away with a tissue and then begin to walk toward me. I put the mic down and walked downstage to meet her. She took a deep breath then said, "I must tell you, I enjoyed your show more than anything I've seen or done all year. Everything you did was so much fun that I couldn't stop laughing—and this is the first time I've laughed in a year. You see, my three-year-old grandson has cancer." I reached out, grabbed her hand, and, with tears in my eyes, wished her luck and told her that I'd say a prayer for her grandson. Now, as I sing the last notes of "Wonderful World," I say that prayer.

At the end of one performance, a gentleman approached me with an outstretched hand and proudly announced that he was ninety-two years old. I told him that he looked terrific, which he did. He leaned over and, in a whisper, gave me some sage advice. He said that in my shows I should speak and sing loudly and keep the show short since folks his age have "old ears and old rears." Seniors—ya gotta love 'em!

YOU MISSED YOUR CALLING!

As I previously mentioned, at the conclusion of many of my shows, I tell my audience about the FBI portion of my life. Invariably, one or two audience members approach me and say, "You missed your calling! You should be on TV!" or "You should be on Broadway. You're as good as the people in those shows!" Of course, I take this all with as much humility as I can muster. Some of them seem to have a tinge of sadness in their voices, as if they are pining for my lost or misspent years. I remember at least one elderly lady who told me that it's too bad that I wasted all those years in the FBI. I politely corrected her, saying that those years were not at all wasted, but were, in fact, a productive period, during which I accomplished a great deal.

Of course, the folks who say that I missed my calling mean well and are being complimentary. However, not one of us has the ability to turn back the hands of time. If we could do this, I'm sure that many of us would grab those hands and grind them back to a critical time in our lives when we made the decision to follow a certain path. This "coulda-shoulda-woulda" thinking is simply an exercise comprised of misspent energy. We are where we are at this point in our lives. We can only forge on and go forward from here.

LESSONS TO BE LEARNED

I believe that all of us can learn a lesson or two from our experiences. In pursuit of my goal of becoming an entertainer, I learned a great deal. I sum up these lessons in two phrases:

Life is not a dress rehearsal.
and
One of these days is none of these days.

Neither phrase was coined by me. I've come across them in a variety of places over the years. Both echo the same message: Do it now.

Life truly is no dress rehearsal. We're not practicing for the big show someday. This is the big show. Every day is a real live performance, and, without any understudies, we must shine. Those who say things like, "One of these days, I'm going to . . ." probably will not do, make, create, or become any of the things that he, or she, is talking about. If you're going to do something, make a plan and do it! But first, take a step back and look at the big picture. The "just do it" philosophy espoused by a major sporting goods company works only when applied sensibly. If you're young and have no real responsibilities, then the "go for it!" mentality is fine. However, if, like most of us, you're responsible for a few minor things such as a mortgage, car payments, and a couple of kids, both of whom consume food on a daily basis, think twice. Perhaps your goal of becoming a full-time professional skydiver is not that practical. Don't, as they say, give up your day job. Instead, ease into your goal. Try it out on a part-time basis. If it's entertaining, join a local community theater group. Audrey and I have a friend who takes cake-decorating courses in her spare time. She's quite talented and will, we're sure, work her way out of the corporate world and into the area of producing creative cakes for affairs and events.

Pursue your goals and dreams with good sense and sound judgment and don't rush it. Above all, don't sacrifice family and friends as you forge ahead. Rather, show them that their love and support, coupled with your enthusiasm and talent, is the driving force that will propel you to reach the stars.

LIVING LA VIDA LUCKY

I've learned that as an entertainer, not every performance is greeted with accolades. There's a fine balance between acceptance and rejection. Every performer must face this dilemma. It comes with the territory. Sometimes it's the fault of the entertainer or whoever wrote the show. Perhaps the material and/or the performance, was not appropriate for a particular venue or audience. On other occasions, it's simply a matter of appearing before a nonresponsive audience. Their demeanor may be the result of any number of things. They could be drunk, rowdy, too young to appreciate the material, too old to relate to the jokes, etc.

Recently, after facing what I regarded as a hostile audience, I mentioned to Paul, a longtime friend of mine, that I was feeling kind of low. Paul, who is an astute observer of the human condition, said, "You know, Rick. You have to keep in mind that you're retired from your first career. What you do now should be fun. If you're not having fun doing it, don't do it." I know that he's right—and I am having fun. But no job, and show business is a job, is all fun all the time. Every occupation has its highs and lows. Although there are appearances where I wish I had called in the understudy, on the whole I am having fun, and part of the fun is in dealing with the challenges I face in this crazy career. I consider myself lucky—lucky to be able to pursue my life's passion in good health and in good spirits. I guess you can say that I'm living La Vida Lucky!

WHAT . . . AND GIVE UP SHOW BUSINESS?

Have I ever thought about throwing in the towel and maybe pursuing something other than show business in my post-FBI years? Oh yeah, but its not because of a lack of love for what I'm doing. It's simply a matter of annoyance with certain aspects of the job . . . mainly the preshow preparations and the equipment schlepping. (Note* Shlepping is a technical term used to describe the transporting of any item which you'd rather see someone else carrying for you.)

My act is basically a one-man vaudeville show. In an effort to please almost everybody (and keep the nursing home audiences awake) I incorporate a variety of techniques including music, dance, magic, and, of course, comedy. My goal is to create a miniature variety show similar to those seen on our TV screens throughout the '50's and '60's . . . programs such as The Ed Sullivan Show, The Glen Campbell Goodtime Hour, The Smothers Brothers Show, and The Carol Burnett Show. On these programs we saw comedy skits, singers, dancers, and, particularly on the Ed Sullivan Show, ventriloquists. To do this type of show effectively requires me to carry an extensive amount of props and equipment. Many ventriloquists carry a case with a few puppets, a stand on which to place them while performing, and, if they're not using the theater's sound equipment, a small public address system. Believe me, traveling light like that has its advantages. When they arrive at their destination, it only takes a couple of minutes to carry their stuff into the theater and set up. I, on the other hand, carry several cases of props and costumes, a sound system, cordless microphone receiver/transmitter, power cables, magic tricks, and several puppets, all of which are lovingly protected in cases designed to ward off attacks from large animals and small children.

When I arrive at the place where I'm appearing, I embark upon what is usually a fifteen-minute attempt to locate the entertainment director who will take me to the room in which my show will be presented. Next comes the process of unloading my equipment onto a flatbed truck, which I carry in my van, and then schlepping it to that room. I then familiarize myself with the room and begin to prepare the stage. Part of this process consists of advising the crew that's setting up the seating arrangement as to the best placement of chairs. This is to prevent someone from sitting to my extreme right or left since all they'll see from that position is a guy with his hand up some puppet's rear end. Sometimes, however, some elderly person will insist on sitting there since it's their "regular" spot in the room and they refuse to change their location. I've made it a policy to simply let them know that the spot they've chosen is not a good one. If they insist on staying there, I don't argue. After all, when you've reached age ninety-six you deserve to sit wherever you want.

Although I get to perform on some great clubhouse stages, I don't always work in an actual theater setting. In nursing homes and assisted living residences, for instance, I often do my show in the dining room. This provides the folks with a nightclub atmosphere (even though the sun is shining through the windows.) Due to a perennial lack of staff in these places, most of the time I have to set up my area by myself. This often consists of moving large dining room tables and chairs around, as well as carrying in and arranging other tables to be used as supports for my sound system. These are usually much longer tables which also form a staging area, behind which I hide my props and puppets. All of this is accomplished while a clean-up crew vacuums up kernels of corn and other food particles around my feet. It takes me about forty-five minutes to set up the show. By this time, exhaustion is setting in and I haven't sung a note or had one puppet tell a joke. At this point, I usually begin to question my reason for doing what I'm doing. I start to think that perhaps I should drop all the extras and simply show up with a puppet or two, or perhaps use only my musical talents and market myself as a singer. How much easier it would be to show up with just my voice and a couple of CD's. However . . . when the folks out there start to laugh and applaud, my mood changes and I'm glad I'm doing what I'm doing. An added benefit, which makes all of these inconveniences worthwhile, is that I get a lot more bookings than many of my colleagues since my show is more than just a vent act. Those that book me often say that they love my show because it's very different from that of other entertainers they hire.

So, do I sometimes question what I'm doing and think of switching to neurosurgery or some other less taxing field of endeavor? Sure. Don't we all at times? Here's another example of why I start to ponder:

For many years, I performed for kids in a summer program sponsored by an inner city school district. Most of the activities were held on the schools' playgrounds. However, in an effort to protect my equipment and to avoid having to compete with the noise of passing traffic and breathe in gas fumes, I insisted that my show be held indoors. This resulted in my having to perform in a non-air conditioned cafeteria where the temperature was often well above a hundred degrees.

One blistering summer day, I arrived at a school quite enthused over the prospect of performing some new magic tricks I had just perfected. As I hopped out of the air-conditioned comfort of my van, I was hit by a shocking blast of heat. Honoring my request to work indoors, the teacher in charge directed me to an art room on the school's first floor. The area where I was to set up was absolutely filthy. I wouldn't even consider putting my equipment down on the floor. Since there was no custodian in sight, I did what I had to do. I located a large push broom, a dustpan, a utility sink, and a mop, and began to work on the floor. When it looked fairly presentable, I dragged one of the large ancient wooden art tables into the area. I needed this to hold my sound system, props etc. I then began to clean the table. Wet paper towels were no match for the clay and lumps of plaster of Paris that had to be removed. As I scrubbed, I became covered with tiny bits of colored glitter left on the table from an art project the kids had completed at the end of the school year. By now, I looked like a reject from a Mardi Gras parade. At this point I began to question why I had gotten myself into this situation. I envisioned myself on Broadway singing and dancing my way into the hearts of American theatergoers. I became infused with self-doubt. But it all changed at the end of the show when those little kids clapped their hands and told me how much they enjoyed Danny's song about reading and how Nick O'tine had convinced them not to smoke.

I now perform almost exclusively for seniors. However, in attendance at some of these shows are adult children (Baby Boomers like myself), grandchildren, and great grandchildren. It's a challenge to perform for these intergenerational audiences as I must include material suitable for those from age two to one hundred and two. As I get older, I'm sure that I'll tire of schlepping, cleaning, and setting up prior to show time. However, for the time being, I'll keep rationalizing by telling myself that there's some inconvenience associated with everything that's worthwhile, and that suffering makes you a stronger person. In show business, a little struggling helps to keep one's feet firmly planted on the ground while reaching for the stars. The struggle keeps your ego in check and can help prevent changes in your attitude and personality . . . changes which can have damaging effects on relationships with family and friends.

Friends who have seen me prepare for a show ask, "Why do you put up with all the inconvenience? Is it worth it? At some point, are you going to stop this insanity?" I answer, "What, and give up show business?"

The extraordinary singer and painter Tony Bennett, in a recent magazine article, was asked by the interviewer about his life's two passions. He explained simply, saying, "It's not that I *want* to paint or I *want* to sing. I *have* to."[6] I understand.

THE WIZARD IN ALL OF US

You may have noticed throughout this book several references to "The Wizard of Oz". Those references were deliberate. You see, if you think about the theme of that story, you'll remember that three of the characters, the lion, the scarecrow, and the tin man were all in search of something they thought they didn't possess. The lion wanted courage, the scarecrow brains, and the tin man a heart. They traveled far and wide to reach the one person who, they thought, could provide these things. But after a long hard journey, when they finally confronted him they learned that there was really no need for the wizard to give them what they desired because they already possessed these treasures within themselves. He was only a messenger who delivered the message, "You always had it."

In my life, I knew I always had it . . . the gift of making others happy through my talents as an entertainer. But I'm not alone. There's a hidden and sometimes unexplored potential in all of us. If you haven't already discovered it, just give it a try. Begin your search. I guarantee, once you discover what you can do, the sky's the limit.

CURTAINS UP!
LIGHT THE LIGHTS!

Well, folks, that's my story, and I'm stickin' to it! Retiring from a career that defined my life for thirty years was a tough and traumatic experience. Redefining my life and goals continues to be a challenge, but the rewards are indescribably delicious.

I hope that along with Ceil, Murray, and the rest of my little family, I get to meet you someday.

For those of you who are young, yet know in your head and in your heart what you want to do with your life, I say, "Give it your best shot." What have you got to lose?

For the oldsters out there, I say it's never too late. In my travels, I see people in their nineties learning how to surf the Web. Why not?

For anyone considering a career change, my advice is to map out a plan, proceed cautiously, and exercise a great deal of patience and planning. Consider the pros and cons, paying particular attention to what effect this will have not only your life but on that of your family as well.

My little friends and I wish you the best of luck. Thanks for coming tonight. You've been a beautiful audience. Good night!

The End

REFERENCES

1 Robinson, Edwin Arlington. *Collected Poems.* New York: The Macmillan Company, 1921

2 Laboy, Julio. "FBI Agent Kills Himself." *Newsday*, December 13, 1994.

3 National Transportation Safety Board (NTSB). NTSB Number AAR-00/03. Aircraft Accident Report: In-flight Breakup Over the Atlantic Ocean Trans World Airlines Flight 800 Boeing 747-131, N93119.

4 Berger, Rick. *It Ain't Broadway.* Littleton Colorado: Maher Studios, 2004.

5 Schoenfeld, Mark and McPherson, Barri. *Brooklyn, The Musical,* 2004.

6 Bennett, Tony. "The New Kid." *AARP Magazine, September/October 2007*